ARABS AND NORMANS
IN SICILY AND THE SOUTH OF ITALY

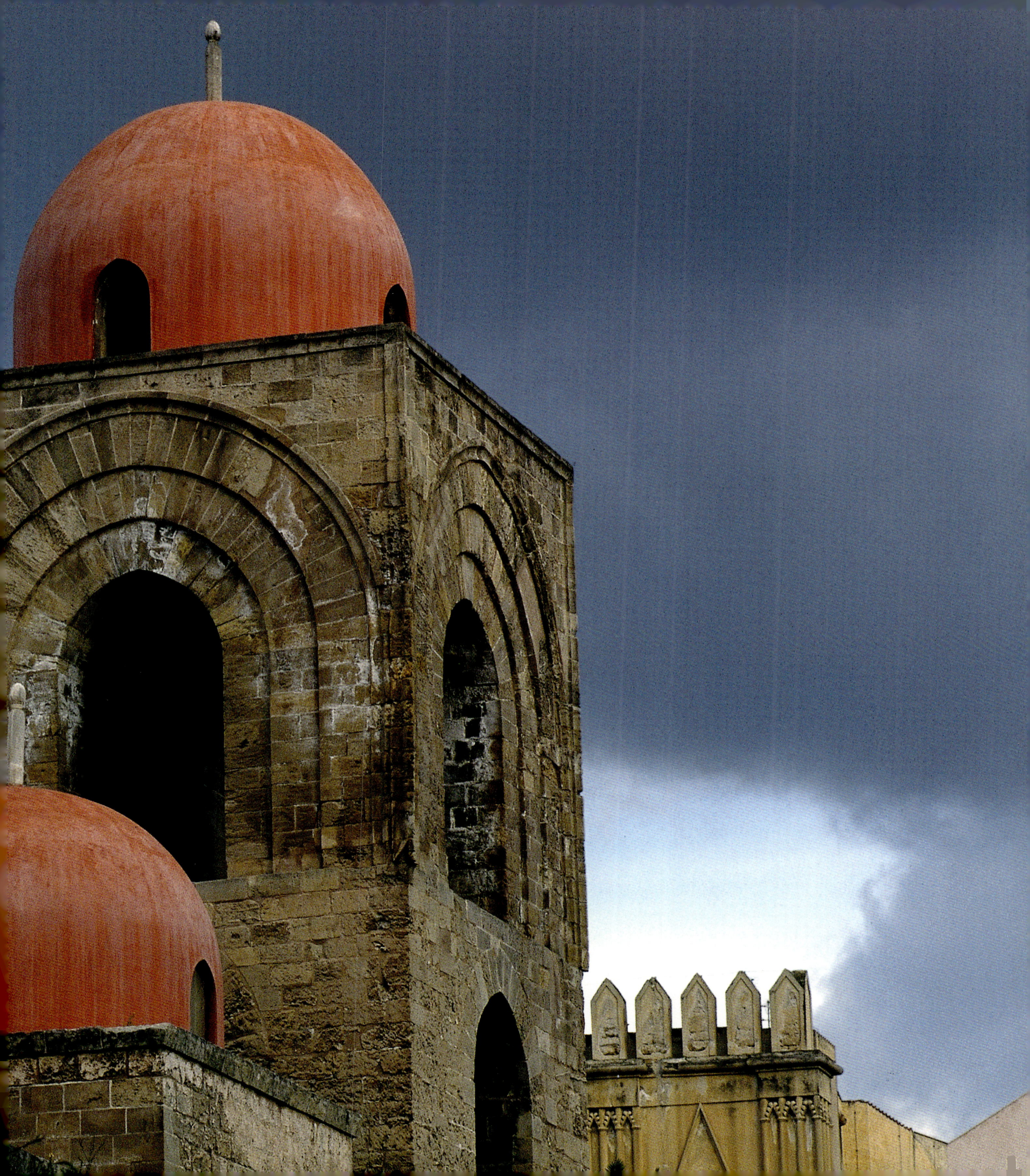

opposite:
The cathedral of Cefalù.

preceding pages:
Detail of a marble slab with figures of flowers and birds, from the pulpit of the cathedral of Ravello, 1272. Museum of the Cathedral of Ravello.

The church of San Giovanni degli Eremiti. Palermo.

following pages:
The cathedral of Palermo.

Detail of the wooden ceiling in the Cappella Palatina. Palermo.

Game of chess between a Muslim notable and his Norman guest. From the Book of Games *by Alfonso X el Sabio. Library of the Monastery of San Lorenzo, the Escorial, Madrid.*

The castle of Pietraperzia in the province of Enna, in Sicily, built by the Normans on top of an earlier Muslim fortification.

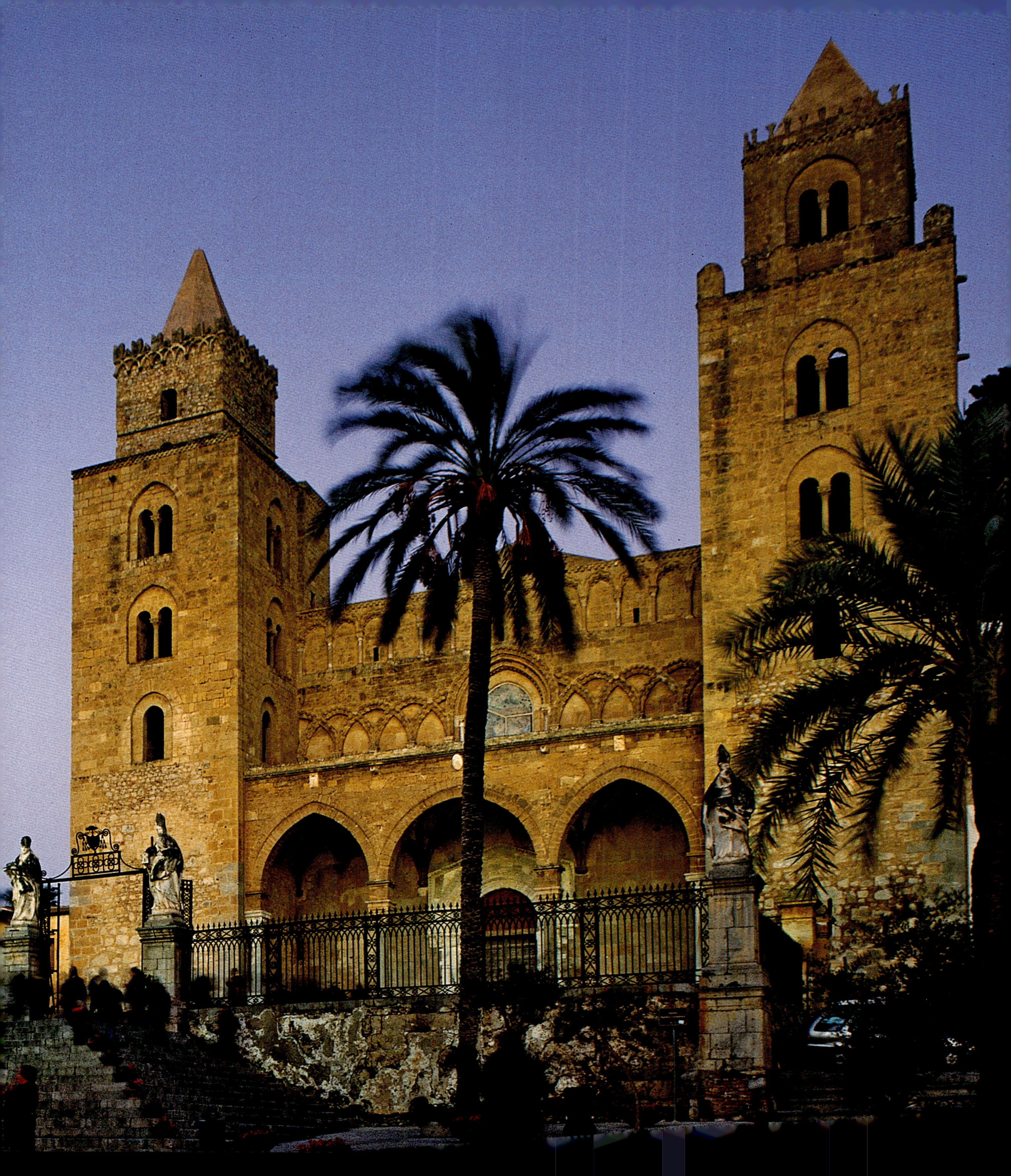

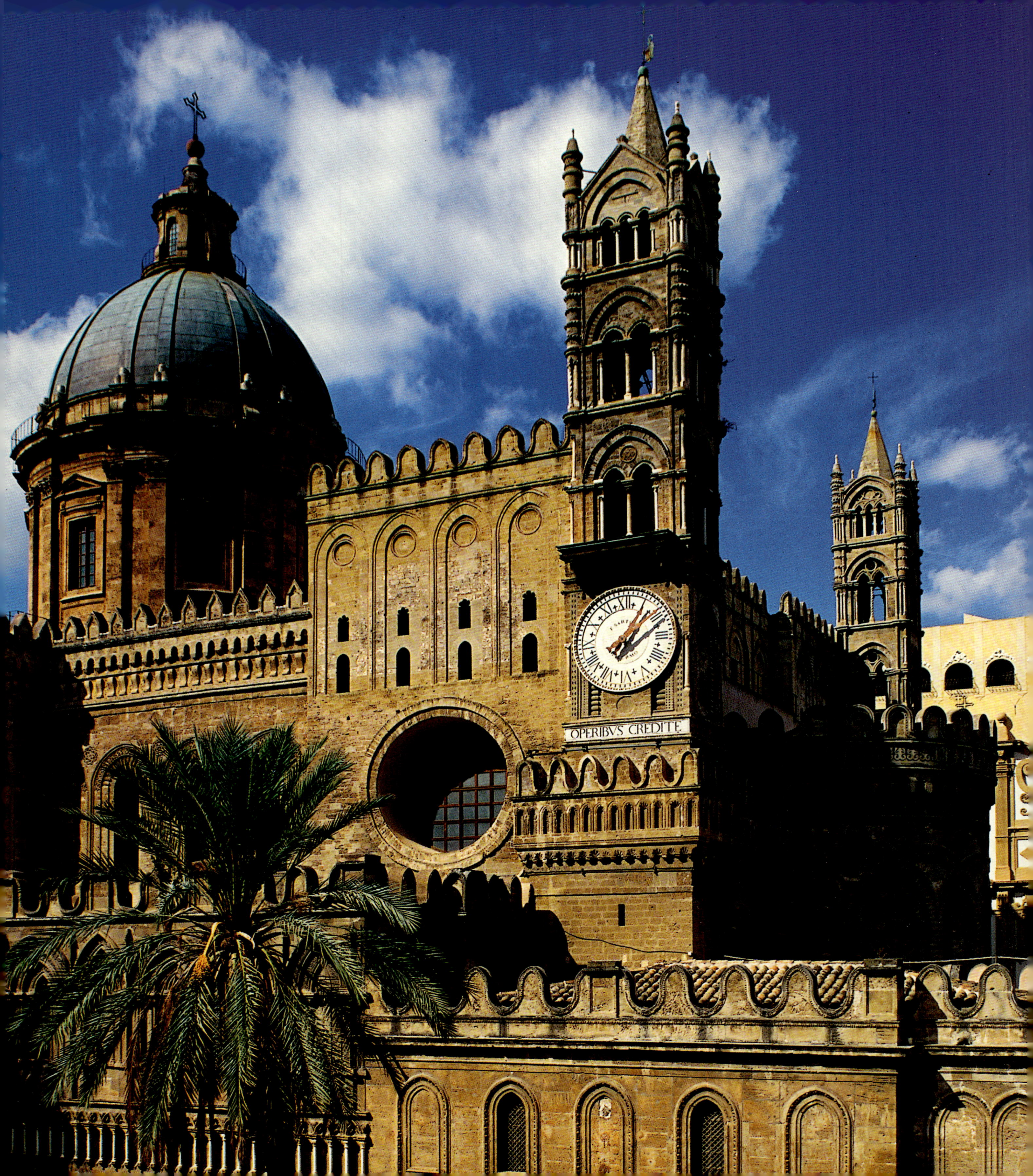
OPERIBVS CREDITE

ARABS AND NORMANS
IN SICILY AND THE SOUTH OF ITALY

TEXTS BY
Adele Cilento
Alessandro Vanoli

RIVERSIDE BOOK COMPANY, INC.

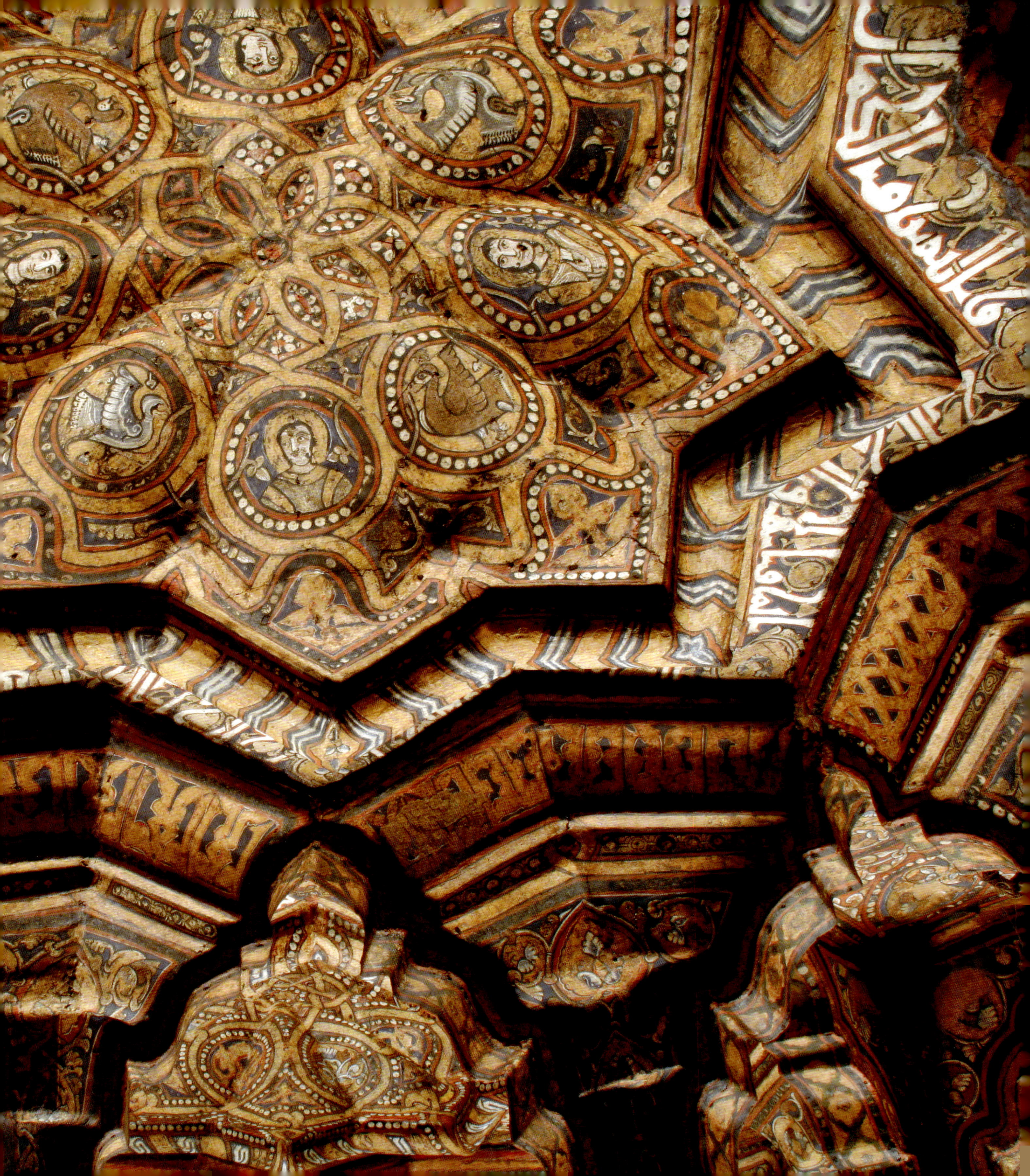

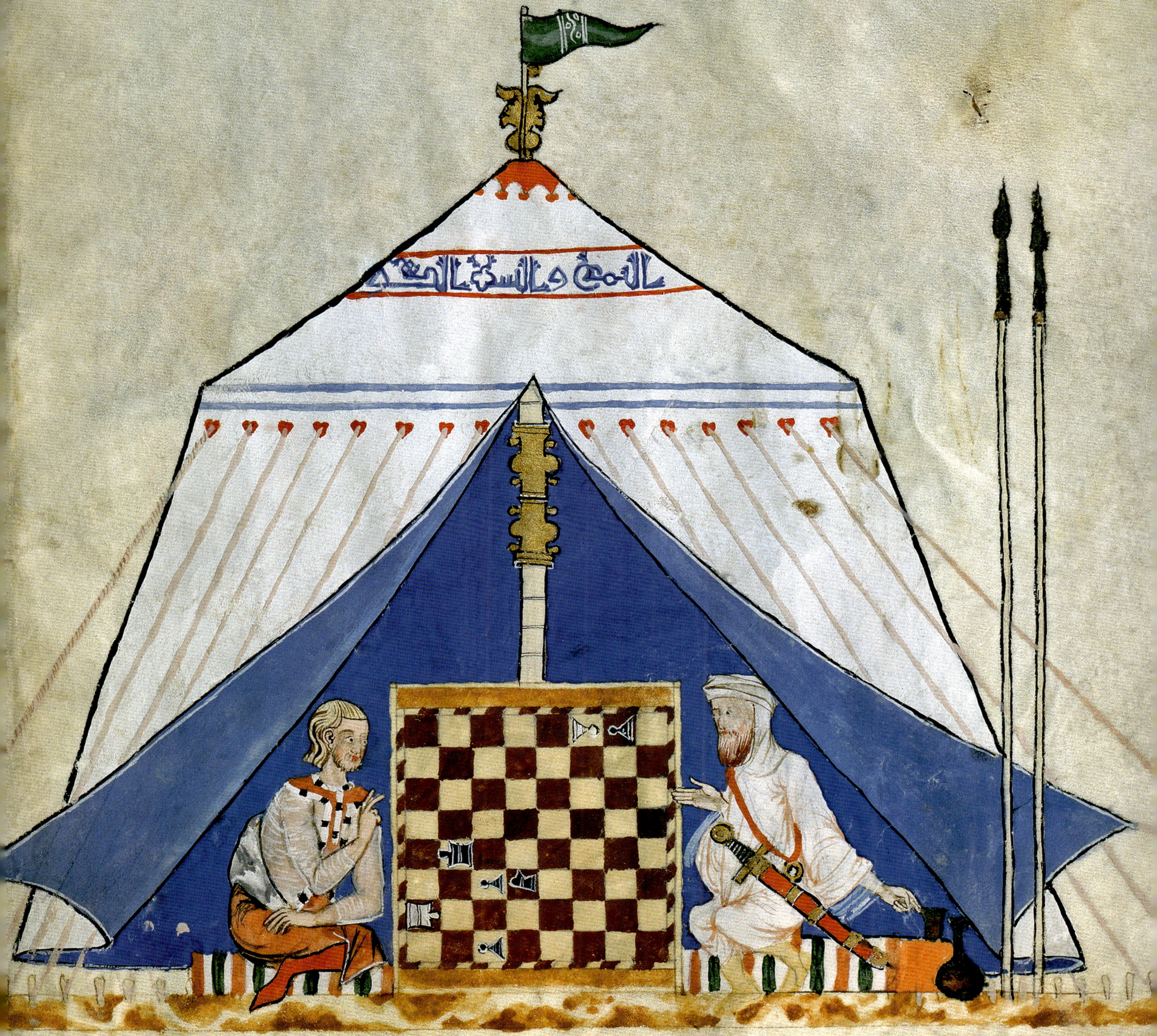

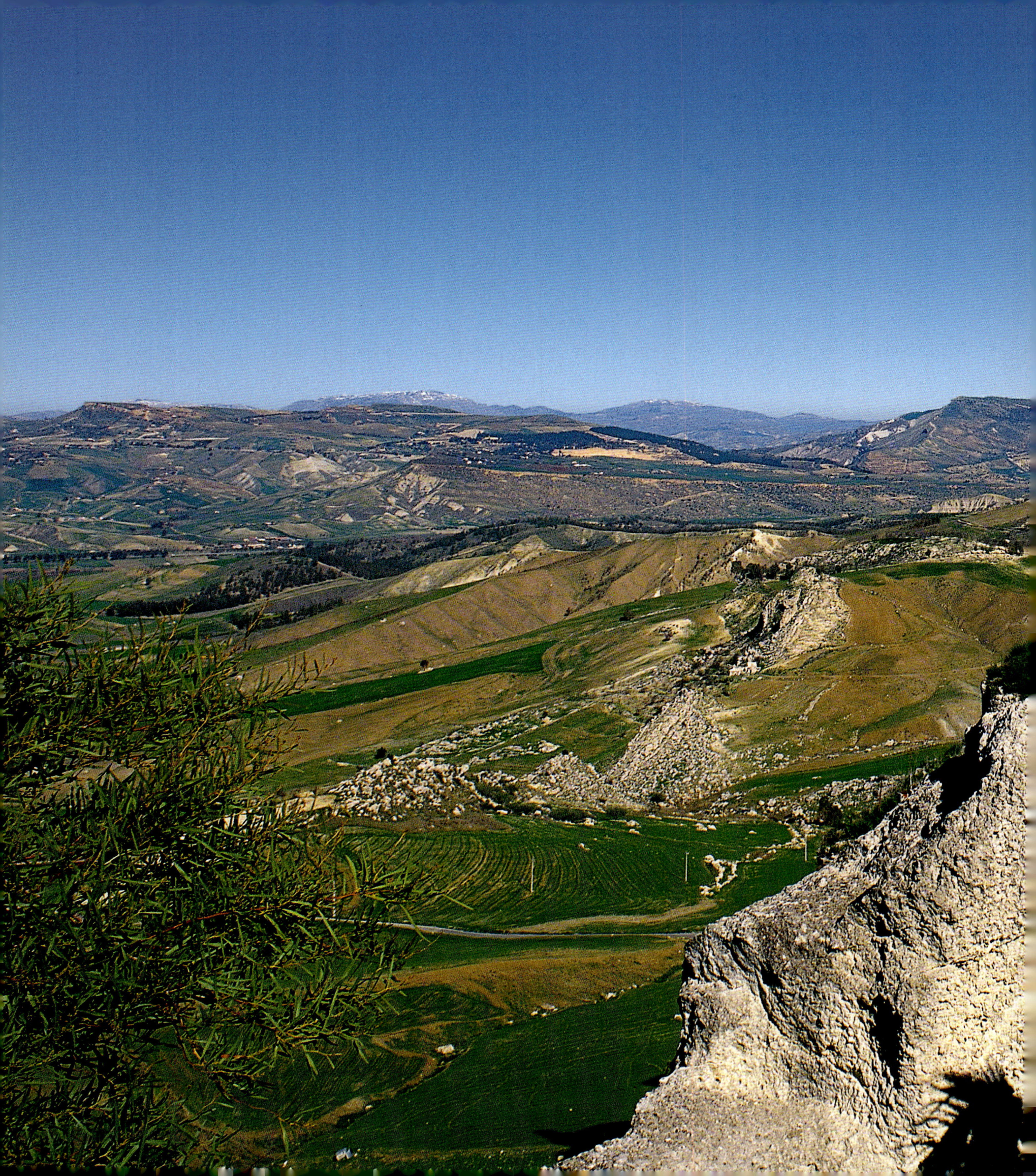

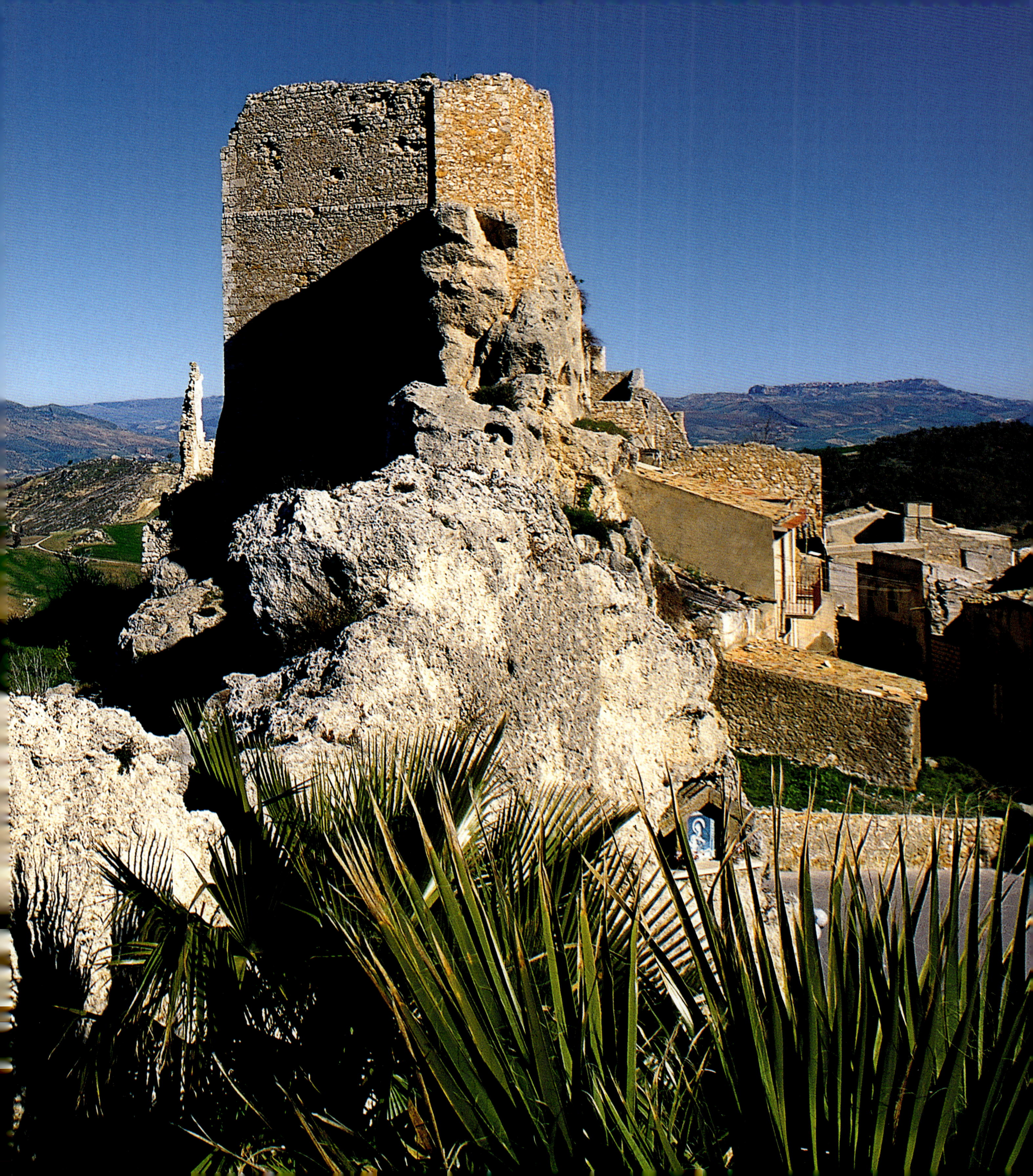

Editorial coordination
Luisa Chiap

Editor
Jessica Basso

Layout and design
Gianfranco Casula

Photolithography
Studio RGB

Printing
Lito Terrazzi

Translation
Brian Eskenazi

Printed in Italy.

© 2007 Magnus Edizioni
SpA, Udine, Italy.

First published in Italian in 2007.

English-language translation © 2007
Riverside Book Company, Inc., New York.

All rights reserved throughout the world.
Reproduction of the text and illustrations,
in whole or in part, forbidden except by
written permission of the publisher.

Riverside Book Company, Inc.
P. O. Box 237043
New York, NY 10023
www.riversidebook.com
info@riversidebook.com

ISBN 10: 1-878351-66-4
ISBN 13: 978-1-878351-66-1

TABLE OF CONTENTS

17   MUSLIM SICILY
by Alessandro Vanoli

21   *The Mediterranean in the Ninth Century and the Arrival of Islamic Rule*
29   **THE CONQUEST**
37   **FROM THE FATIMIDS TO THE KALBIDS**

49   *Sicily and the Expanse of the Islamic Mediterranean*
60   **THE SOCIETY OF MUSLIM SICILY**
76   **POWER AND MILITARY ORGANIZATION**
83   **MUSLIM SICILY AND OTHER CULTURES**
92   **ARAB CULTURE AND SCIENCE IN SICILY**

107   *The Memory of Muslim Sicily*

141   NORMAN SICILY
by Adele Cilento

143   *The Peoples of the North in the Ninth and Tenth Centuries: From Scandinavia to Italy*
144   **THE MEN OF THE BAYS AND FJORDS**
145   **SEAMEN AND MERCHANTS, FARMERS AND WARRIORS**
153   **THE DISCOVERY OF NEW LANDS**
157   **FROM NORMANDY TO THE SOUTH OF ITALY**

165   *Knights in Conquest of the South*
166   **FROM MERCENARIES TO PRINCES: THE BEGINNINGS**
171   **THE STAGES OF THE CONQUEST: APULIA, CAMPANIA, AND CALABRIA**
176   **RELATIONS WITH THE CHURCH AND THE ALLIANCE WITH THE POPE**
185   **THE CONQUEST OF SICILY AND THE RULE OF THE GREAT COUNT**
197   **WOMEN AND POWER**
200   **CATHEDRALS, CITIES, AND CASTLES**

239   *The Kingdom of a Thousand Colors*
240   **THE REUNIFICATION OF THE KINGDOM OF SICILY**
246   **THE IMAGE OF THE SOVEREIGN**
251   **A COSMOPOLITAN AND ELEGANT COURT**
258   **STYLES: NORDIC SHAPES, ARABIC LINES, BYZANTINE LIGHT**

287   *Heirs and Descendants*
288   **THE LAST NORMAN RULERS**
294   **THE LAST RADIANCE OF AN EXTRAORDINARY ARTISTIC ADVENTURE**

308   *Bibliography*

MUSLIM SICILY
Alessandro Vanoli

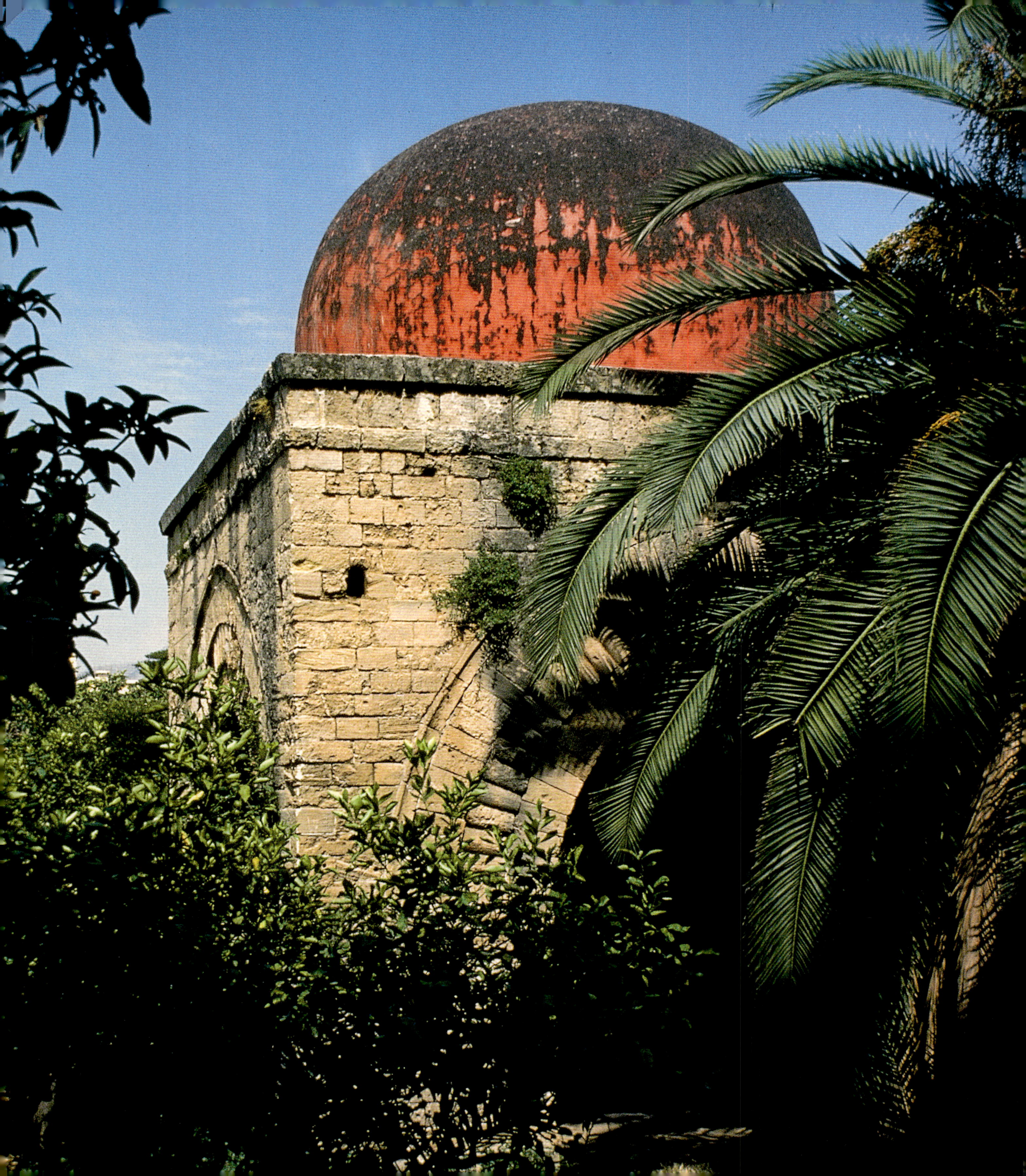

I think of Sicily and the memory brings pain to my heart.
A place of youthful folly, now desolate;
    enlivened once by the flower of noble minds.
If I am expelled from paradise, how do I tell of it?
If my tears were not bitter,
    I would believe them to be the rivers of that paradise.

These lines are by the Arab poet Ibn Hamdîs. The island of which he sings was his native country. Over the course of the eleventh century Sicily fell almost completely into Norman hands and there were many like him who sought refuge elsewhere, to the south and the east, in Muslim territory. Nothing of that Muslim world is left except ruins and ancient memories. For a long time, the Christian rulers of Sicily would welcome Muslim art and culture. In the history of its cities and countryside, and in its language, Sicily would hear the echo of its Arab past to a greater extent, perhaps, than even Ibn Hamdîs could have imagined. But that is quite understandable. Two centuries had passed since the arrival of the Arabs in Sicily, and during that time new cultural ideas took root, new customs came in contact with older traditions, and a new Mediterranean-based outlook contended with other, older, ways of looking at the world.

The pages that follow will speak of all these things, beginning two hundred years earlier when the island was still Byzantine territory and the southern and eastern coasts of the Mediterranean witnessed great and rapid change.

opposite page:
One of the distinctive small bright red cupolas on the church of San Giovanni degli Eremiti that adorn Palermo, a city known as "La Felicissima" and "La Splendida" ("the most fortunate" and "the splendid") during the time of Arab and Norman rule from 831 to 1189.

preceding page:
Bottom of a glazed ceramic cup made from artificial silica paste, specially cut and inserted as an ornament on the ambo, or pulpit, of San Giovanni del Toro in Ravello, Salerno. The dense ornament contains the blessing or praise of God known in Arabic as al-baraka, *with letters in Kufic script.*

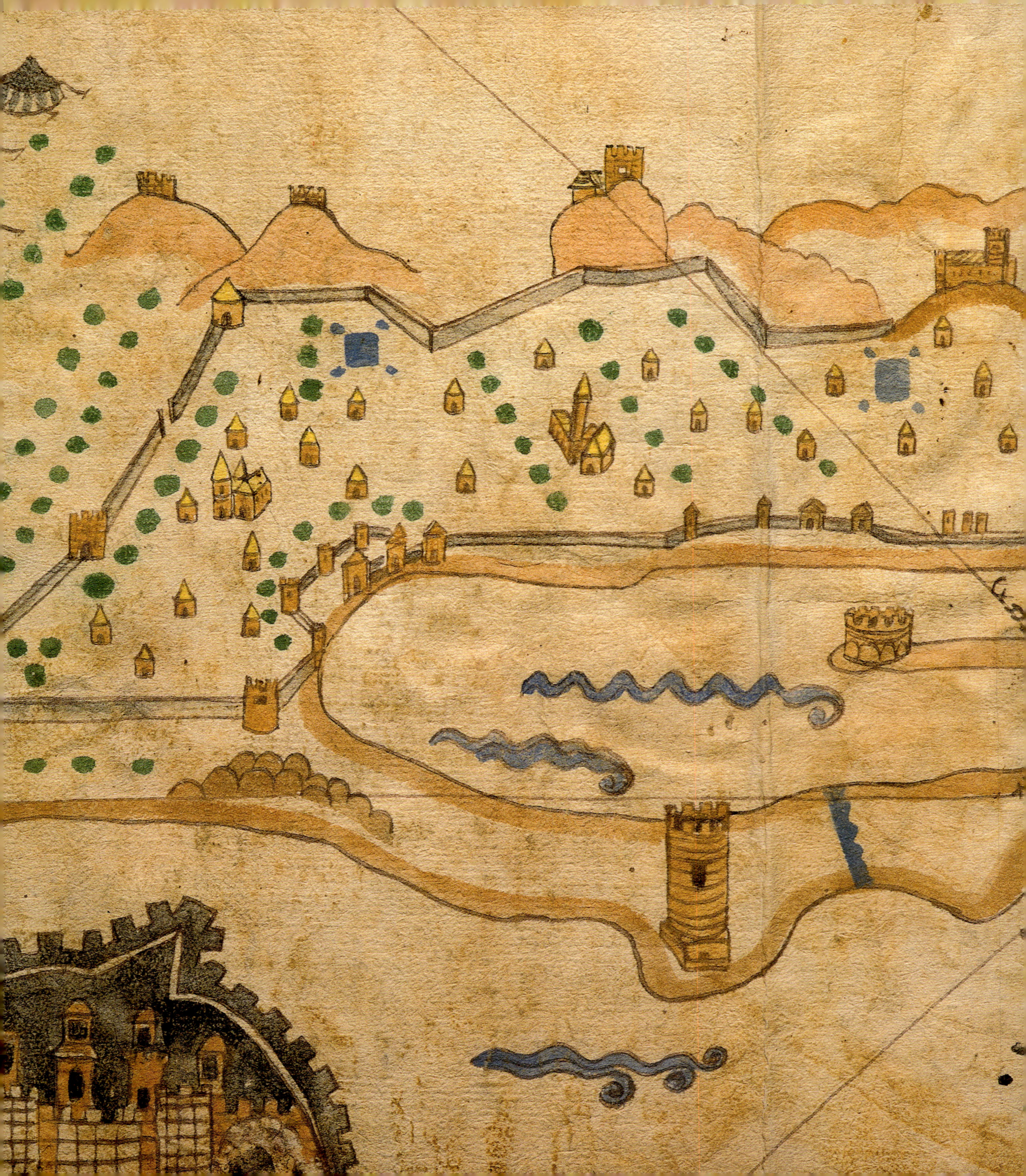

THE
MEDITERRANEAN
IN THE NINTH
CENTURY AND
THE ARRIVAL OF
ISLAMIC RULE

THE MEDITERRANEAN IN THE NINTH CENTURY
AND THE ARRIVAL OF ISLAMIC RULE

First a Roman sea and then a Byzantine one, and the destination of Germanic tribes from the north in search of conquest, the Mediterranean between the sixth and seventh centuries was many things simultaneously. It saw and helped make possible dramatic transformations, but also experienced considerable continuity. For a long time, the emphasis was on what had survived from the Roman empire. In the Mediterranean of the early Middle Ages, some have seen a coherent world that was basically a single unit, deeply marked by the heritage of Greece and by a new, emergent Christian identity. Others more readily find evidence of progressive splits and breakups, and in the Gothic hordes of North Africa and Spain have preferred to see a foreshadowing of the arrival of Islam.

However one looks at it, events in the East were destined to change many aspects of the status quo in the Mediterranean and elsewhere. The preachings of Muhammad culminated in the establishment of the first, restricted Muslim community, centered on the Arab oasis of Yathrîb, which would later be known as Medina: the city, par excellence, of the Prophet. It was the year 622, and within little more than a century Islam would reach the entire known world.

Muslim expansion was swift. In 639 the Byzantines were defeated on the Yarmuk river near the Sea of Galilee. Two years later a victory at Fustat, near present day Cairo, opened the door to North Africa. The conquest of Visigothic Spain began in 711, while a defeat at the hands of a Chinese army on the Talas river in 751 marked the limits of Islam's eastward advance. These few dates are enough to give the measure of an epochal change: in the space of a century the Islamic world had become an empire.

In this phase of rapid expansion, two dynastic caliphates were preeminent, one following the other. The first dynasty, that of the Umayyads (651-750), transferred the center of Muslim power eastward from Arabia and made Damascus its capital. The dynasty of the 'Abbasids, which came to power in 749 after a bloody internal struggle, moved the political and economic center still further east. The founding of Baghdad as their new capital in 763, on the order of Caliph al-Mansûr, was a clear sign of this trend. Under the 'Abbasids, the Islamic world solidified itself. Its external borders

Fustat: the Fatimid cavalry attacks a fortress. Painting on paper, fragment, from the end of the eleventh century, British Museum, London. Al-Fustat was the name of the early urban center that, beginning in the tenth century, became Cairo. Similar to Kairouan, it was a misr, *which in Arabic indicated a fortified camp.*

preceding pages:
A depiction of the Muslim siege of Messina in the year 843 from a handwritten map of the twelfth to thirteenth century. Collezione Giulio Torta, Palermo.

were strengthened, and internal threats, both political and religious, were contained. At the same time a centralized political structure took shape ever more clearly, one which owed not a little to the earlier imperial models of Byzantium and Persia. It began to be thought of as an empire. The world was divided into two areas: a *dâr al-islâm*, or House of Islam, within which Muslim law was safeguarded and in force, and a *dâr al-harb*, or House of War, consisting of all the lands in which Muslim law was not in force and toward which should be directed all that effort of attraction, persuasion, and assimilation understood by the term *jihâd*.

Within such a large political area, the southern Mediterranean along the African coast was considered a distant province. Heading west from Egypt, the Arab conquerors entered the region of *Ifrîqiya*, which the Romans had called *Africa Proconsularis* and was located between Libya and Mauritania. From there, along the parallel strips of the mountain chains, relatively easy roads opened up and led to more western regions, the furthest of which was Maghrib al-Aqsa in present-day Morocco. The advance was rapid, but not always easy, not so much due to the weak defense of the Byzantines as to the protracted and stubborn resistance of the Berbers, who from

A page from the Kitab al-masalik wa al-mamalik, *or Book of the Roads and the Provinces, compiled between the tenth and eleventh centuries by the Arab geographer Abu Ishaq Ibrahim al Istakhri and today in the National Museum in Cairo. It shows the Tigris River, the Persian Gulf, and Baghdad. The points of the compass are represented by precious inscriptions in gold in Kufic characters at the corners of the manuscript.*

Damascus of the Umayyads, with the Great Mosque, one of the best and most famous examples of early mosques, built between 705 and 715 by Caliph al-Walid I.

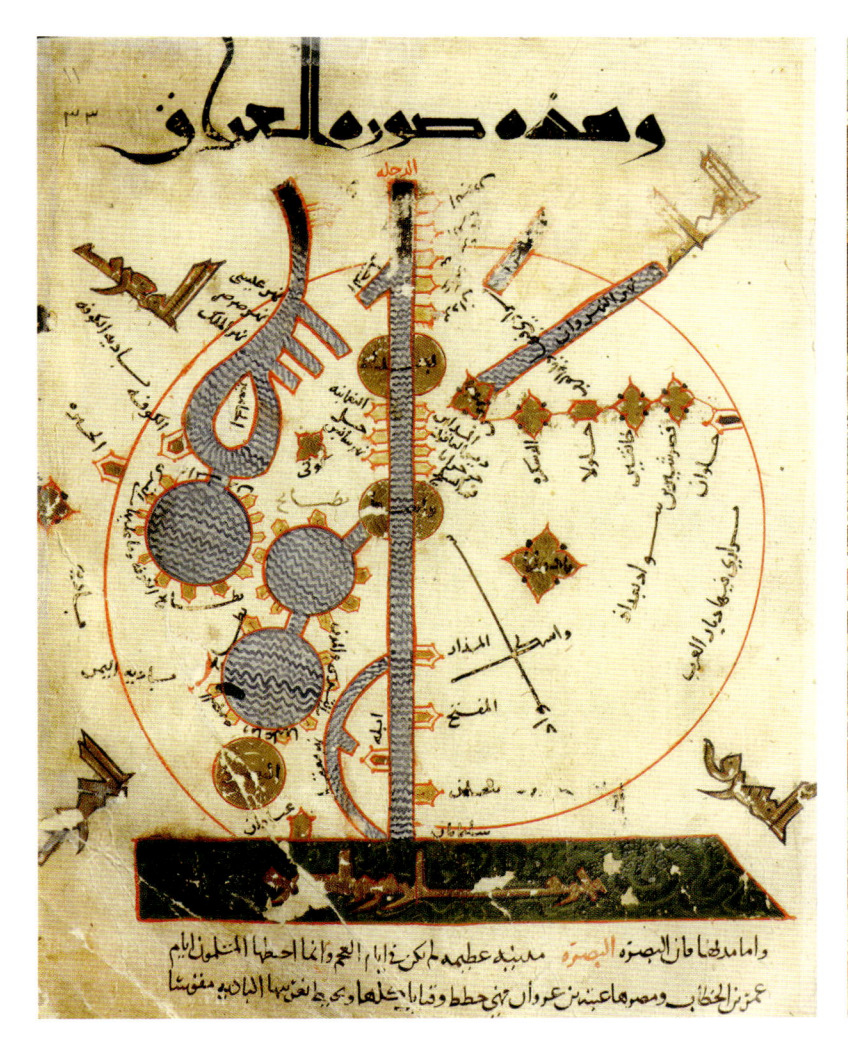

■ *in the 7th century*

■ *in the 8th century*

■ *in the 9th century*

■ *in the 10th and 11th centuries*

■ *temporary conquests*

The Arabian peninsula, already an important stop on the route between the Mediterranean and India, opened itself to the world with the advent of Islam. The biography of Muhammad reveals that his preaching took root and developed in a society devoted to trade and commerce. Given this environment and their wish to bring Muhammad's teachings even to the ends of the earth, as well as a desire for riches, Muslims became great scholars and travellers. They benefited from the heritage of the classical world and the Orient, drawing on Egypt, Greece, Iran, and India, thus becoming the official intermediary between antiquity and the modern world.

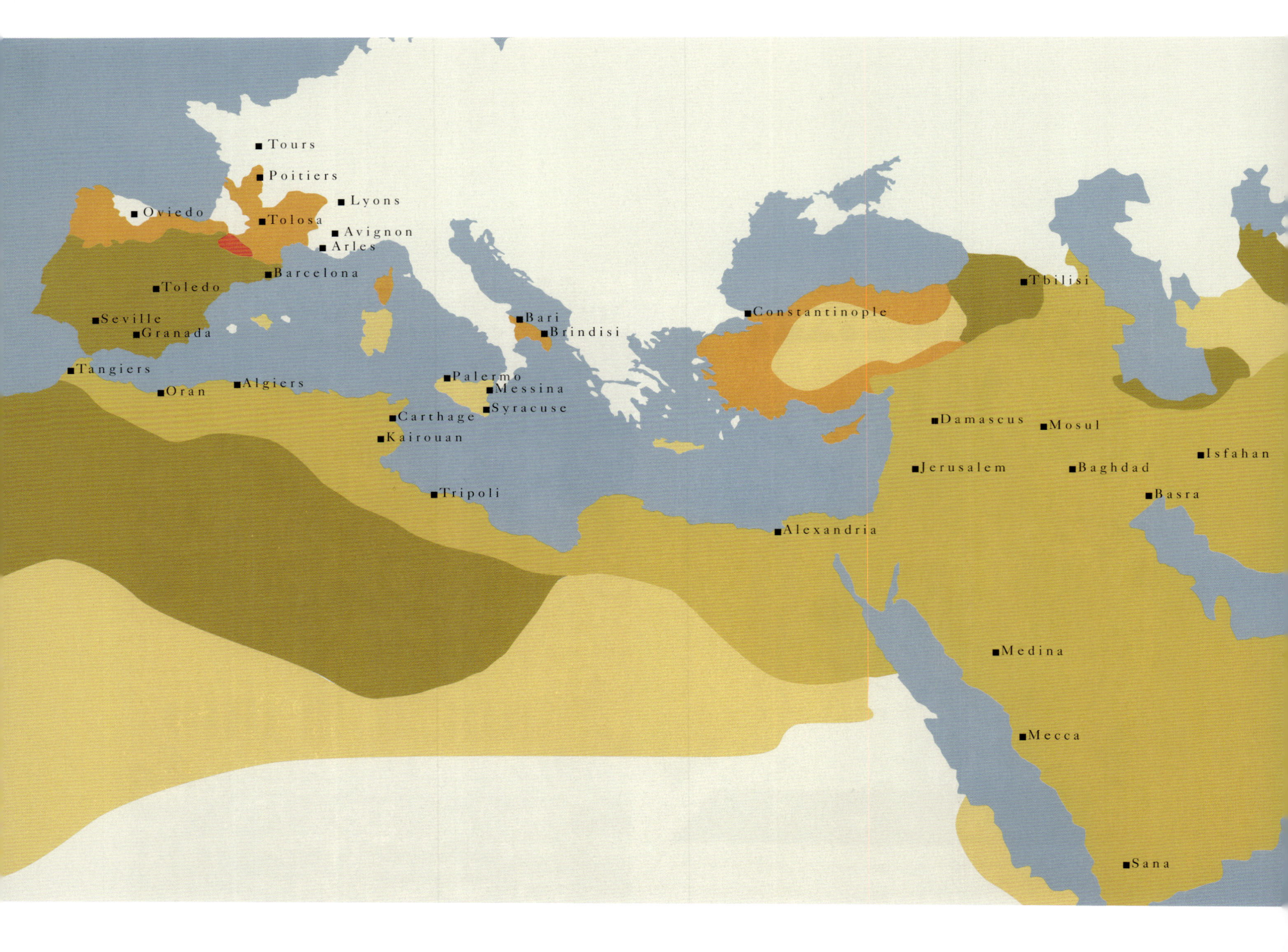

time immemorial had occupied the long strip that extends from Egypt to the Atlantic Ocean. The Arabs told and spread a legend according to which the Berbers had in Biblical times been subjects of Goliath, and that after Goliath had been killed by King David the Berbers emigrated westward. They were called *barbar*, or Berber, after the Greek word *bárbaros*, for barbarian, due to what seemed to be the inarticulate and incomprehensible sounds of their strange speech.

With a tribal structure that split them into many small groups, and an animist faith, the Berbers would never be completely assimilated. While the Arab conquerors retreated to their cities and developed a refined civilization, from time to time among the mountain tribes and the tribes of the desert there arose groups determined to resist, sometimes with arms, their absorption by Islamic culture. In this, the history of Sicily would be no exception.

From the start, commerce fed the growth of the cities of the interior, especially those built on the caravan routes that crossed the Sahara such as Fez and Sijilmassa. The coastal areas grew more slowly, even though ports such as Alexandria, Mahdia, Tunis, and Bugia gradually became more important. Close by arose an extensive system of coastal defenses, meant to protect against attack by *Rûm*, or Rome, as the Byzantines were known. There was an uninterrupted chain of *rîbât*, fortifications whose inhabitants dedicated themselves to war as well as prayer. Near these structures numerous small ports sprang up, all mostly dependent on fishing, but also, more and

The ribat *of Susa, one of the most important ports in Tunisia, part of the region known as* Ifriqiya *during the Arab period. It was from here that Asad ibn al-Furàt sailed with his troops in order to conquer Sicily, accomplishing the last of the* futùh, *or conquests made in the west in the name of the religion of Muhammad.*

A true jewel among the places dedicated to prayer is the Zaouia di Sidi Sahab, *or the Mosque of the Barber, dedicated to the saint who accompanied Muhammad when he preached, and embellished on all its walls with stuccos, inlays, and majolica.*

more, on trade. Some stuck to coastal navigation, but others would steadily improve their ships, taking advantage of the two-masted rigging with a lateen, or triangular, sail that was used especially in the Mediterranean, and also of new techniques being developed by sailors on the Indian Ocean.

The population that went back and forth along these roads and sea lanes was necessarily mixed. Muslim domination led to the progressive Arabization of a heterogeneous world composed of descendants of the Romans and Greeks along with Berbers and Jews. Even more than the others, the Jews were linked by a reliable network of communication that covered the entire Mediterranean. These men and these Mediterranean connections would, at the start of the ninth century, become part of the history of Sicily.

Ship with a lateen sail, from a late thirteenth-century manuscript in the Museo de la Torre del Oro, Seville.

opposite page:
Arab galley, a miniature from Las Cantigas de Santa Maria *by Alfonso X el Sabio (1221–1284), in the Library of the Monastery of San Lorenzo, the Escorial, Madrid.*

Como os mouros sacaron o Conde da soutá da galea.

C. os mouros tornar o Conde a ssa ermida.

28 . ALESSANDRO VANOLI

THE CONQUEST

The actions that preceded the arrival of the Muslims are well-known, and they have their counterparts in the great events taking place along other coasts. In 526 the Goths lost Sicily for good, and the Byzantines arrived in force. For a long time, Sicily looked east to Byzantium and north to Rome. It was a frontier for both the soldiers of the emperor and for the church, which was very anxious about the religious life of the island and also about its great landed estates, as may be seen in the correspondence of Gregory the Great. This balance of power would long remain undisturbed, at least until the beginning of the eighth century when events came to a head with the struggle over iconoclasm, the ensuing clash with the papacy, and finally, in 751, the annexation by the patriarchate in Constantinople of the churches of Sicily and Calabria. The following years would thus witness a change in the liturgy from Latin rite to Greek, while the relationship between Sicilian monasticism and its Byzantine counterpart became ever closer. It is well-known but worth repeating that the Greek culture which permeated Sicily at that time would for many reasons survive the Islamic invasion. On the landed estates and in the organization of the church, its traces would be so deep and long lasting as to make some historians imagine a re-emergent Greek culture in Sicily of even greater antiquity and undiminished strength.

To the south, on the African coast, the situation in those years remained troubled. During the middle of the eighth century, while the caliphate was passing to the 'Abbasid dynasty, the Berbers continued their revolts, often linked to the spread of Kharijism, a strict schismatic movement that maintained, among other tenets, the right of Muslims to choose their own leaders, and which therefore allowed the Berbers to accept the new religion of Islam while at the same time rejecting domination by the Arabs.

It would take time for this world to stabilize itself. In 800 the 'Abbasid caliphs entrusted the emirate of Ifrîqiya to the head of the al-Aghlab family. The new governor and his heirs organized their kingdom according to the administrative practices of the Arabs as well as to the fiscal and monetary policies of the Byzantines. In the court were descendants of the invading Arabs, Islamicized Berbers, black slaves, and probably even some Christians and Jews. Under their rule, the region that ran from modern Libya to Algeria was notably prosperous: hydraulic works furnished water for agriculture and the cities, the great trans-Sahara trade routes were strengthened, and, naturally, expansion to other areas and coastal regions increased.

Since the start of Islamic expansion, Sicily had suffered various naval attacks originating first in Syria and then in Ifrîqiya. Towards the end of the eighth century, however, the

opposite page:
St. Gregory giving a benediction, from the Liber Regulae Pastoralis, *or* Book of Pastoral Rule, *by St. Gregory, in the Bibliotheque de Valenciennes.*

A page from the oldest and most important manuscript on Islamic engineering, the Book of the Knowledge of Mechanical Works, *compiled in 1206 by Al-Jazari, showing the invention of a water pump. Topkapi Museum, Istanbul.*

situation would grow relatively calm, due perhaps to the strength of Byzantine forces on the island and an improvement in its defenses. There may also have been an increase in offensive capability, if it is true that the great *rîbât* constructed at Monastir in Tunisia in 796 was meant to defend against Greek ships. The ninth century, in fact, opened with a truce meant to protect mutual commercial interests. Paradoxically, however, when an unexpected political act suddenly brought matters to a head, these mutual interests would result in war.

In the year 827 a Byzantine soldier of middle rank, a provincial official or *turmarch* named Euphemius, rebelled against the empire, sent a fleet that was under his command against Syracuse, and proclaimed himself emperor of Sicily. The chronicles of the time, both Greek and Latin, say that he did it for love of a nun, but the truth was presumably less romantic and had more to do with a period of great tension and revolts that Byzantium experienced in the first half of the ninth century. In any case, what is most important for us is that, in the end, Euphemius sought military aid at the court of the third Aglabid emir, Ziyâdat Allâh (d. 838), and asked him to intervene in Sicily.

According to the historical sources, the request was received with some perplexity, especially in view of the truce which, at least as a formality, remained in effect. The

The majestic ribat *in Monastir with its characteristic crenellated walls and watch tower, built in 796 and many times remodelled in order to make it impregnable to attack by enemy fleets.*

problem was resolved by the *faqîh*, or law experts, of Kairouan, in Tunisia, in particular by one Asad ibn al-Furât. He justified military action against Sicily on the basis of numerous treaty violations, injuries caused by Byzantine merchants, and harm done to Muslim prisoners. The result was a decision to conduct *jihâd* against the Byzantines in Sicily. This war allowed the Aglabids to employ the unruly Berber forces someplace other than Africa, and in a wider sense it became part of Islam's struggle with Byzantium for control over that part of the Mediterranean.

The invasion force was composed of Arabs, Berbers, and Andalusians. It would be commanded by that same Asad ibn al-Furât, and perhaps this was a way to assure the strict observance of the rules of *jihâd*. On June 18, 827 the Muslims disembarked in Sicily at Mazara, and the Arab chronicles, perhaps exaggerating a bit, relate that there were almost one hundred ships and some ten thousand men.

It is almost certain that their first encounter with Byzantine forces was on a plain to the west of Corleone. Shortly after came the start of the exhausting siege of Syracuse, which would be resisted for almost fifty years with the help of the navies of Byzantium and Venice. But meanwhile, in the years that followed, the Muslims spread out over the rest of Sicily. Palermo fell in 831, after almost a year of siege which decimated the population. According to the rules of *jihâd*, the governor of the city

The Arab occupation of Sicily.

following pages:
Battle scene between Christians and Muslims, in folio 4 of the thirteenth-century Latin manuscript Secreta Fidelium Crucis *by Marino Sanudo. Biblioteca Nazionale Marciana, Venice.*

...tem ... dicas na...
...sta ... ṗpanoꝛū...

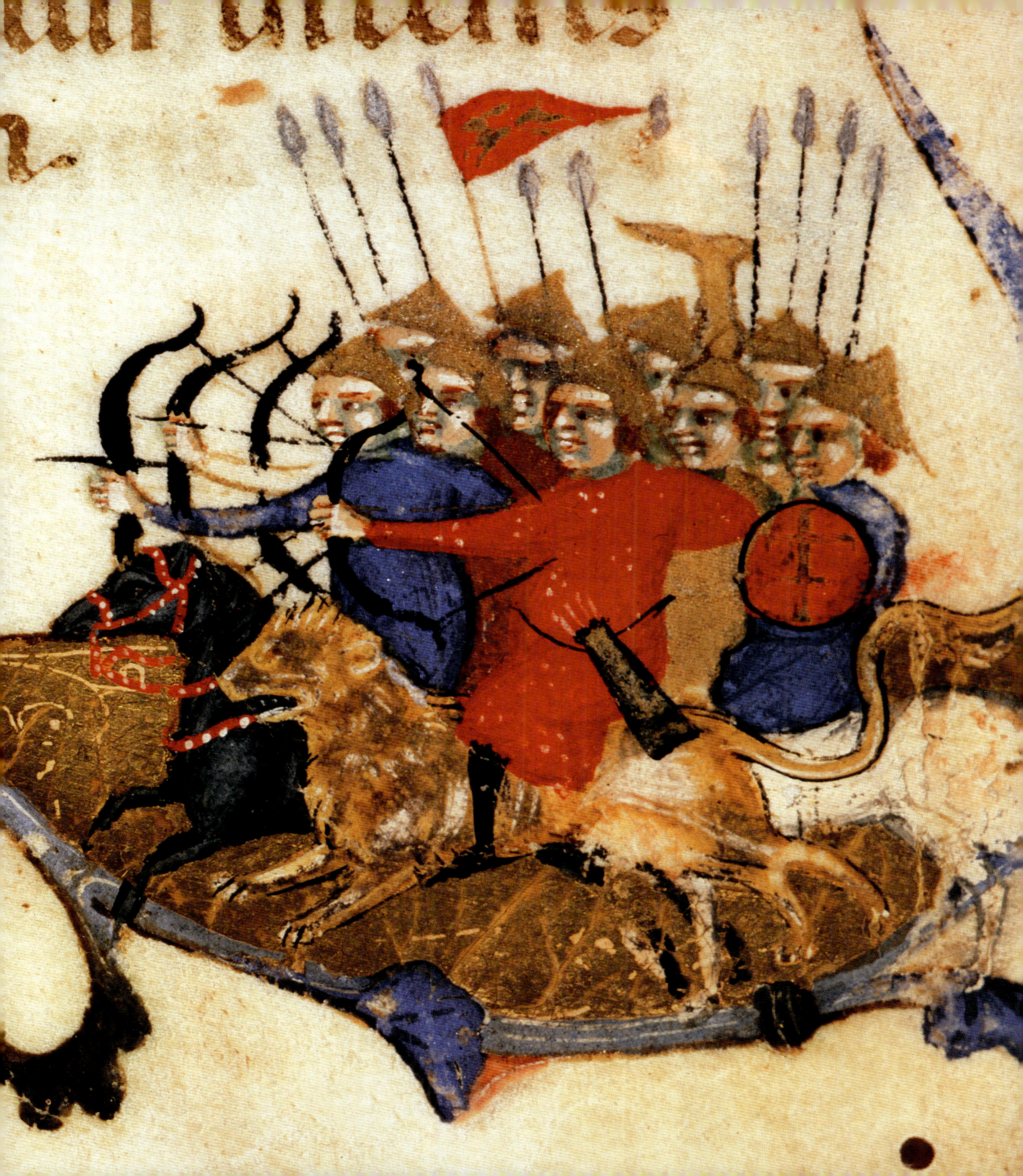

asked for and received the *amân*, or capitulation terms, and then, along with a bishop named Luca and others, he left for Greek territory. According to the historian Ibn al-Athîr, there were some sixty thousand men in Palermo at the start of the siege, and little more than three thousand when it was over.

Making their capital in Palermo, the Muslims set up their first new institutions and the governor, Muhammad ibn 'Abd Allâh (832-835), a cousin of the emir of Kairouan, began to coin money. Meanwhile, military activities elsewhere in Sicily continued and sieges were laid to the cities of Castrogiovanni and Cefalù. Sometime around 842 Arab control of western Sicily became secure. It was in this period that the Muslims began to raid the Italian mainland, entering almost immediately into the political intrigues of the time. Among the first on the mainland to deal with the new rulers of Palermo was probably Andrea, the duke of Naples, who obtained assistance against his rival Sicardo, the prince of Benevento. The Muslims pushed to the Tyrrhenian Sea and the southern Adriatic. Around 838 they sacked Brindisi and, some two years later, occupied Taranto. During this period they made heavy use of naval forces and sometimes plundered the Italian coasts. Still remembered are the sacks of Ponza and Ischia, and, above all, the sack of Rome that took place on August 23, 846. The brief existence of the emirate of Bari also dates to this period, and not by chance: it was as independent of Palermo as it was of Kairouan, and survived on the mainland from 847 until 871.

Meanwhile, in Sicily, the conquest continued. Castrogiovanni, one of the strongest of the Byzantine fortresses, capitulated in 859. In 864 it was the turn of Noto, and, the year following, of Troina. These were years of conquest but also of internal turmoil. In 869 the Muslims occupied Malta and secured a strategic naval base, but in the same period the chronicles note the death of several governors. Murders and upheavals were

Gold solidus *coin with Sicard of Benevento, recto. Sforza Castle, Municipal Numismatic Collections, Milan. Sicard became prince of Benevento in 832 and was its last ruler before it split in two. The principality included a large part of southern Italy known as Langobardia Minor. After Sicard's assassination in 839, Benevento descended into a dark period of civil wars that lasted until a final breakaway from Beneventan rule by the new principality of Salerno.*

opposite page:
The Great Mosque of Kairouan, Tunisia, built during the ninth century. After its surrender to the Muslims in 831, Palermo became the seat of the new military and civil government, although all of the officials were chosen in Kairouan and then sent to Sicily.

MUSLIM SICILY . 35

Arab cavalry; a panel from Las Cantigas de Santa Maria *by Alfonso X el Sabio (folio 112r).*

perhaps connected to revolts by the Berbers; the historical sources for this period are full of gaps.

Despite this disorder, the Muslims were subsequently able to consolidate their positions. On May 21, 878 the siege of Syracuse finally ended. This last great Byzantine stronghold on the island fell after tremendous suffering, as told by the Byzantine chronicler Teodosio Monaco and confirmed by the Arab chronicler Ibn Athîr:

> "…they besieged the city for nine months; then they stormed it, killed many thousands of men, and took much plunder, more than in any other city. Of the Christians of Syracuse there survived only a few."

The Muslim troops proceeded to occupy the Val Demone, in the northeast corner of Sicily, despite continued internal disorder. In 900 a new and more violent clash between Arabs and Berbers broke out. The revolt was put down by the arrival on the island of Abû l-Abbâs 'Abd Allâh, the son of the Aglabid emir Abû Ishâq Ibrahîm (d. 901). The rebels were crushed and the new ruler took possession of Palermo on September 18, 900. By now the invasion was for the most part finished. Somewhat less than two years later, in 902, the fall of Taormina at the hands of Ibrahîm II would mean that all of Sicily had been delivered to the Muslims.

FROM THE FATIMIDS TO THE KALBIDS

By the start of the tenth century, the 'Abbasid caliphate was already in decline, and from a political point of view the Muslim world began to break up into a series of relatively independent territories. North Africa saw the rise of the Fatimid dynasty (909-1171), which came into being on a current of religious Ismailism. This doctrine, which derived from Shiite Islam, had strong political and social elements as well as religious ones. Its adherents were in expectation of a renewal of Islam through the appearance of a *mahdî*, an eschatological guide who would lead Islam into an era of greater justice. This idea would meet great acceptance throughout the *dâr al-islâm*, especially in North Africa. The Aglabids there, who supported the 'Abbasids, gave way to an onrush by the Kutâma Berbers, who supported the Fatimids and their proclamation of an independent caliphate in Baghdad. This launched a new polity in the Mediterranean, one which found its strongest adversary in the emirate of al-Andalus in Spain. It was not an accident that the Muslims of Spain proclaimed their own independent caliphate just a few years later.

The first Fatimids arrived in Sicily in 910 and they soon found it necessary to deal with revolts by those Muslims who, especially in Palermo, had remained loyal to the preceding Aglabid dynasty. The rebellion, as usual, turned into a battle between Arabs, who were loyal to Baghdad and the Sunni tradition, and Berbers, who in large part were loyal to the Fatimids. It was during this struggle that a man named Ibn Qurhub rose to prominence. He was a well known native of Palermo loyal to the Aglabids who placed himself at the head of an uprising against the Fatimids. The uprising was initially, at least in the city, supported by Arabs as well as Berbers. For a brief period, fealty to the caliphate in Baghdad was restored and the government was back in Sunni hands. But it was only a brief period: already by 915 and 916 the Muslims of Agrigento had begun to challenge his authority. The revolt spread rapidly, and, finally, for Ibn Qurhub his fate was clear: departure from the city, perhaps voluntarily, and then, in 917, death at the hands of the Fatimids. But the uprisings continued. In 937 there was a new rebellion in Agrigento and also one in Palermo. It was precisely because of this turbulent situation that the new Fatimid ruler of the capital, Khalîl ibn Ishâq, considered it wise to build new fortifications. So, in 937, he began construction of the Khalîsa ("the chosen one," or "the one reserved for the ruler") in an area near the port. It was a new residence for the Fatimid governor and a barracks for the military garrison. With an area of some twenty acres, set between the old city and the sea, it soon resembled a separate city with its own palaces, baths, and mosque. As is well known, it survives today as "la Kalsa," the name of a neighborhood in Palermo.

The history of those years is complicated and marked by new hotbeds of revolt and the corresponding reactions of the central government. In 939 Khalîl ibn Ishâq took

Two Arab soldiers; detail of a panel from Las Cantigas de Santa Maria *by Alfonso X el Sabio (folio 139r).*

Muslims attack Messina in 843; a page from the *Synopsis Historiarum* by John Skylitzes, twelfth century. Biblioteca Nacional, Madrid.

ποσερημίαν κεκαυμένος· τριαλοσίοισιν ἀπὸ τοῦ
οἱο·   αὐδον πεζῶν ὁρμησάντων μὲν δὲ βαίων
Φαλαντηριω· παρά τε τὸ πτολουκηνοσαιδιά
λουκαρχάδδονίων· ἀπελθόντες ἐμμεσονύκτι τὸ

σαρακηνοί

Καὶ μηδεραγαπὸ πολιν δὲ ἐξωρτοῦτο τιῆς πάδρον· ἀλ
λορισαν περὶ σαρακηνοί· ἀπεσωπεισκεδαζω·
μιλοισο καὶ κυκεμαφοροσιων· ειστό ϟ απ ο
ιεβολαδὲ τηγάρτη· καθ υγιειω ταμελκπε
καμιπιραμελεδανκοι ῥαδμιαντοσαρι

Caltavuturo, Collesano, and Sclafani by storm, occupied Mazara, and laid siege to Caltabellotta. In 940 he accepted the surrender of Agrigento. Just these few dates give some idea of how complicated those years of Muslim rule were. In fact, this situation ended with a change in the ruling dynasty. In 947, in the face of continued rebellion, the Fatimid caliph decided to send emir al-Hasan ibn 'Ali al-Kalbî to Sicily. This was the start of the hereditary emirate of the Kalbids (948-1053), under which Sicily enjoyed a period of relative peace and considerable prosperity, along with great building and city planning projects and a flowering of literature and art.

Within a few years the situation on the island had stabilized and al-Hasan resumed the *jihâd* against Byzantium with great vigor, both in Sicily and on the Italian mainland. Between 962 and 963 he subdued the mountainous region south of Messina for good. Then it was the turn of Taormina, which had earlier come under Christian control. The city fell in December 962 and was renamed al-Mu'îzziya in honor of the Fatimid caliph. To the north, the Christians of Rametta (today's Rometta) asked the Byzantine emperor Nikephoros Phokas for help. The Byzantines clashed with the Muslims on the outskirts of Messina and suffered a disastrous defeat. Not long after, in 965, Rametta was taken by storm. That which followed, it has been said, was a

A Muslim fighting in Sicily; detail of a thirteenth-century fresco in Tour Ferrande, Pernes les Fontaines, France.

opposite page:
Illustration for the maqamat *(a collection of adventure stories in rhythmic prose) in the tenth-century Arabic manuscript of al-Hariri Abu Muhammad. Osterrichische Nationalbibliothek, Vienna. In the Muslim world the most widespread and practical form of pictorial art was manuscript illustration. The oldest and richest miniatures that have come down to us are those that accompany the tales of al-Hariri, the fables of the* Panchatantra, *and Arabic translations of Greek scientific texts. These works, distinguished by their lively descriptions and charming naivete, also recall the carved caricatures of Romanesque architecture.*

MUSLIM SICILY . 41

وَقَالَ الْأَجَلْسَ إلَى أَن نَرُوقَ فَاكِهَةً وَنَشُوقَ مُفَاكَهَتِهِ جَلَسَ لَا غَنَامَ مَعَاشَرَ

لَا لَا لَنَا مَا يُحْضِرُهُ فَحِينَ سَفَرَ عَنْ أَدَابِهِ وَشَرَعَ فِي أَنْبَائِهِ عَرَفْتُ أَنَّهُ أَبُو زَيْدٍ

يَحْسُنُ مَلْهَى وَمَهُ قَلْبِهِ مَعَادَ مَا حِينَئِذٍ وَجَفَتْنِي فِي رُجْحَانِ سَاعِدٍ وَلَمْ أَدْرِ

بِأَيِّهِمَا أَنَا أَضْحَى وَجَهَا وَأَوْرَى مَرْجَى أَبَاسْفَادِهِ مِنْ دُجْنَةِ أَسْفَادِهِ أَمْ خَصِيبَ

رَحَالَهُ بَعْدَ إِمْحَالِهِ وَمَا قَفَتْ نَفْسِي إلَى أَنْ أَوْضَحَ خَتْمَ سِرِّهِ وَأَبْطَرَ دَاعِيَةَ بِشْرِهِ

A duel; *miniature from the Fatimid period. The miniature is particularly interesting as the means by which artists avoided the iconoclasm of Islam. The rules regarding the subjects that could be illustrated, which included plant life as well as both real and imaginary animals, are contained in the* hadith, *the oral traditions of Islam, and recall the laws regarding iconoclasm developed in Byzantium during the eighth century.*

opposite page:
Bowl with a painted glossy metallic decoration. This piece dates to twelfth-century Egypt and the Fatimid era. Removed from the church of San Sisto in Pisa, it is now in the Museo Nazionale in San Matteo. Its decorative technique was invented in Samarra. A metallic solution was spread out on the baked clay and then the piece was fired again under medium heat, producing brilliant red, brown and green tints. Here, the refined portrait of a drinker recalls the agreeable and elegant life at court that had such a great influence on the tastes of the Norman kings and which was depicted many times, especially in the muqarnas *on the ceiling of the Cappella Palatina.*

happy season: the Kalbids dedicated themselves to the fortification of some of the more important cities in Sicily and to their administrative organization. In 967 an armistice with Byzantium was signed. Furthermore, the Fatimid caliphs in Cairo were more and more preoccupied with matters in the East and therefore, while not loosening their hold on the loyalty of the Kalbids, they paid less attention to Sicily. In this way governors in Sicily such as the cultured Abû l-Futûh Yusuf (989-998) and his son Jâ'far (998-1019) were able to surround themselves with a court that was basically independent, with its own *wazîr*, ministers, and poets whose job it was to sing the praises of the governor (who they ever more frequently, and not by chance, addressed with the title *malik*, or king).

Nevertheless, that happy season was brief. At the beginning of the eleventh century, the Muslims began to suffer their first setbacks in southern Italy: at Bari in 1004 at the hands of Byzantium and Venice, and at Reggio in 1005 at the hands of Pisa. Then it was the turn of the internal rebellions which had never been completely suppressed and which for a long time had continued to flare up at regular intervals. This was the case with an uprising that broke out in Palermo in 1019 following a

MUSLIM SICILY . 43

44 . ALESSANDRO VANOLI

heavy increase in taxes and which led to the removal of Jâ'far and his replacement by his brother Ahmad al-Akhal (1019–1038).

Further complicating the picture was a clash with the Zirid dynasty, which arrived from North Africa where they ruled on behalf of their Fatimid overlords. During this period the Byzantines renewed their attacks. In 1038 Syracuse was taken after a siege and the Zirid ruler 'Abd Allâh asked for help from Berber mercenaries in Africa, making things even more chaotic.

It was in this turbulent political climate that various small independent states were formed. This was similar, if on a smaller scale, to what was occuring in Spain with the *reyes de Taifas*, the small kingdoms that came into existence following the civil war and fall of the caliphate there. After a series of battles and fratricidal disputes, Sicily was divided among various military commanders, an arrangement that lasted from 1040 to 1050. Trapani, Marsala, Mazara, and Sciacca were ruled by the *qa'id* Ibn Mankûd; Castrogiovanni and Agrigento were in the hands of Ibn al-Hawwas; and Catania and Syracuse were ruled by Ibn al-Thumnâ. According to the chronicles, it was Ibn al-Thumnâ, because of his thirst for power, who would deliver Sicily to the Normans.

It was in 1061, from Messina, that the new invasion began, although this time it was by men from the north. But the Muslim adventure in Sicily did not end with its conquest by the Normans. If it is true that some Muslim scholars left for North Africa, Spain, and the East, it is also true that many Muslims remained in Sicily. Besides the common people of Arab and Berber origin, these included intellectuals, men of letters, scientists, and jurists who would find prominent roles even in the new

A copper coin known as a follaro, *from the time of William II (1166-1189), produced in Messina. On the front is the head of a lion, on the back a palm tree with dates. The presence of large* follaro *coins in Syria allows its production in Messina to be linked to coins issued by the Turkoman princes of Asia Minor. Starting in the mid twelfth century, they minted a copper coin known as a* dirham *with the same diameter and weight of the* follis *minted in Byzantium, many of which have been found in Sicily, and of the large* follaro *with palm tree and lion of the Normans. The lion is a perfect symbol for the de Hautevilles, especially in contrast to the eagle of the Swabians. Museo Archeologico Nazionale, Naples.*

opposite page:
A fable from the Panchatantra, *in a precious Arab manuscript from the eighth century. Bibliotheque Nationale de France, Paris.*

opposite page:
Silk fragment, imitation Byzantine, made from cloth of Sassanian origin; eighth century. There are Mesopotamian motifs such as the lions and the Tree of Life; Islamic motifs such as birds of prey and the hunt for large feline animals; and Christian motifs such as the cross that ornaments the diadem worn by the hunters. Museo Sacro, Vatican City, Rome.

this page:
Detail of the oldest lining of the mantle of Roger II (1133-1134), definitely the product of a Sicilian workshop. There are three linings, all of red silk interwoven with silver and gold threads. The embroideries that decorate the hem embellish the garment, which opens as the wearer moves about. The figurative themes are connected to the ancient symbolic traditions of the Near East filtered through Christianity: the Tree of Life becomes the Tree of Good and Evil in which the serpent hid, and the birds remind us that we are in the Garden of Eden with Adam and Eve. Kunsthistorisches Museum, Vienna.

government. Other scholars would arrive later, some on the invitation of the new kings. Yet again, in other words, the history of Sicily coincided with the larger story of the Mediterranean. In the twelfth century, Arab-Islamic culture began to circulate widely, from one coast to another, originating in the Levant and using Spain and Sicily as its channels. It is well-known that to Arab travellers of the twelfth century Norman kings such as Roger II and William II gave the appearance of Muslim rulers: they used Islamic titles, spoke Arabic, and supported a refined court that bore the marks of Muslim culture and was frequented by Arab as well as Sicilian poets. The world that would later belong to Frederick II looked back on a past that was by then centuries old, and over an expanse that for some time had been much larger than just one island. Let us now speak of that large expanse, beginning again with the preceding Muslim centuries.

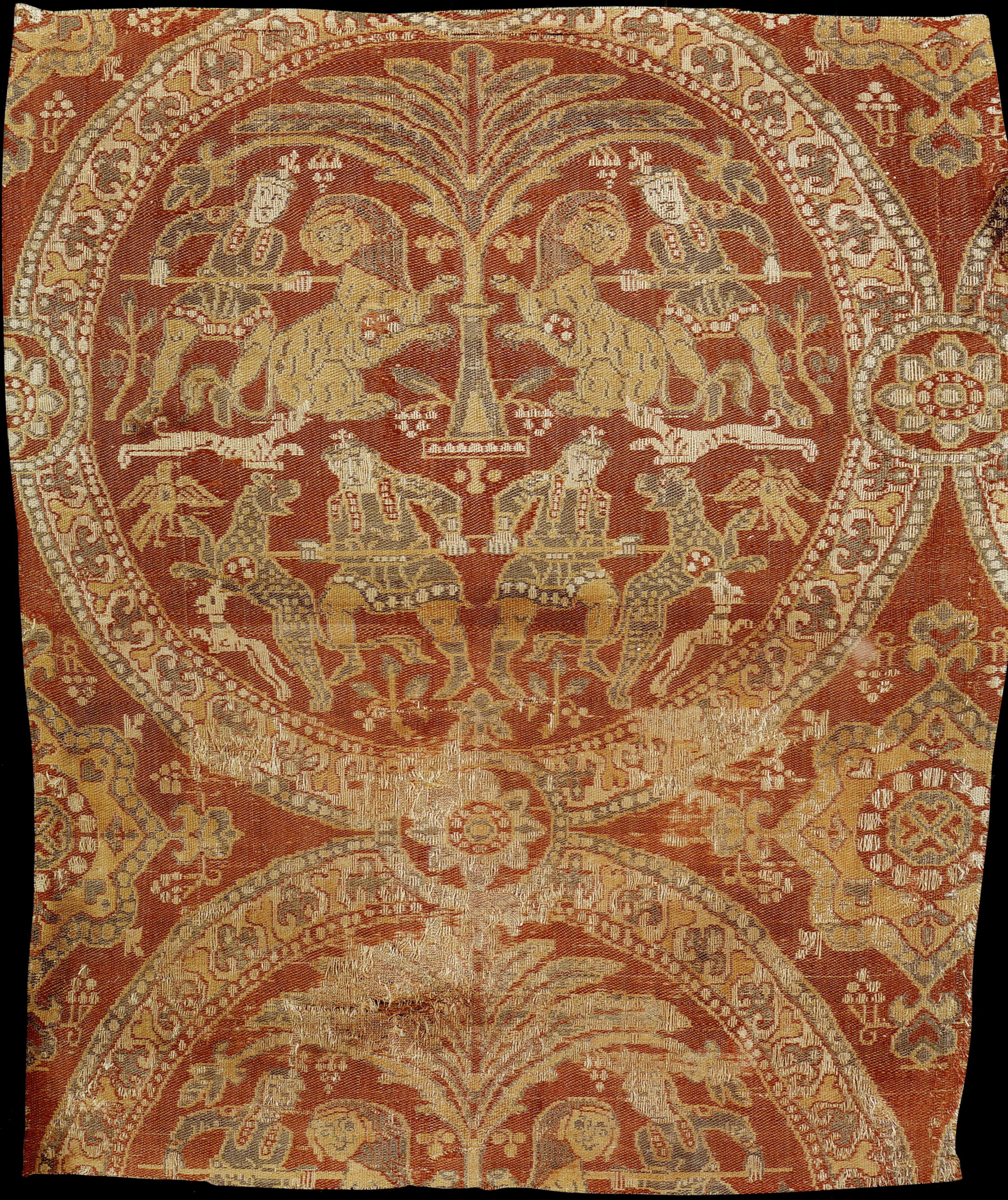

مشرق

صعاله راورال

حبر الاح كىز

النس الهند
الصعر
كمار الدل

SICILY AND THE EXPANSE OF THE ISLAMIC MEDITERRANEAN

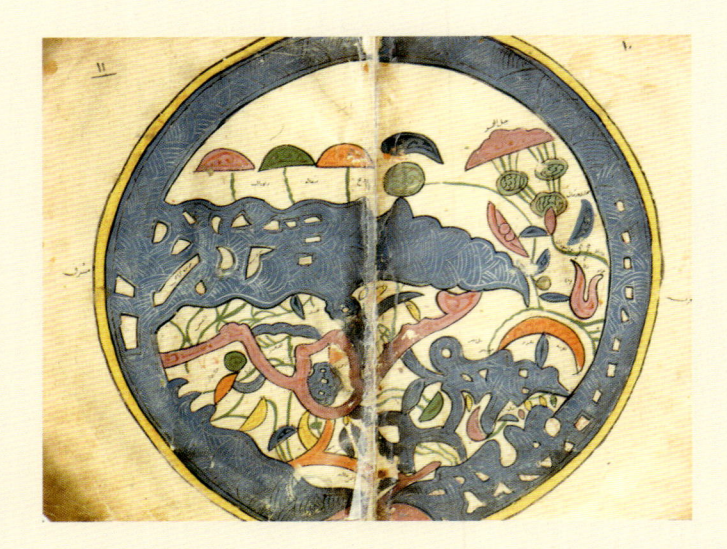

SICILY AND THE EXPANSE OF THE ISLAMIC MEDITERRANEAN

As we said earlier, following the Muslim conquest Sicily became part of the *dâr al-islâm* and was absorbed by an empire that stretched from India to the Atlantic Ocean. In a narrow geographic and administrative sense, however, the island became part of a zone that encompassed the entire strip north of the Sahara and extended to al-Andalus, the part of the Iberian peninsula that was under Muslim control. The Arab geographers called these areas *iqlîm* (sing. *qilîm*), after a word that was originally Greek. Sicily was therefore known as the *qilîm al-maghrib*, the western province of the Muslim world. Here in its entirety is a description of that zone by an important traveller of the tenth century, al-Muqaddasî:

> " It is a province of particular beauty, large, and rich; it possesses many cities and villages, its estates and vacation places are wonderful. Here the frontiers (*thughûr*) are secure, the fortifications (*husûn*) extensive, and the gardens places for amusement. There are many islands: among them al-Andalus, the excellent and marvelous; Tâhart, with a sweet and pure climate; Tanja (Tangiers), the far-off country; Sijilmâsa, the favorite and incomparable one; Isqiliyya (Sicily), the island that is the greatest of gifts; its people are in constant *jihâd*, but the wealth of the place remains intact. In the Maghreb, cities such as al-Basra are numerous, the inhabitants wish only prosperity for them, the ruler (*sultân*) is just, benevolent, and highly esteemed. "

Apart from any further investigation, it would be worthwhile to continue his suggestion (and that of most of his contemporaries) and strive to think in a coherent way about the history and institutions of an area that encompassed the Maghreb, Sicily, and Spain. This area was cohesive not only due to its geography but also because of its merchants, jurists, and men of culture, and even because of the Jews and Christians who at that time lived under Islam.

For many of them, as al-Muqaddasî again quickly reminds us, Sicily was always a *thaghr*, or frontier territory, that functioned as a kind of passageway, one of those special areas that bordered on the *dâr al-harb* and therefore on potentially hostile territories that were subject to Muslim attack, territories of, in a word, *jihâd*. In this period, around the tenth century, the term *thaghr* referred above all to two areas, at

Map of the world, by Abu Abdallah al-Idrisi (1099-1165), the famous Arab geographer active at the Norman court. The atlas is dated in the year 560 of the Hegira, or 1182 A.D., and is oriented to the south, in accord with a rule of Arab cartography that derives from Iran. National Library, Cairo.

preceding page: detail.

Map of Italy according to Idrisi. Contrary to modern practice, Arab geographers put south at the top.

opposite ends of the Mediterranean. In the east, it referred to areas north of Syria and in Mesopotamia that were opposite defensive lines established by the Byzantines in the Taurus mountains in modern-day southern Turkey. In the west, it referred to the area of al-Andalus that bordered on the northern Spanish kingdoms. But even Sicily was part of this group: opposite Messina was the province of Calabria, and further north loomed parts of the Longobard kingdom. From the Arab point of view, Sicily was the last region before the *dâr al-harb*. Al-Muqaddasî further emphasized that its inhabitants were in continual *jihâd*, even though, he added, it did not undermine the island's wealth.

The deep connection, or at least the perception of one, between Sicily and that part of the Muslim Mediterranean can also be seen in the meagre accounts of their travels that geographers such as al-Muqaddasî have left us. Lists of cities follow one after the other, each city seemingly the same, characterized perhaps by some sign that they are Muslim, above all by the minarets of the mosques, but more often noted for the presence of some source of supply for water or for the city walls. Fortresses, wells, and cisterns were perhaps the very foundation of the urban Islam which made its way along roads and caravan routes that were marked, in the geographers' accounts, by long days of marching:

> Atrâbinush (Trapani) is a city on the sea, situated in the west, and it is surrounded by walls; the inhabitants drink from a stream.
> 'Ayn al-Mughattâ (Canicattì) and Mazara are two cities situated in the west.
> Qal'a l-Ballût (Caltabellotta) is a fortified city situated high up; the inhabitants obtain water from a spring that flows in that place.
> Jirjant (Agrigento) is a city on the sea that is surrounded by walls; it drinks thanks to its wells.

الحر... بن... يكون على ساحله الأوجه الى... بنصل بطرطوسه الى بلاد الأندلس
وممتد على بلاد اني و... ما... لا... ترجي وادي اليمين يجزره جبل طارق
ثم ممتد على البحر المحيط الى سرس و... الى بلد... البحر ولوان زجلا سارس من
الصره على الساحل حي يعود الى الما... جاد به من ارض الاندلس حي اخلج ان يعبر هذا او خلصنا
ام كذا ع
وهذه صوره بحرالروم

MUSLIM SICILY . 53

Map of Italy according to Idrisi. In this detail, Sicily is clearly shown, in detail and complete, while the Italian peninsula is misshapen and difficult to make out. This is a result of the Ptolemaic system of the seven atmospheres, or heavenly zones, which makes it difficult to describe a country that lies in more than one zone.

opposite page:
The Mediterranean as seen by the Arabs in the eleventh-century manuscript of al-Istakhri. National Library, Cairo.

Buthîra (Butera) is a city on the sea, situated in the west, and surrounded by fortified walls, as if it were a fortress (*qal'a*).

Saraqûsa (Syracuse) consists of two attached cities; it has a magnificent port and is surrounded by a moat that is full of sea water.

Lantînî (Lentini) is surrounded by walls and is located on a stream, and it is near the sea; the buildings are all of stone.

Qatânia (Catania) is a city on the sea, situated in the south, and surrounded by walls. It is also known as Madînat al-Fîla (City of the Elephant).

Al-Yâj (Aci) is a city on the sea in the south that is surrounded by walls; it has running water.

Batarnû is a city in the east; it is at the bottom of the mountain where the fire flows.

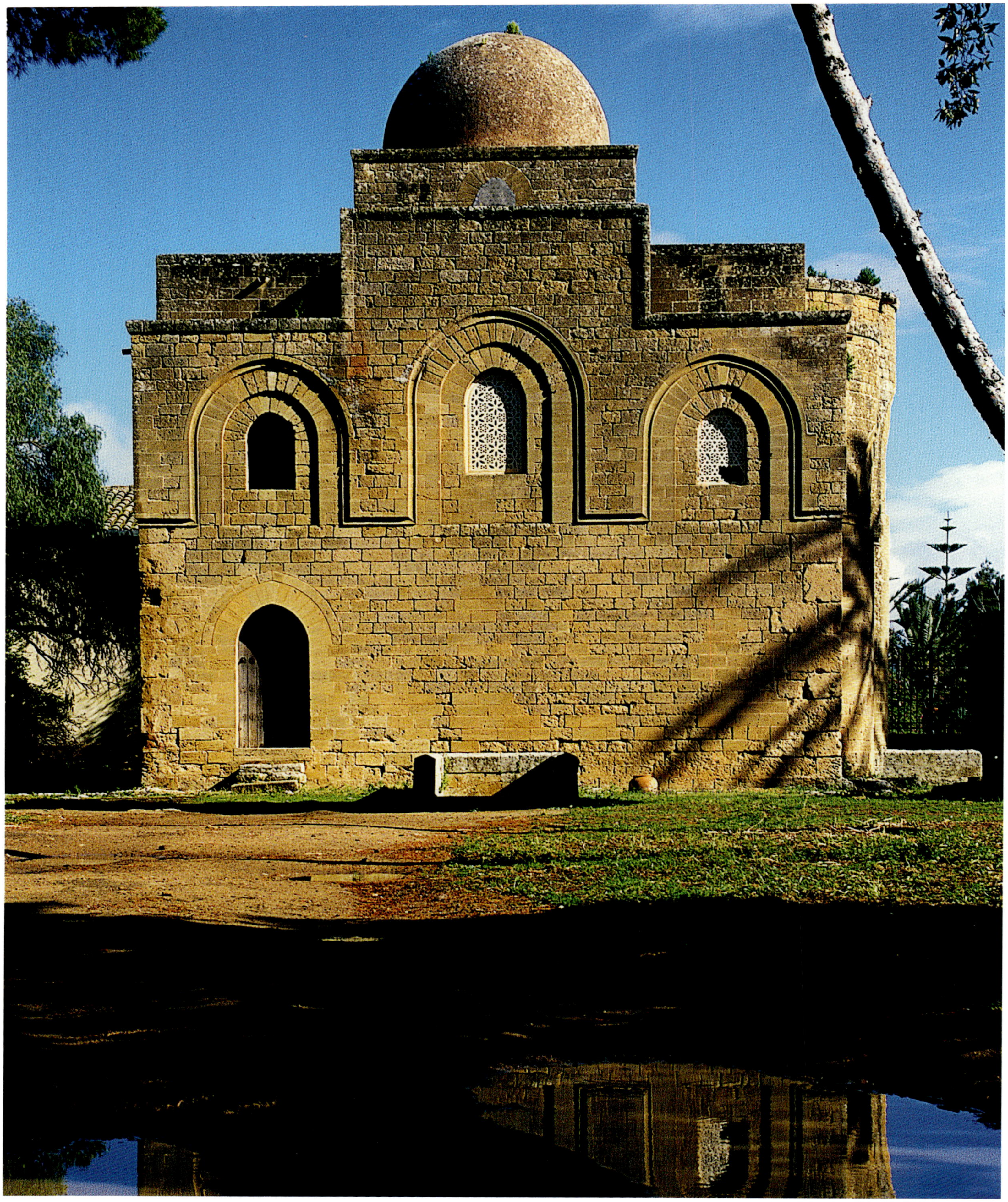

The Bridge of the Saracens in Adrano, Catania, looms over the Gorge of Simeto in a harsh landscape of volcanic rock. It rests on four unequal arches, two of them round and two pointed. Traditionally thought to have been built by the Arabs, it was probably built later, an indication of the influence that the innovations and construction techniques of the Orient had throughout the Middle Ages.

opposite page:
The Norman church of Santissima Trinità di Delia in Castelvetrano, Trapani. Built in the twelfth century, it preserves all the typical Muslim architectural features, such as the cupola, which is always red, and the indented frames that surround the windows.

following pages:
The sea at Trapani, where the Arabs first landed in Sicily.

Aci Castle and the ruins of a fortress that looks out over the sea from a cliff made of volcanic rock. Mentioned by the Arab chronicler Ibn al-Athir, the fortress was the center of Byzantine resistance against the invading Arabs. The castle was built in 1076 by Roger I on the site of the earlier fortification destroyed by the Arabs.

    Tabarmîn (Taormina) is a city on the sea located in the east; it faces the country of *Rûm*; it has a fortress of stone and a port on the sea.

    The remaining cities in the east number ten, except for Qal'at al-Sirât, which is situated on high ground.

    Batarliya (Petralia) is a city of the inland regions, situated in the south; it is surrounded by walls and in its center there is a fortress which contains a church.

    Bartinîq (Partinico) is not a city on the sea; it has an abundance of henna; it is located, same as Akhyâs e Balja (Bilici) on the plain.

    Sicily is a large and important island; the Muslims possess none other which is more famous, more populous, or with a greater number of cities. Its length is twelve days' travel and its width four."

    It is the Mediterranean itself that runs through these brief notes for the use of later travellers. As encountered in the geography book of al-Muqaddasî, Sicily appears similar to all the other regions in which he travelled on his journey to the west: an island of vast extent but one that is also part of a social, cultural, political, and economic continuum that links it to the Maghreb and to Spain. We must now speak about this society and culture, with closer attention, even within those city walls.

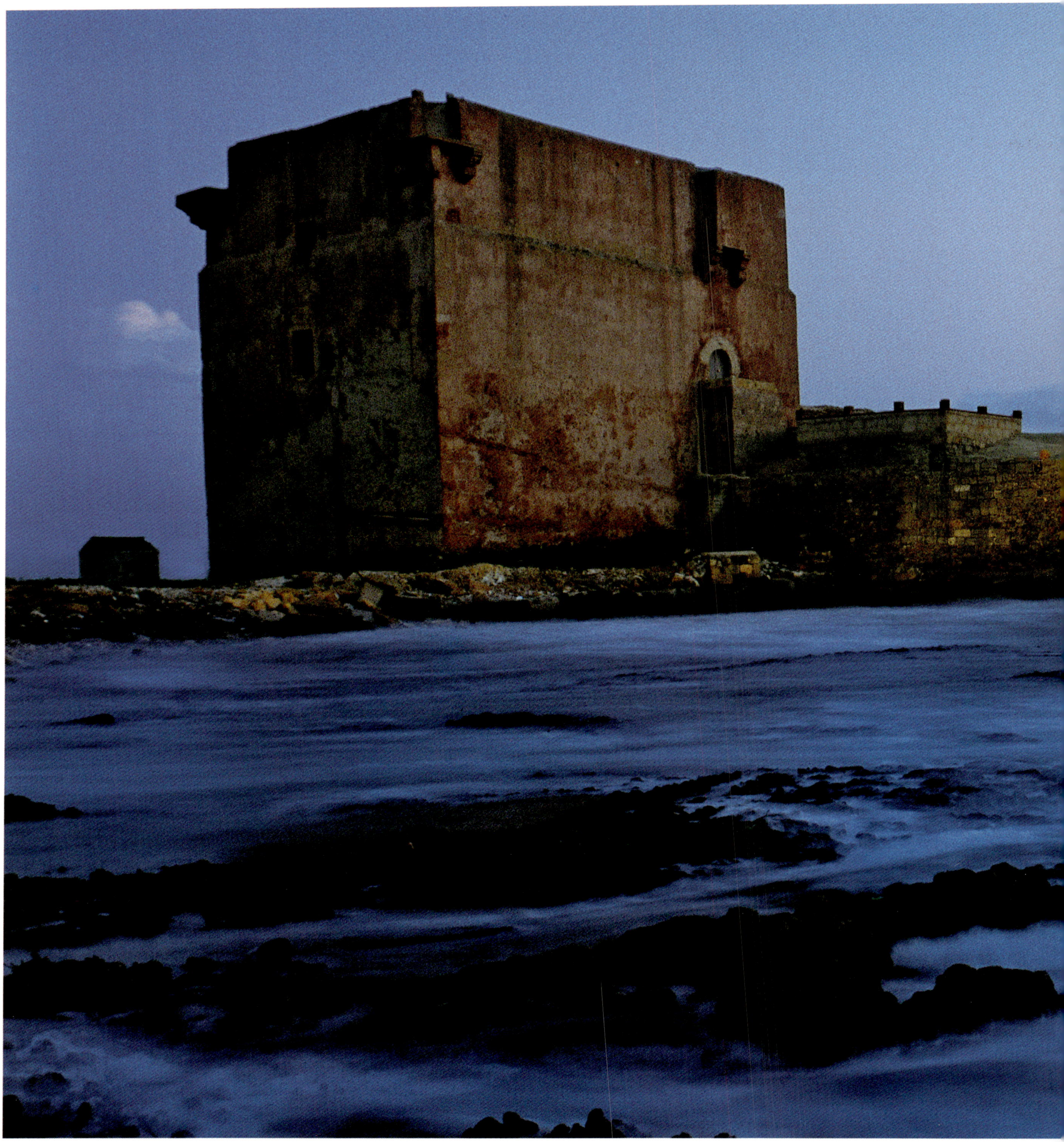

MUSLIM SICILY . 57

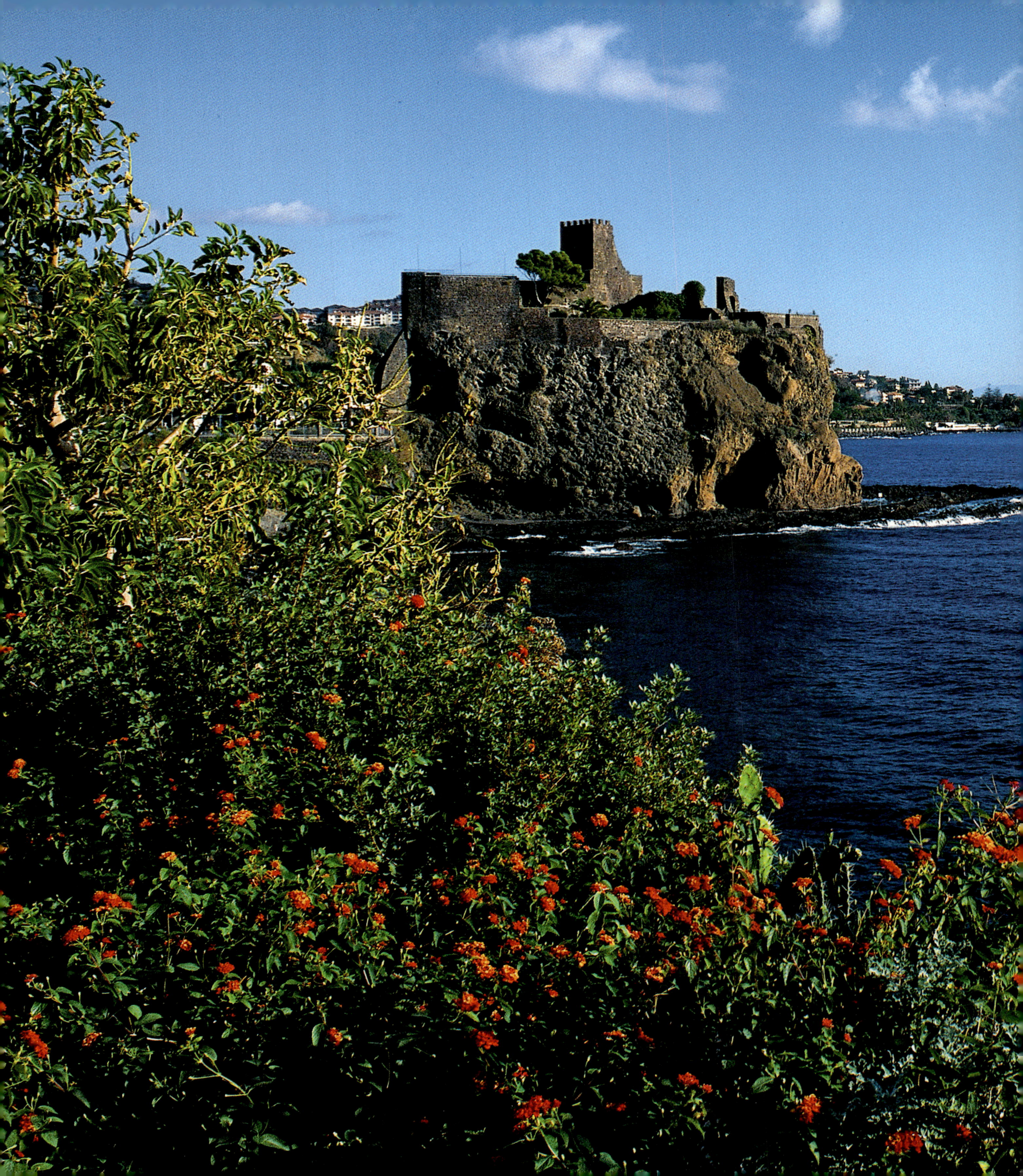

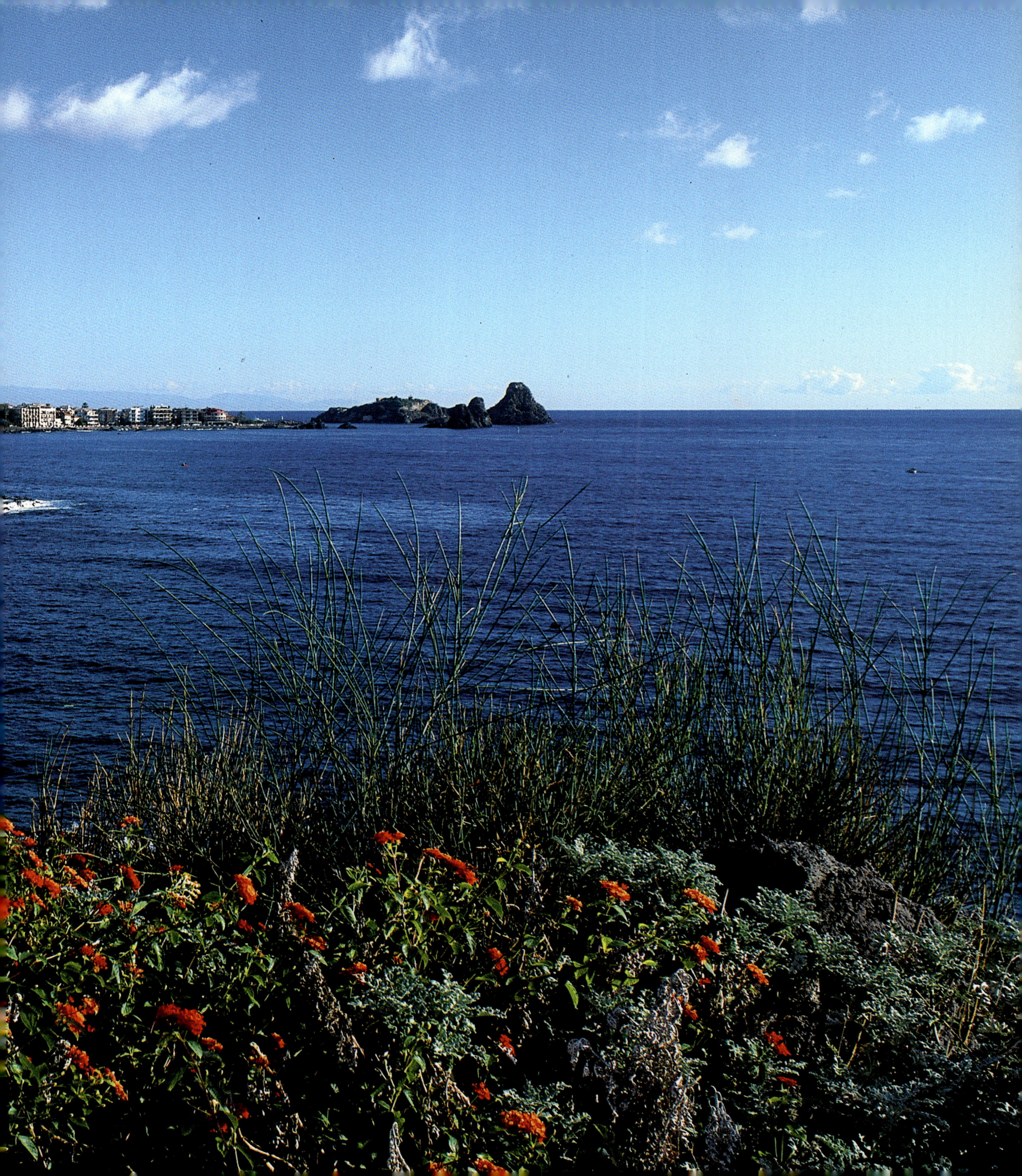

THE SOCIETY OF MUSLIM SICILY

In its early centuries the world of Islam was relatively homogeneous, and it was not a question of faith so much as of language and institutions: how the inhabitants of an area that stretched from Morocco to India felt a common belonging and participation in a common order that was defined by shared language, laws, customs, and daily practices.

Thus, when Sicily became part of Islam, the cultural unity provided by the Muslim religion and the Arabic language linked it to a larger region and to a social, political, and commercial network that extended throughout the southern Mediterranean and from there to the Orient. We know less than we would like regarding what the island became once it was called, in Arabic, *Siqiliyya*. Based on the available sources, we can reasonably imagine a heavily urbanized mercantile society in which power was based more on lineage than on land ownership. And the institutional and communicative unity to which we have alluded was found, naturally, even in the alleys and piazzas of the new Islamic cities of Sicily, because the city was (and is) a culturally connoted space in which political power and the needs of societal living assert themselves with great force. That is where the men who administer the laws are found, along with the institutions and the basic structures of community life, similar, presumably, to every other city in the Islamic world. These include a mosque, a school (*madrasa*), the public bath (*hammâm*), the market (*sûq*), and also, at some distance from the public areas, the seat of local power, which usually included the residence of the governor and the government offices (*dîwân*).

Even the religious environment of Sicily's cities was, naturally, the same as in most of contemporary Islam. The mosques and religious sites had to spread out rapidly: according to Ibn Hawqal, a geographer of the tenth century to whom we shall return later, in Palermo there were some three hundred neighborhood mosques plus one large main mosque. Perhaps that number is a bit exaggerated, but it does give an indication of profound change. The main mosque, the *jami'a*, was now the main gathering place, above all for Friday prayers. For daily observance and for many community activities there was a neighborhood mosque, the *masjid*, often of smaller size and constructed with funds that the Muslims reserved for pious works, the *waqf*. For the most part they were simple places with a rectangular hall that was covered with mats and oriented according to the *qibla*, that is, toward Mecca. They also had a small internal court with a well for ritual ablutions. Besides the adherence to a new religious faith, the most important aspect was above all the sharing of a new culture, a sharing that obviously included not just the traditions of Islam and the Arabic language but also allowed a deep mix of ethnicities that extended, as we shall see, to other religious environments and different cultural contexts.

Arab inscription carved on a column in the Cappella Palatina.

opposite page:
Mecca, in a detail from a ninth-century Koran painted on wood belonging to the Turkish Sultan Osman III. Museum of Islamic and Turkish Art, Istanbul.

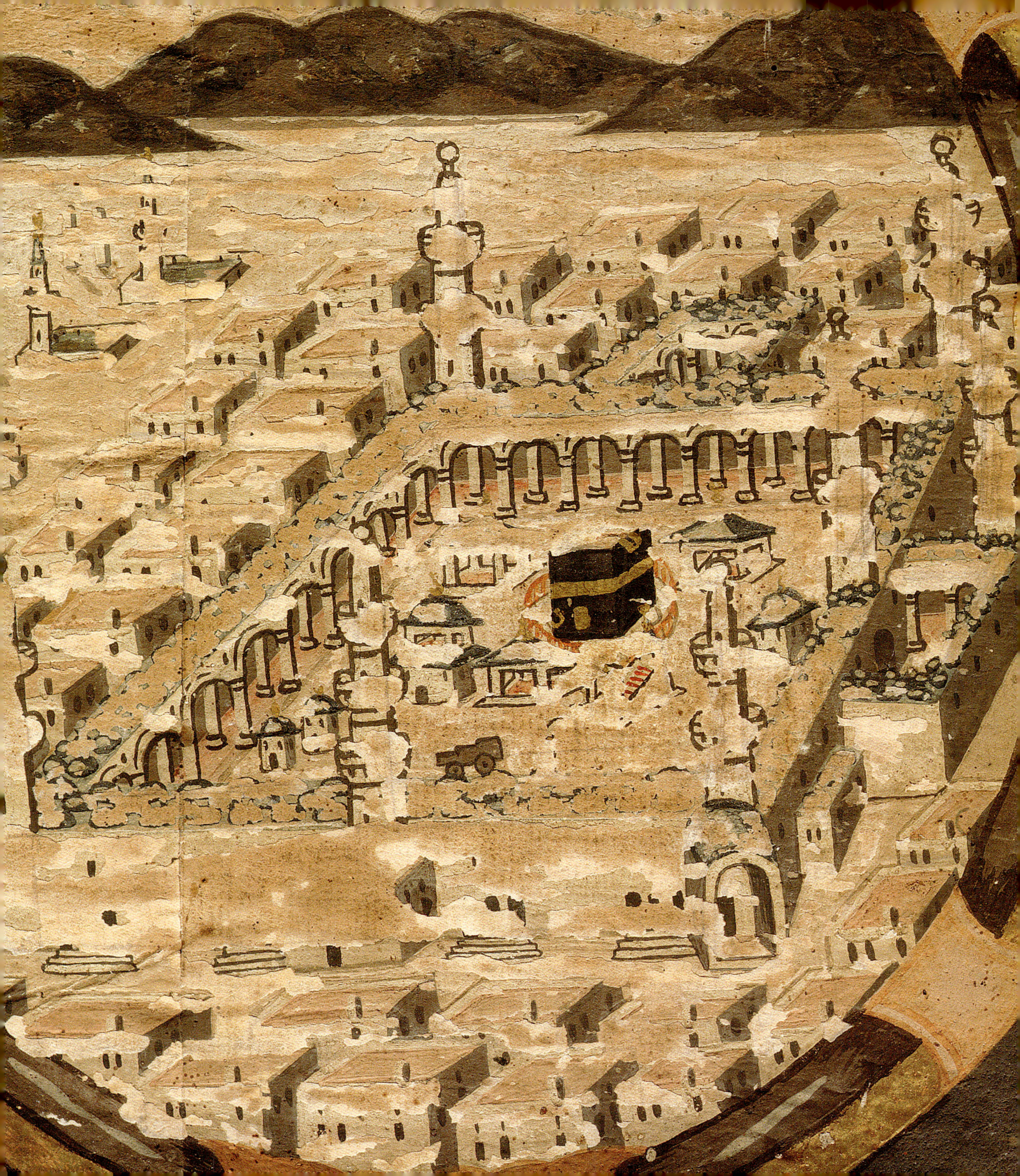

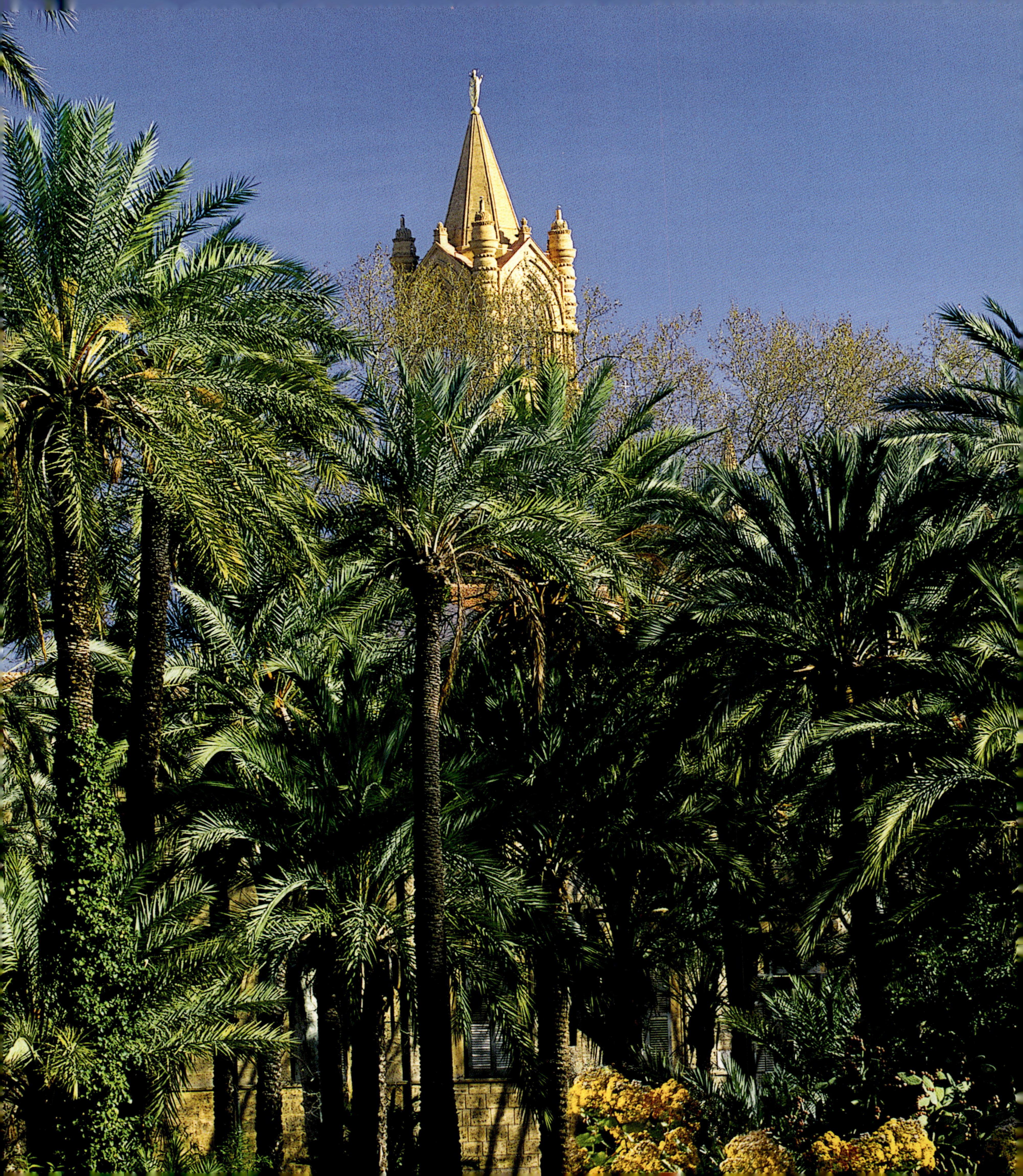

A description of Palermo by Ibn Hawqal:

> The great city of Palermo is surrounded by a magnificent and impregnable wall of stone. It is inhabited by merchants and contains the Great Mosque that was a church of the *rûm* before the conquest and has an impressive chapel.... Opposite the capital is the city known as al-Khâlisa. It possesses a wall of stone that is not, however, comparable to the one of Palermo. The *sultân* lives there along with his court. There are two public baths, but no merchants or caravanserai. Instead there is a small mosque in a modest style, a military garrison, the *dâr al-sinâ'a* (the arsenal, or dockyards), and government offices. The city has four gates, two on the north and one each on the south and west, while on the east is the sea and the walls have no gate. One of the neighborhoods of Palermo is known as Hârat al-Saqâliba, the Quarter of the Slavs. It is one of the most populous and important in the two cities that I have mentioned. It has a seaport and several streams that run between it and the capital, and the water marks the border between the two. Another quarter is known by the name of the mosque of Ibn Siqlâb. It is also quite large but does not have any running streams and the inhabitants drink from wells. At one end is the river known as Wâdî 'Abbâs, which is of considerable size and contains many mills, in addition to orchards and gardens which do not, however, produce any profit. The Hârat al-Jadîda, or New Quarter, is near the quarter of the mosque and there is no dividing line between them. Nor does the Quarter of the Slavs have any walls.

The cathedral of Palermo was built in 1184 by the archbishop Gualtiero Offamilio on the site of an older church that the Muslims had turned into a mosque and which was later restored to Christianity by the Normans. Even after its ornamentation and decoration were complete, it remained a work in progress up until the eighteenth century with additions and restorations that were in harmony with and preserved the original structure.

opposite page:
The cathedral of Palermo and one of the many gardens which adorn the city even today.

following pages:
Detail of the battlement that runs along the right side of the cathedral of Palermo.

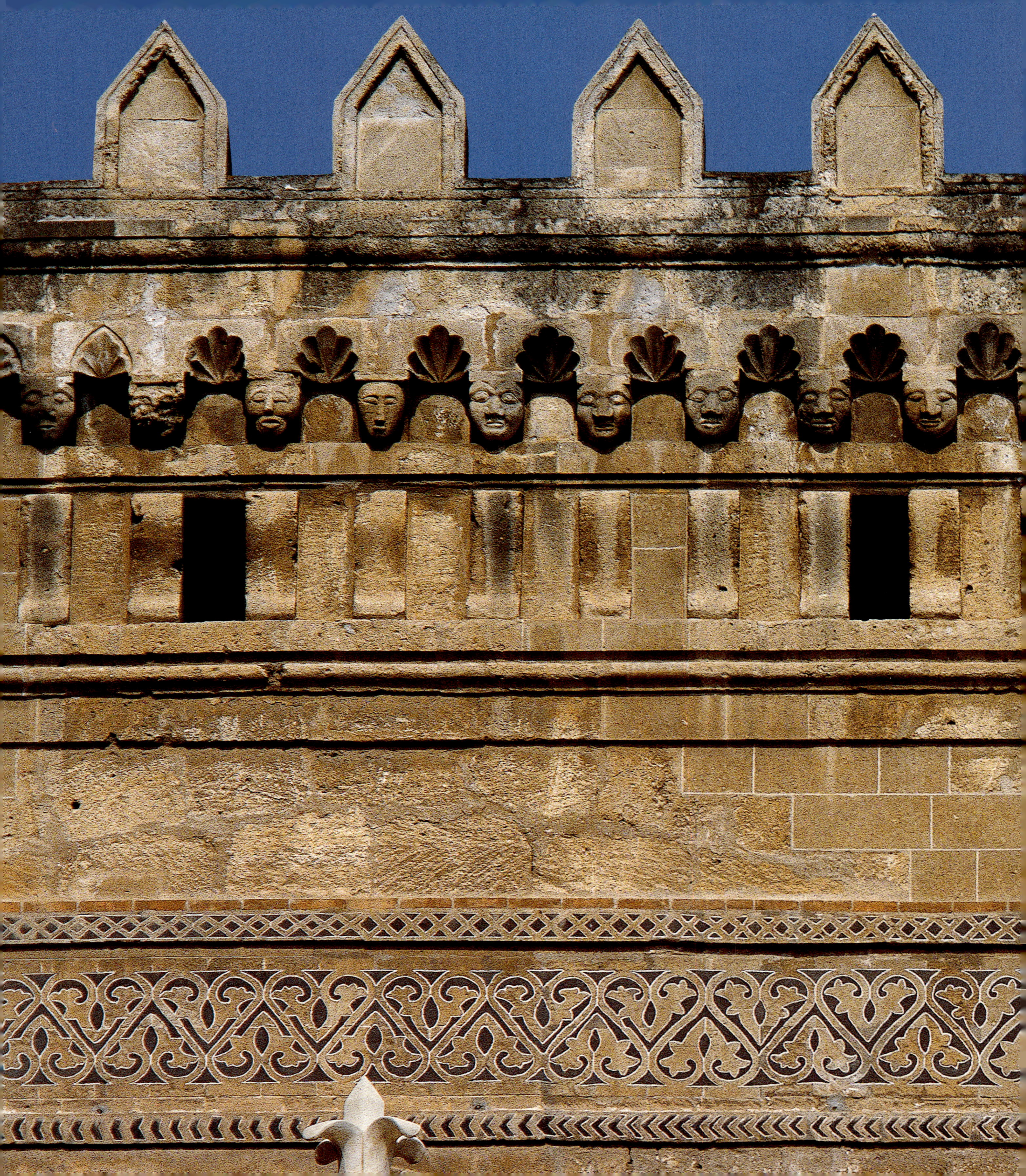

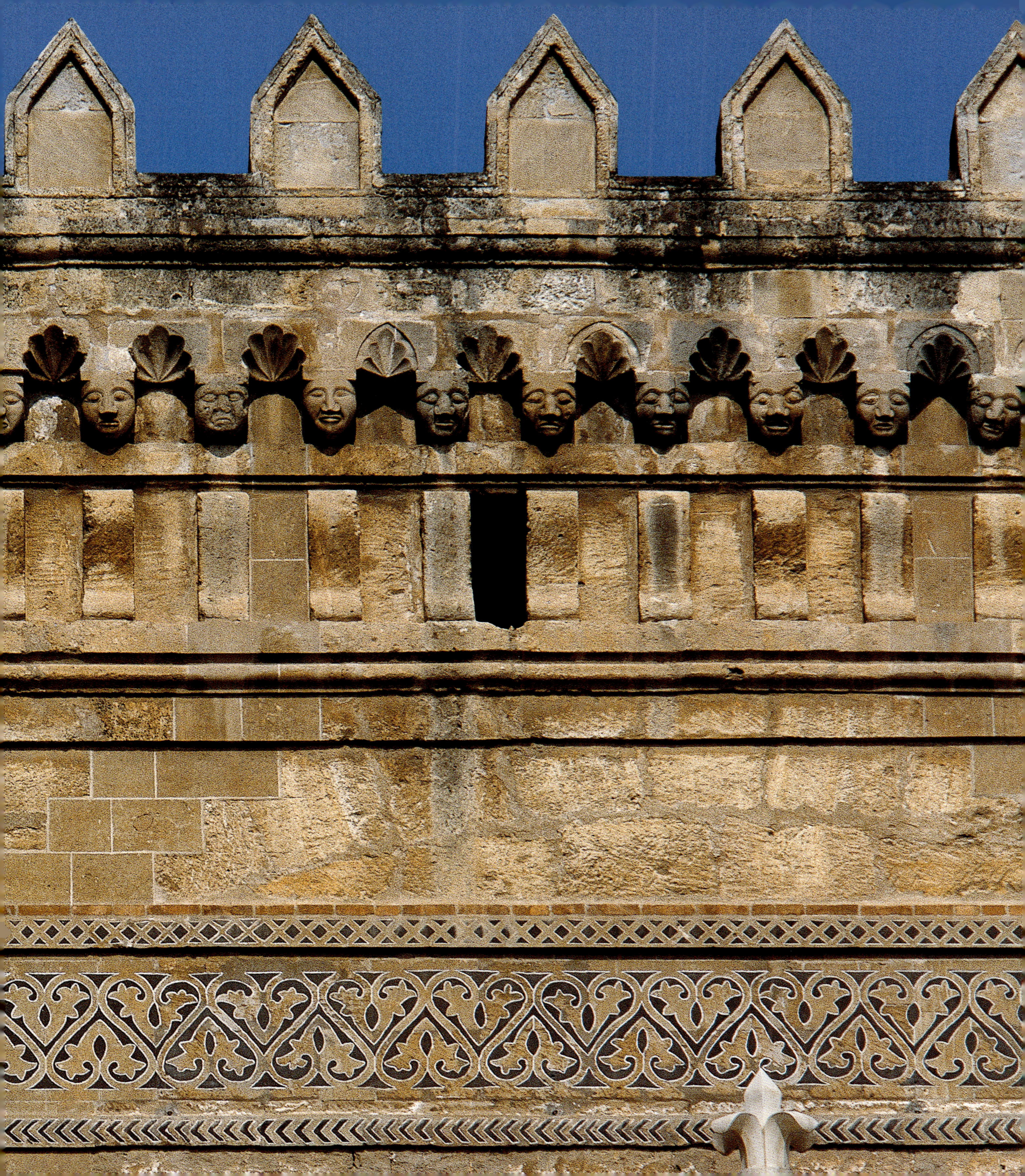

Northwest facade of the mosque of Ibn Tulun, built in 876. Cairo. Today considered to be an Egyptian imitation of the mosque in Samara, in ancient times the mosque of Ibn Tulun was thought to be a unique example of its genre. The geographer al-Yaqubi, who had lived in both places, did not see any resemblance, and the historian al-Qudai mentioned the unusual choice of brick, instead of the plundered stone generally used by Egyptian builders, for its construction

opposite page:
Tympanum of the mosque of Ibn Tulun. Cairo. The pillars that support the balcony of the prayer hall, like all the others in the mosque, are all of brick dressed with stucco, in order to differentiate them from the columns made of stone used by the infidels. The choice of this material, alongside carved wood, allowed the entire building to be embellished with elaborate ornaments and inscriptions.

Most of the markets are found between the mosque of Ibn Siqlâb and the New Quarter, such as the market for all those who sell oil, the market for flour, the money-changers, the grocers, the blacksmiths, and the armorers; also the markets for grain, the one for the tailors, and the one for the fishmongers...."

If these Islamicized urban spaces produced a class of merchants, artisans, and small proprietors, it also saw the birth of a class of religious authorities, the *ulamâ* and the *faqîh*. It is notoriously difficult to distinguish between these two figures. Each was an interpreter of *sharî'a*, the divine law, and the guardian of an elaborate set of rules of behavior. They sometimes had great influence on political decisions, as can be seen in the role assumed by the *faqîh* Asad ibn al-Furât at the time of the invasion of Sicily. Just as in North Africa and Spain, the form of law adopted in Sicily was the Malikite, one of four schools of law recognized by Islam and based on the teachings of Mâlik ibn Anas (d. 795), a jurist in Medina and author of the oldest compilation of Islamic law, the *Kitâb al-Muwatta'*, or Book of the Levelled Road.

From a political point of view, there was always a dependence on Africa, even if that link, at least starting in the last years of Kalbid rule, became progressively weaker. The governor, or *wali*, was usually named by the emirs in Kairouan, afterwards by those of al-Mahdiyya, and still later by those of Cairo. In the Aglabid and Fatimid periods, the *wali* carried out both civil and military duties, even if in the Kalbid period there was a progressive distinction between the two functions and therefore also between the physical location of their respective officials. Especially prominent in

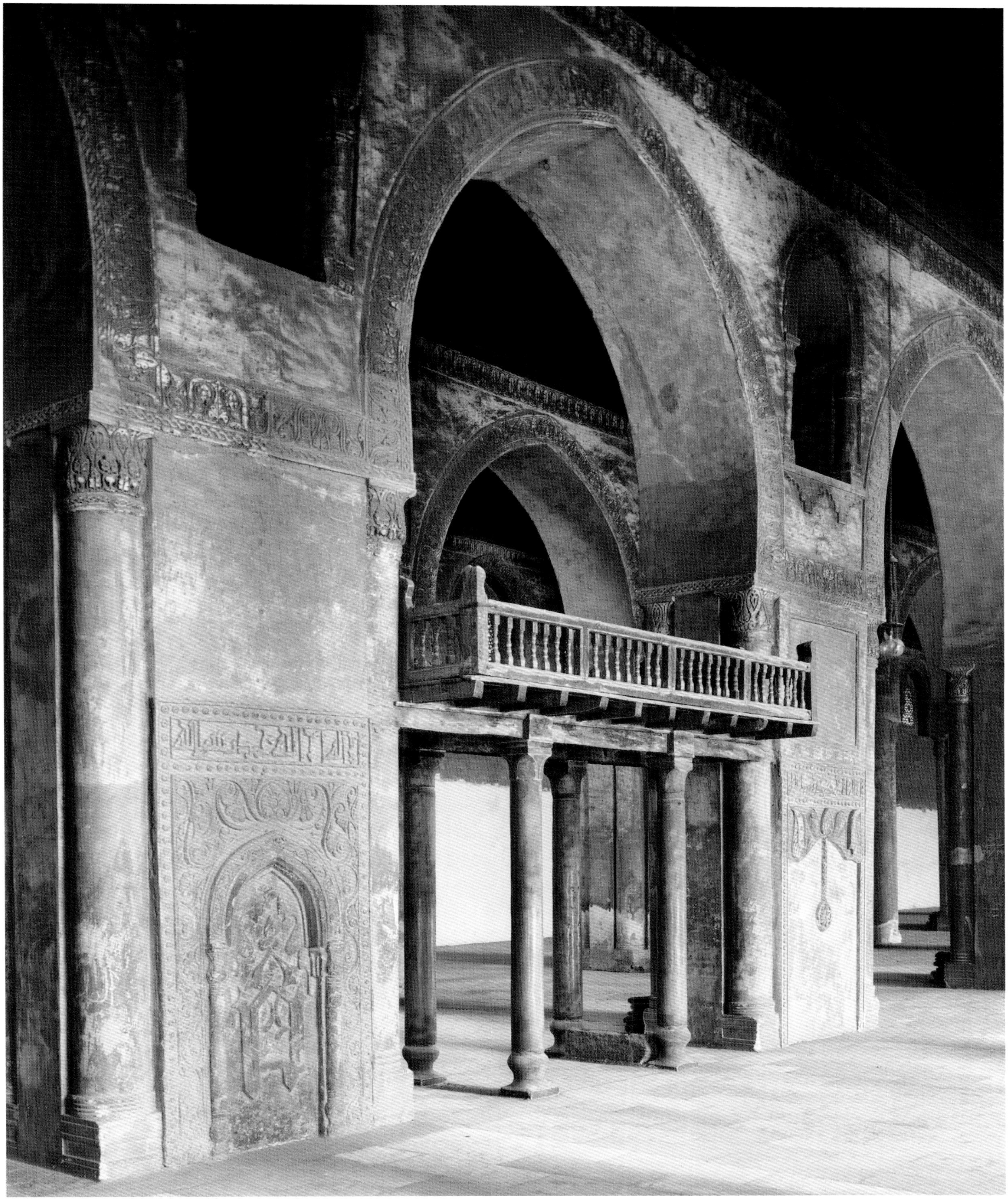

Sicily was the *jama'a*, or assembly of notables, which was very active in the affairs of certain areas of the country, above all in Palermo and Agrigento. It was probably similar to an analogous institution active in Ifrîqiya: a body that was sometimes consultative and sometimes deliberative that supported the emir (or the subordinate governors appointed by him). In Sicily the importance of the *jama'a* was often considerable, and sometimes, in the absence of the *wali*, it had the legal right to assume his authority, and even to challenge it.

Military power was maintained by the *jund*, the armed troops that, in accord with Islamic practice, were paid and participated in the division of booty according to the rules of *jihâd*. These soldiers were often paid with plots of land, or *iqta'*, which speeded the transfer of landed property from the vanquished to the victors. In fact, this problem is connected to that of land regulation, of which we should give an account, if only because it deals with a subject relating to which there is specific documentation in a treatise by al-Dawudi (d. 1011) in his *Kitâb al-amwâl*, or Book of Possessions. On the whole, one can say that in Sicily there were many different systems of land use, at least in comparison with the types of ownership provided for by classic Islamic law. In this regard the great discretion with which the central authority, or *al-sultân*, could either grant or deny the lawful possession of land to settlers is often emphasized. In any case, the great upheaval in land ownership caused by the Muslim conquest remains obvious: existing large landholdings by both church and laity were annulled as a result of their confiscation by the Muslims as spoils of war; the concentration of wealth in the hands of previous individual owners was eliminated; and, as a consequence, the ownership of land was split into many small holdings. The fate of lands acquired as the result of treaties, transfers, and peaceful agreements, known as *fay'*, was instead decided by the head of the community, which controlled their use and distribution based on the common interest. This difficult-to-interpret text, in other words, is evidence of the breakup of large estates into small plots for the specific purpose of increasing the value of

Olive trees, the cultivation of which was improved by the Muslims.

opposite page:
Wheat, the precious gold of antiquity, made Sicily the nugget that shines at the center of the Mediterranean.

following pages:
Orange trees with Mount Etna in the background.

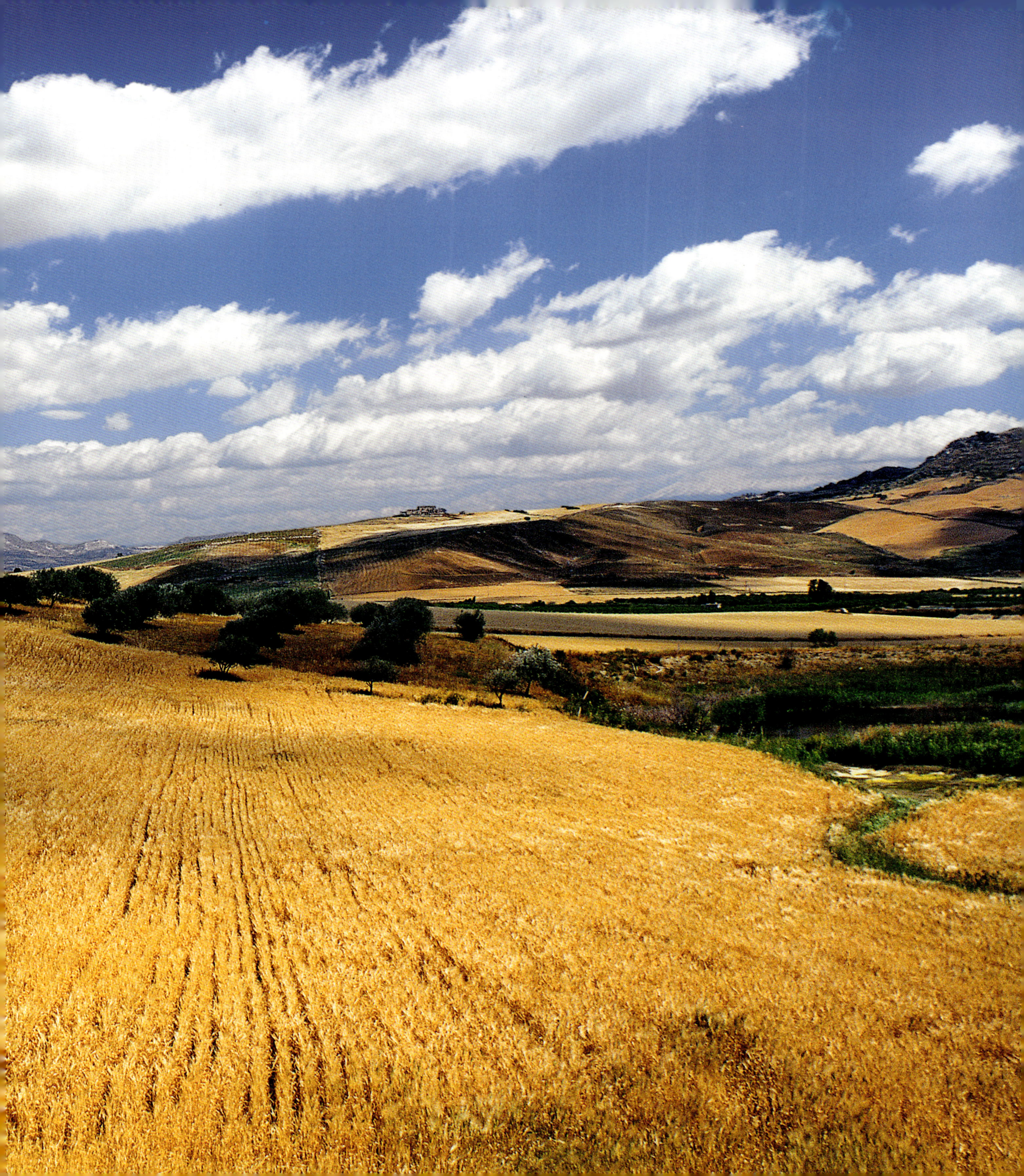

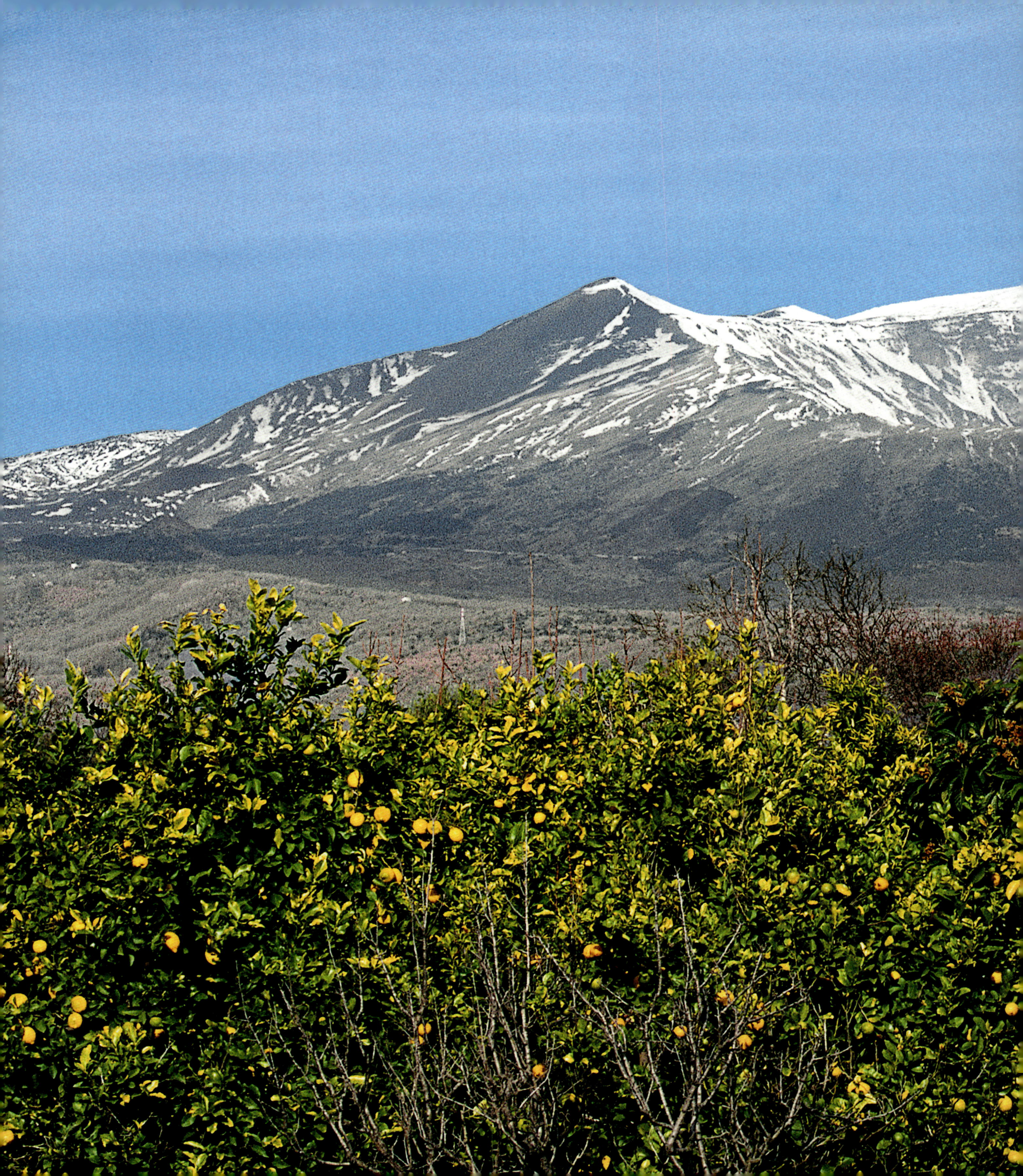

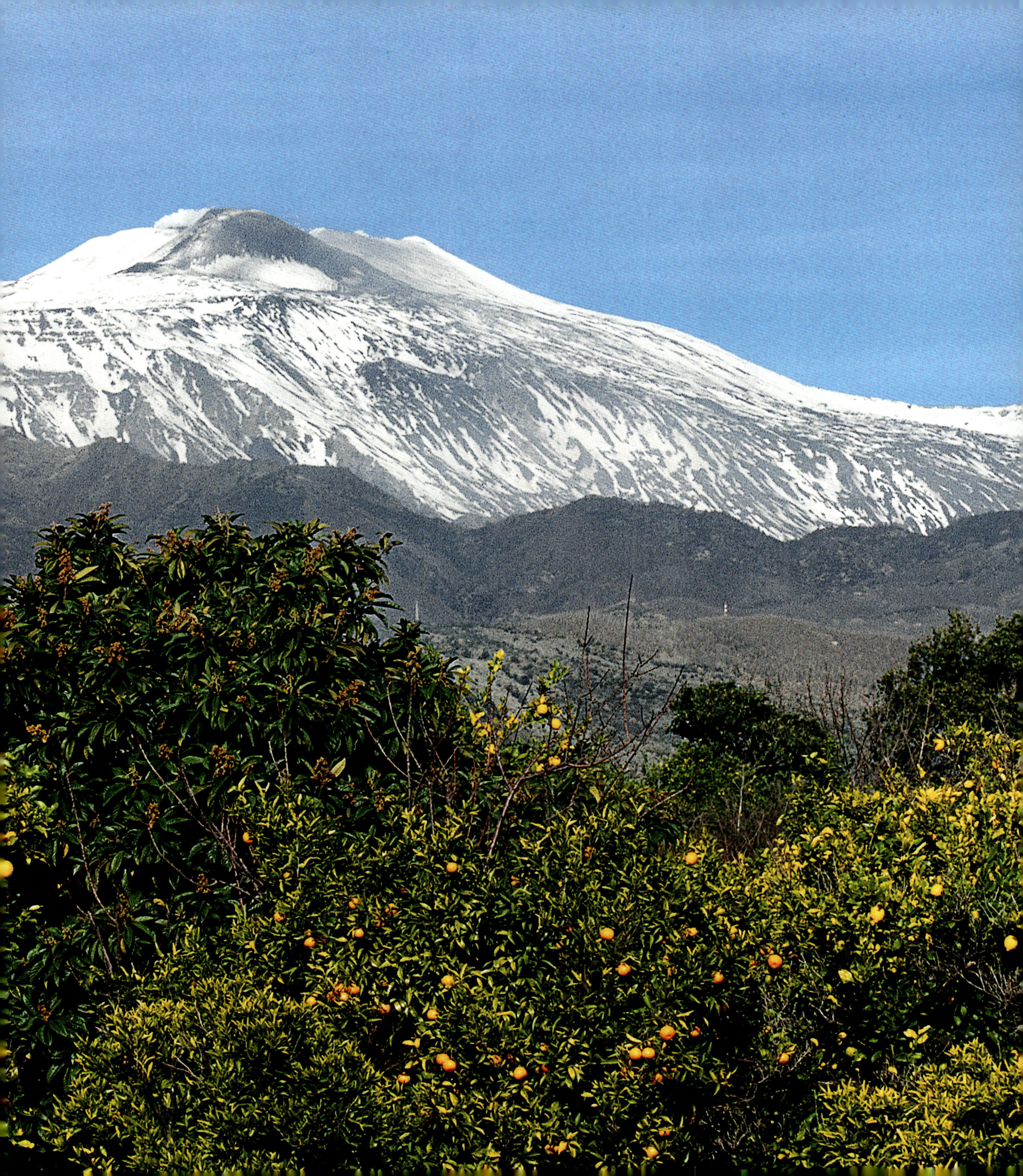

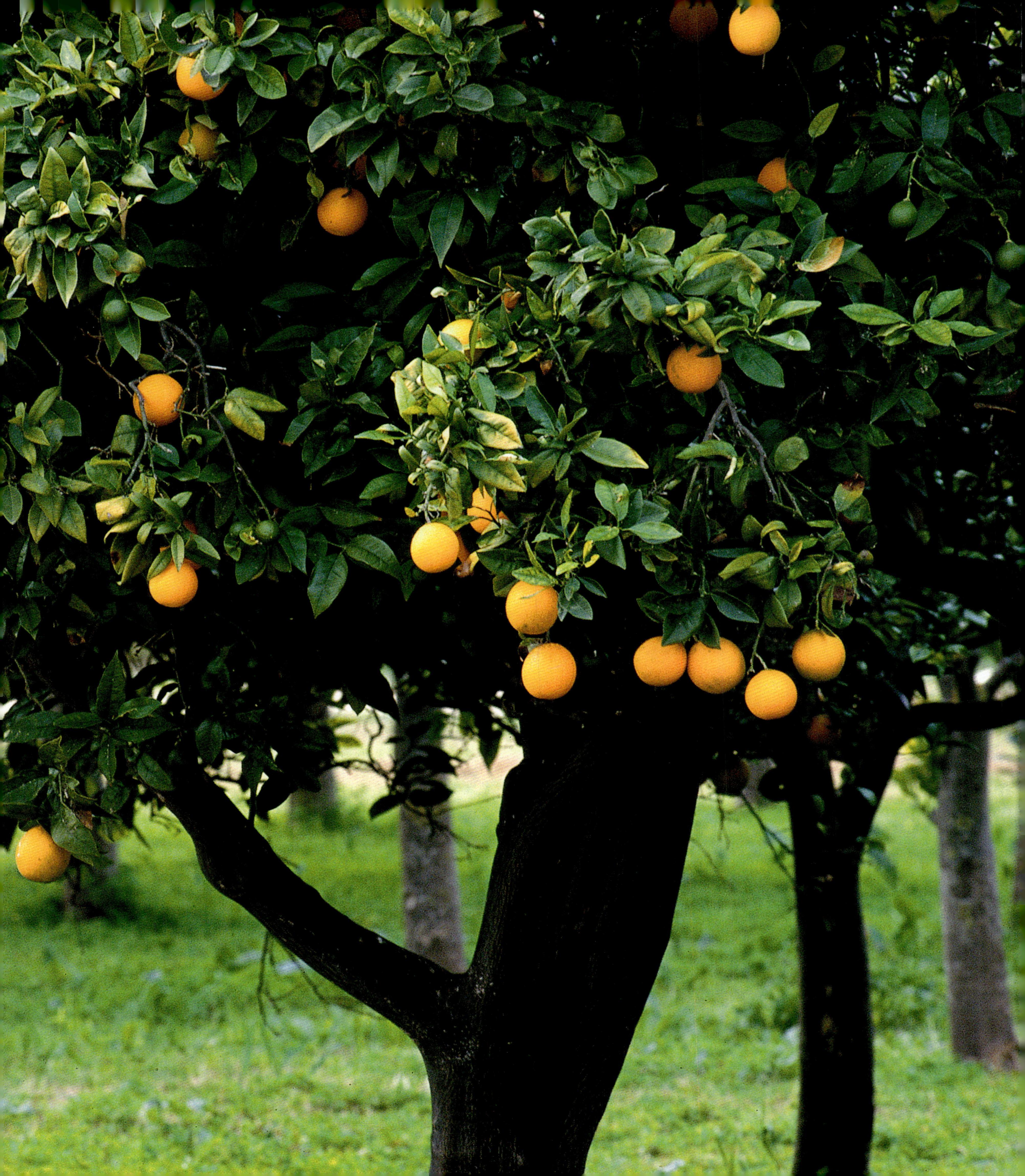

Waterwheel located near the tenth-century Mill of the Abulafia, in Cordoba. This is a special type of hydraulic mill consisting of a wheel equipped with vanes, besides those that were receptacles for the harvest, that were driven by the force of the water, without the need for human or animal effort.

opposite page:
Sicilian oranges.

that same land, although it also bears witness to the great complexity and legal difficulties involved in the redistribution of land that was conquered slowly over time on an island in which a state of *jihâd* continued for almost the entire duration of the Muslim presence there.

Beyond these problems, however, Arab rule benefited agricultural activity in many ways. It seems that the introduction of new irrigation techniques, with a consequent improvement in the cultivation of hemp, cotton, and vegetables, dates to this period. Even if the introduction of citrus in the Mediterranean goes back—in a sporadic way—to the Roman period, it experienced an intensification with the arrival of the Muslims. Starting in the tenth century, the Arab sources speak with reference to other areas of the *dâr al-islâm* about the cultivation of a bitter species of orange (*naranj*, from its Persian name) that spread throughout the Mediterranean by way of trade routes that began in Iraq and Egypt, and also about lemons imported from India at around the same time. Regarding Sicily, the Arabic texts provide general evidence of the fertility of an island rich with woods, forests, and, especially, water. The most valuable voice is still that of Ibn Hawqal, who alludes to the cultivation of watermelon, papyrus, "Persian" reeds, cotton, hemp, vegetables, and vines, as well as the production of high-quality linen, even if he does not speak explicitly of citrus. The only direct references to citrus in Sicily are those of Ibn Makki (d. 1107), who

A page from the thirteenth-century Arab manuscript The Tale of Bayad and Riyad. *Biblioteca Apostolica, Vatican City, Rome. The arrival of the Muslims brought an end to a long social and economic depression caused by the Roman and Byzantine system of large landed estates. They divided the land, placed it under cultivation, and then gave it to the peasant class that worked it and was dependent on it. All the lands taken by the Muslims flourished with new types of vegetables that were able to develop thanks to innovative irrigation systems and new ways to use water.*

opposite page:
Detail of the vertical vane of the waterwheel.

wrote about the linguistic errors of the Sicilians in a work to which we shall return later. That work mentioned, for example, a popular mispronunciation of the words *laranj* and *aranj* that resulted in the word *naranj*, the source of the modern Italian word *arancia*, or orange. There was also the term *laymuna*, or lemon, which was used in place of *lumia* and *limuna*. As concerns the excellence of agricultural methods in Sicily (was it due to the natives, to the Berbers, or to the Arabs?) a clue might be found in the praise for methods of planting vegetables "in the Sicilian style" found in a Spanish manual of agriculture from the eleventh century. Even Ibn Hawqal confirms the high level of agriculture when he speaks of the water supply in the countryside outside Palermo, rich with fenced-in farms (*mahall*) and streams with numerous mills placed over flowing water. He also says that there were many wells in the various neighborhoods of Palermo, indicating the existence of a large subterranean network of *qanât* ("canes," or "pipes") which today are studied extensively and in some places can be visited. The water in these "canals" was carried to the surface, using methods developed in Arab and non-Arab areas of the Near East, by a system of wells and then used for drinking and irrigation. This flowering of new agricultural methods also opened Sicily to the larger commercial world of the Mediterranean. The port of Palermo received ships loaded with spices and jewels, and those ships would then sail to ports in Europe, Africa, and the Levant loaded with the pastes, wheat, dried fruit, sugar, raw silk, and cotton of Sicily. This trade and commerce often remind us of a complex society in which the Arab element was not always, or even necessarily, dominant.

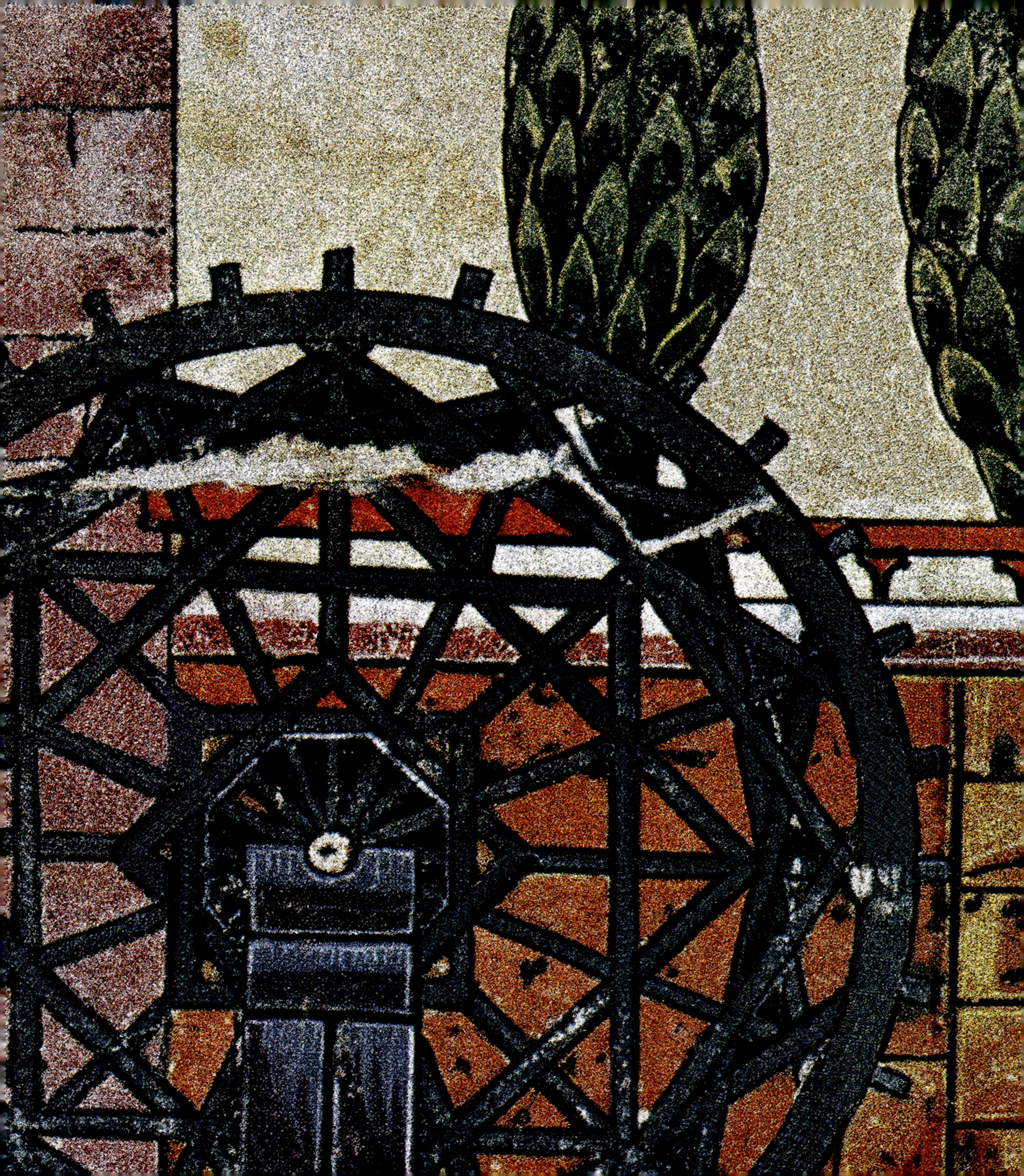

POWER AND MILITARY ORGANIZATION

After the death of Muhammad, it became ever more clear that Islam needed to be a politically homogeneous territory whose inhabitants followed a single faith with laws and institutions in common. This territory was governed by a single man, the Caliph, who held temporal power due to his role as a deputy, or vicar (*khalîfa*, in Arabic), of Muhammad. Muslim expansion was rapid, and some territories were conquered permanently. But it was only with the arrival of the 'Abbasid dynasty that the Muslim world became well organized. Nevertheless, this stability was short-lived. Just a century later, in fact, with the arrival of the Muslims in Sicily, the first signs of weakness in the empire became apparent. Each regional commander, or *amîr* (emir, in English), began to work more for his own benefit than for the empire, and new dynasties began to claim ever more personal power for themselves.

War was one of the simplest and most important ways to demonstrate the extent of one's political power. On this, the doctrine of the caliphate was clear: there was an explicit link between temporal power and the wars that were fought with non-Muslims who were outside the *dâr al-islâm*, or House of Islam. This particular type of conflict was known as *jihâd*, a very complicated term that referred both to an individual's personal struggle to reach out to God, employing his mind, his body, and everything he owned, and also to an actual war fought to defend the territory of Islam and to propagate the faith. The greatest enemies in this struggle were known by two specific terms: the *kâfir*, or infidel, who, according to the Koran, mocked Islam, and the *mushrik*, or associationist, who placed other gods alongside the one true God. It was also by means of this political and legal mechanism that the Muslim armies arrived in Sicily.

We know less than we would like about the military practices of the time. Of great importance was the cavalry, while the infantry was used mostly for sieges and guarding fortresses on the frontier. Each horseman was accompanied by a squire who led a beast of burden, either a horse or a mule (*zamîla*), which carried his equipment. This included a tent made of leather, wool, or linen for the two of them. The army, at least in North Africa, used camels for the transport of heavy items.

The weapons used by the Muslim armies were in fact extremely similar to those employed by Christians. The cavalry used a lance (*rumh*) and a double-edged axe (*tabarzîn*, a word of Persian origin). Foot soldiers usually fought with a dagger, a sling (*wadhaf*), and a javelin (*mizrâq*). The bow (*qaws*) was used on foot and on horse, and there were three types: Arab, Turkish (*qaws turkiyya*), and Frankish (*qaws ifranjiyya*). Starting in the eleventh century, a type of crossbow that was stretched with the feet was used. Even though the most commonly used weapon was probably the lance, the sword (*sayf*) was likely held in greater esteem throughout

Fifteenth-century battle-axe made of steel damascened in gold. Museo Nazionale del Bargello, Florence.

opposite page:
Arab warrior on horseback in full armor. Fifteenth-century painting in the Sala de Los Reyes, Alhambra, Granda.

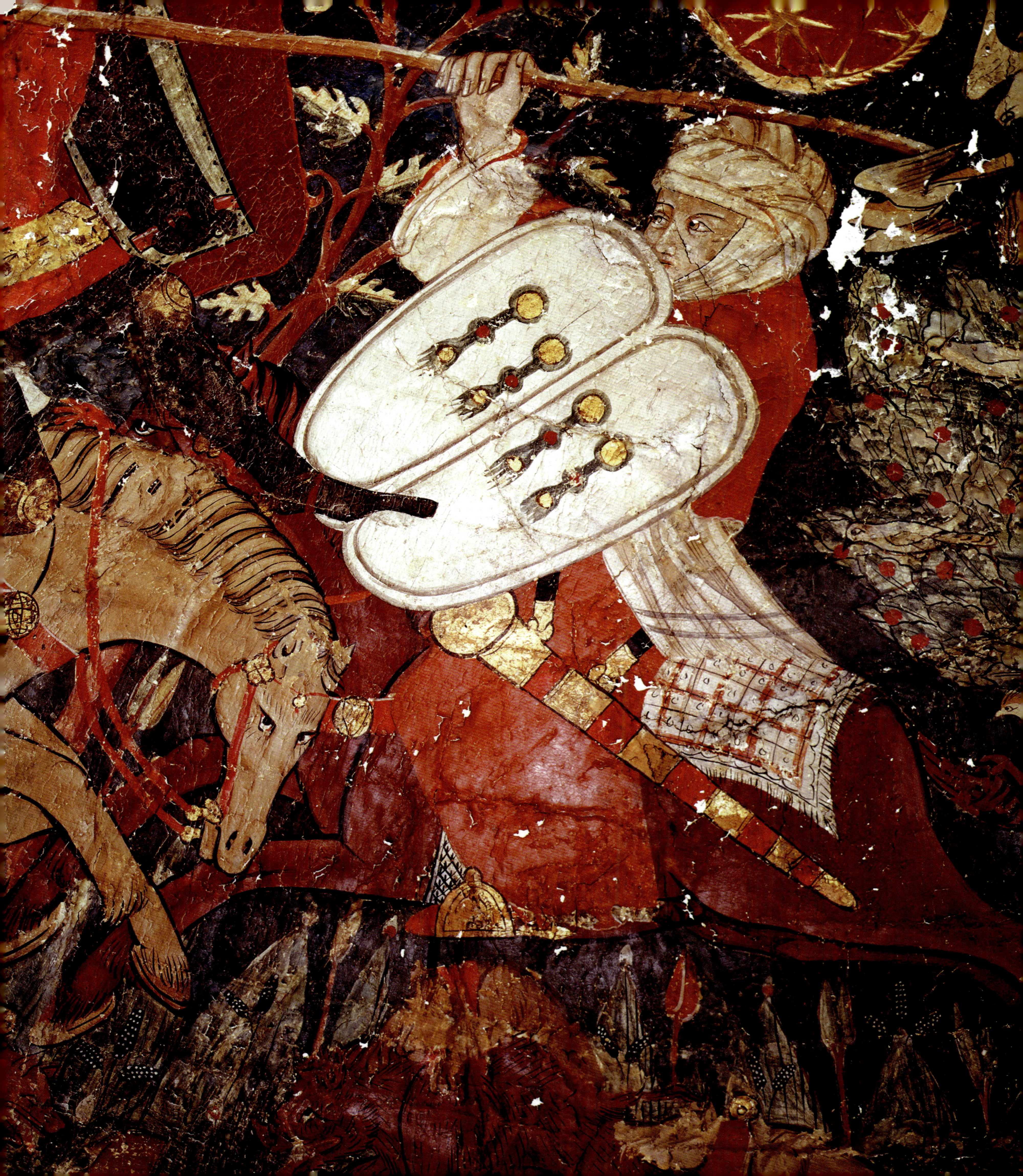

78 . ALESSANDRO VANOLI

the Islamic world, if indeed it is true that by the ninth century the Muslim philosopher al-Kindî had already written two works about swords.

The main means of defense was a coat of mail, usually long enough to protect the legs of a man on horseback. There were other types of mail, made of extremely fine metal links, which conformed perfectly to the shape of the body and were mostly copied from similar models used by the 'Abbasids. In the tenth and eleventh centuries the head was protected either by a metal helmet with a visor (*baida*, or *khudha*), a hood of mail (*mighfar*), or a headpiece made of iron (*tishtaniya*, from the Latin *testinia*). The defensive weapon used most by the army of Andalusia was naturally the shield. The one used by a horseman was called a *daraq* and made of leather. Often mounted on a wooden framework, it was small and very light. The shield used by the infantry was called a *turs* and there were three types: the *'amirî*, *hafsunî*, and *sultanî*. It was made of wood, and sometimes plated with iron in order to deflect the blows of an enemy.

As far as military tactics are concerned, information is again scarce. In the early days of Islam, the Arab armies waged war in flat country. And if one of their classic maneuvers remained the *karr wa farr*, consisting of cavalry charges followed by abrupt retreats, they often favored more complex tactics with encircling movements and sudden raids on the enemy's rearguard. The army's order of battle was as follows: in front were the various rows of infantry, with their shields and their lances planted solidly on the ground at an angle and pointed directly at the enemy; in front of them was a raised banner. Behind them were archers (*ramî*) whose arrows could pierce a coat

opposite page:
Leather shield, Arab, tenth century (?). Armeria Real, Madrid.

this page and following pages:
The Arabs attack a Christian city, from Las Cantigas de Santa Maria *by Alfonso X el Sabio (folio 43v)*, in the Library of the Monastery of San Lorenzo, the Escorial, Madrid.

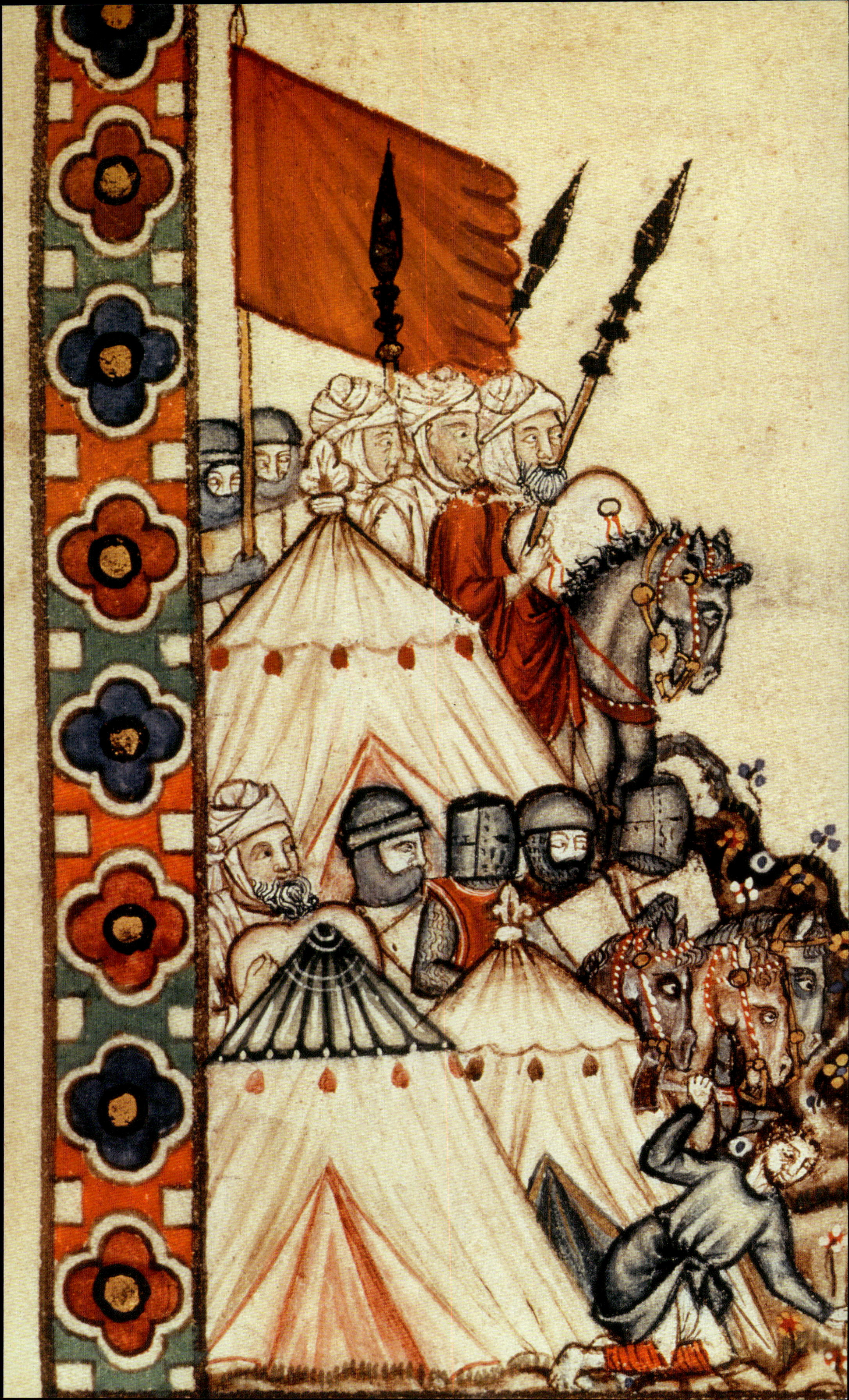

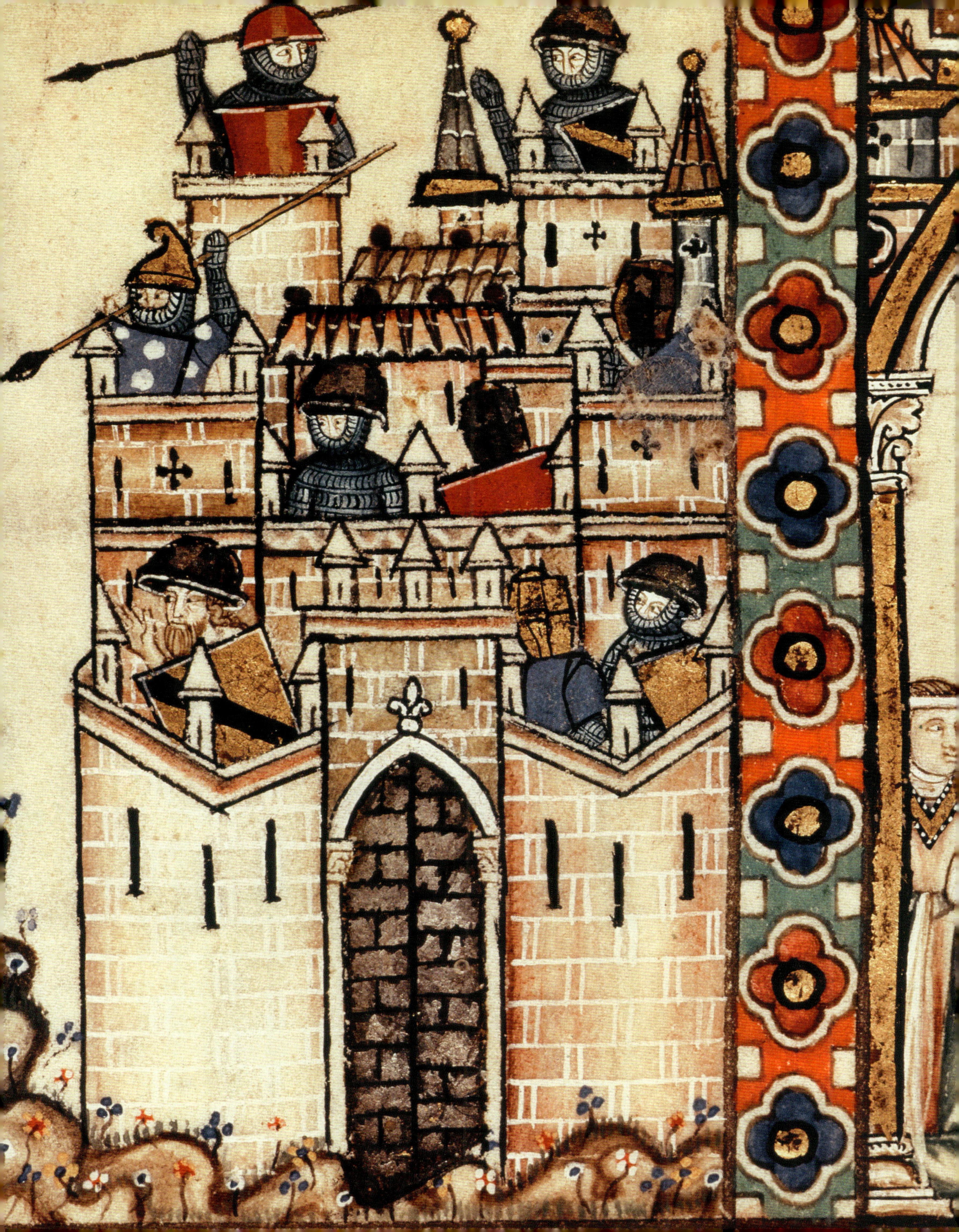

of mail. At the back was the cavalry. When the Christians charged, the Muslim archers would stay in place, confronting them with a wall of arrows. Only later would the infantry and archers open their ranks, moving obliquely to the right and left, leaving an open space for the cavalry to hurl itself against the enemy. The roll of the drums (*tûbûl*), which beat a rhythm during the entire battle, sent a message that travelled quickly in two senses: the signals that frightened the enemy served at the same time to strengthen and give new life to the Muslim ranks. Right after the first attack, while the front ranks continued to fight, an encircling maneuver would be started, a traditional tactic used by armies from the Maghreb.

Mobile warfare was accompanied, even for Muslim armies, by siege tactics (*hisâr*). An expedition sent to the frontier could often have as its purpose the liberation of a castle taken by the Christians, or the laying of a siege to a fortified town. The besieging troops would sack the surrounding countryside with forces large enough to prevent reinforcement by the enemy. Then, with hunger and thirst as weapons, they would proceed to capture the town or castle. At the same time, specialized groups of soldiers would begin to dig underneath the walls, hoping to breach them. A powerful battering ram (*kabsh*) would be used to shatter the gates. Specialized archers would send burning arrows inside the fortress. Finally, if possible, they would use a catapult (an *'arrâda*, or a *manajanîq*). Usually, the Christian garrison would defend the fortress inch by inch. But if they capitulated, their lives would be spared and they would become slaves along with their women and children, exactly as would have happened to the Muslims if the situation were reversed.

*In games of chess played by Arabs, the elephant (*al-fil*) is the equivalent of the bishop. Ivory, tenth century, from Iraq.*

Certificate of pilgrimage to Mecca, dated 1193. The sacred pilgrimage is one of the five Pillars of Islam. Museum of Islamic and Turkish Art, Istanbul.

MUSLIM SICILY AND OTHER CULTURES

By now it should be clear that the Islamic conquest of Sicily was neither brief nor systematic. Many areas remained independent for a very long time, and many places that were conquered suffered reverses accompanied by often violent internal revolts. As we have seen, Islam brought a heterogeneous society composed of Arab conquerors, Berber soldiers, and Levantine merchants to Sicily. All these blended, more or less easily, with the equally heterogeneous society already present there that was composed of the island's former Byzantine rulers, its landowners of mostly Roman origin, monks who followed either the Latin rite or the Greek, and, of course, Jews.

Unfortunately, the sources that would allow us to narrate a history of the social and cultural relations between victors and vanquished are very scarce. It is probably best to start with some of the laws of conquest that governed the behavior of Muslims. According to the theory of *jihâd*, the *ahl al-Kitâb*, or People of the Book, which meant monotheists such as Christians and Jews, who found themselves in Islamic territory as the result of conquest had the right to a form of institutional protection known as *dhimma* that allowed them, with certain limitations, to practice their own religion,

The Mosque of Omar, Jerusalem. During the first two years of his ministry, Muhammad believed that the qibla, *the direction in which Muslims should face during prayer, was towards Jerusalem. Later, after a revelation, he determined that it should be towards Mecca. Since that time all mosques have been built on that axis.*

as long as they paid a tax. In the law codes, the statutes pertaining to *dhimma* had certain fixed rules for non-Muslims: they were required to offer three days of hospitality to every travelling Muslim; they could not ring bells (*nâqûs*) or raise their voices except in prayer; they were not allowed to build new churches or synagogues, could only repair those which were damaged, and could not enlarge them; they could not gather in groups with their coreligionists in Muslim neighborhoods; they could not display any outward sign of their faith or work at converting others to it; they could not learn the Koran or teach it to their children; they could not prevent others from converting to Islam; they could not resemble Muslims in dress or appearance; they had to bear a distinctive mark; they could not use a saddle when riding a horse; they had to honor and respect Muslims, and stand in their presence; they could not make their own houses higher than the houses of Muslims; they could not carry arms; they could not own Muslim slaves or own slaves which had previously belonged to Muslims.

That was the theory. The practice was probably often more accomodating and less rigid. It is certain, for example, that in addition to the property taxes paid by all landowners, taxes paid by *dhimmî* as the price for being allowed to follow their religion were an important source of income for the Muslim treasury. The rest can be intuited from other sources, often just simple hints, and often voices from afar, well beyond Sicily.

Concerning the Jews especially, their history was long and it preceded Islam by a great deal, and here it can only be summarized. For a number of centuries, the Jews had lived outside the land of Israel. As is well known, the final blow was delivered by Rome in the year 70 A.D. when, in response to continued Jewish revolts, Titus, the son of the emperor Vespasian, destroyed the temple in Jerusalem. Deprived once and for all of their place of worship, of the place where the commandments given by God on Mt. Sinai could be fulfilled, Jews adjusted to the situation by means of deep reflection on the fundamental nature of their religion and its future prospects. Now far from Jerusalem, often on the great trade routes of the era, the Jewish world defined itself more and more as the entirety of a Mediterranean community whose members were connected to each other. One aspect of their condition was not new for the Jews: as has been well-known since Biblical times, at least since the period of the second temple, the Jewish people were dispersed in foreign lands, in a movement known as the Diaspora, expressed in Hebrew, with a more negative meaning, as *galut*, or exile. In any case, during the centuries that followed, the Jewish community in the Mediterranean experienced considerable growth, helped by Muslim expansion. It was defined by a network of social, cultural, and commercial ties that extended to all the ports of the Mediterranean and beyond. There was, however, no "Jewish" Mediterranean as such, but rather a Jewish adaptation to the commercial life of the Mediterranean, something which involved in equal measure the Christians of Europe and the Muslims of North

Detail of a sculptural ornament on the family tomb of the Norman priest Grisanto. Twelfth century. Galleria Nazionale della Sicilia, Palermo.

Funerary stone with inscriptions in the four languages spoken in Sicily at the time: Arabic, Hebrew, Greek, and Latin. Commissioned in 1149 by the Norman priest Grisanto, "priest to His Royal Majesty," and dedicated to his mother Anna, who died in that same year. The dates carved on it are expressed according to the custom and in the alphabet of each language. Galleria Nazionale della Sicilia, Palermo.

الفرآن ثم وأبعد اساطير ملاها وزخارف جللها وقال اركبوا فيها بسم الله مجراها
ومرساها ثم تنفس نفس المغمين أو عباد الله للكرمين وقال اما انا

Africa and the Middle East. The unity of this Jewish society in the Mediterranean was the result of family ties, strong commercial relationships, and, above all, the shared religious beliefs and legal practices that were defined in the centuries that followed the destruction of the temple.

The same is true of the sources available to us for describing this world. Much information about the Jews in Sicily comes from the *genizah* of Cairo. That is the Hebrew term for a place set aside for the preservation of sacred materials that are no longer used. This place could be in a synagogue, a warehouse, a cave, or often a cemetery. In this sense, the *genizah* of the Ben 'Ezra synagogue in Fustat, or Old Cairo, preserved a treasure for many centuries. In its interior lay hundred of thousands of documents, including letters, account books, rabbinic rulings, collections of poetry, and treatises on science and philosophy. These were the written remains of an entire world, compiled for the most part between the eleventh and thirteenth centuries. The presence of so many secular texts is presumably due to the fact that almost all the documents were written in Hebrew characters and that those in charge of the *genizah* would have extended the definition of sacred to anything written in the language of the Bible. The preservation of these documents is not just rare, but unique, something that unexpectedly allows us to gaze on a world of great cultural liveliness that embraced the entire Mediterranean and of which Sicily was an integral part.

The delivery of letters between Sicily, the Maghreb, and Egypt was accomplished by a system of couriers that followed shipping routes at sea as well as caravan and pilgrimage routes on land, supporting a thick network of family and mercantile relationships that ensured the religious and legal unity of the various communities. Likely also in this way, a process of Arabization spread among the Jews of the Islamic Mediterranean, to an extent that even their personal names, such as Ibrâhîm, Da'ûd, Fadlûn, Ishâq, and Mûsâ, were often no different than Arab ones.

From a legal point of view, according to the laws of the *dhimma*, even the Jewish communities of Sicily, as in the rest of the Islamic world, governed themselves. Each *jama'a*, or community, was governed by a *Bet Dîn*, or rabbinic court, administered by its elders. It had its own tribunal and was responsible for communal goods and property, including the cemetery. The existence of a Jewish quarter in Palermo goes back at least to the end of the tenth century. We know little about their houses and whether they had commercial buildings, but we do have evidence of a Jewish quarter, a *hârat al-yahûd* in the area of today's Piazza Meschita. We also know of settlements in other cities such as Mazara, Messina, Ragusa, and Syracuse.

Later, well after the Norman conquest, the Jews would continue to function as an intermediary in the Arab world, or, in another way of looking at it, in the southern and eastern Mediterranean. This is attested by letters found in the *genizah* and the few narratives by Jewish travellers that have survived. The most famous of these was written by Benjamin of Tudela, a Spanish Jew who began his journey in 1160 and who, on his return trip more than ten years later, stopped in Sicily, which had only recently returned to Christian hands.

opposite page:
Arab ship, in a thirteenth-century manuscript by al-Hariri (folio 119v). Bibliotheque National de France, Paris.

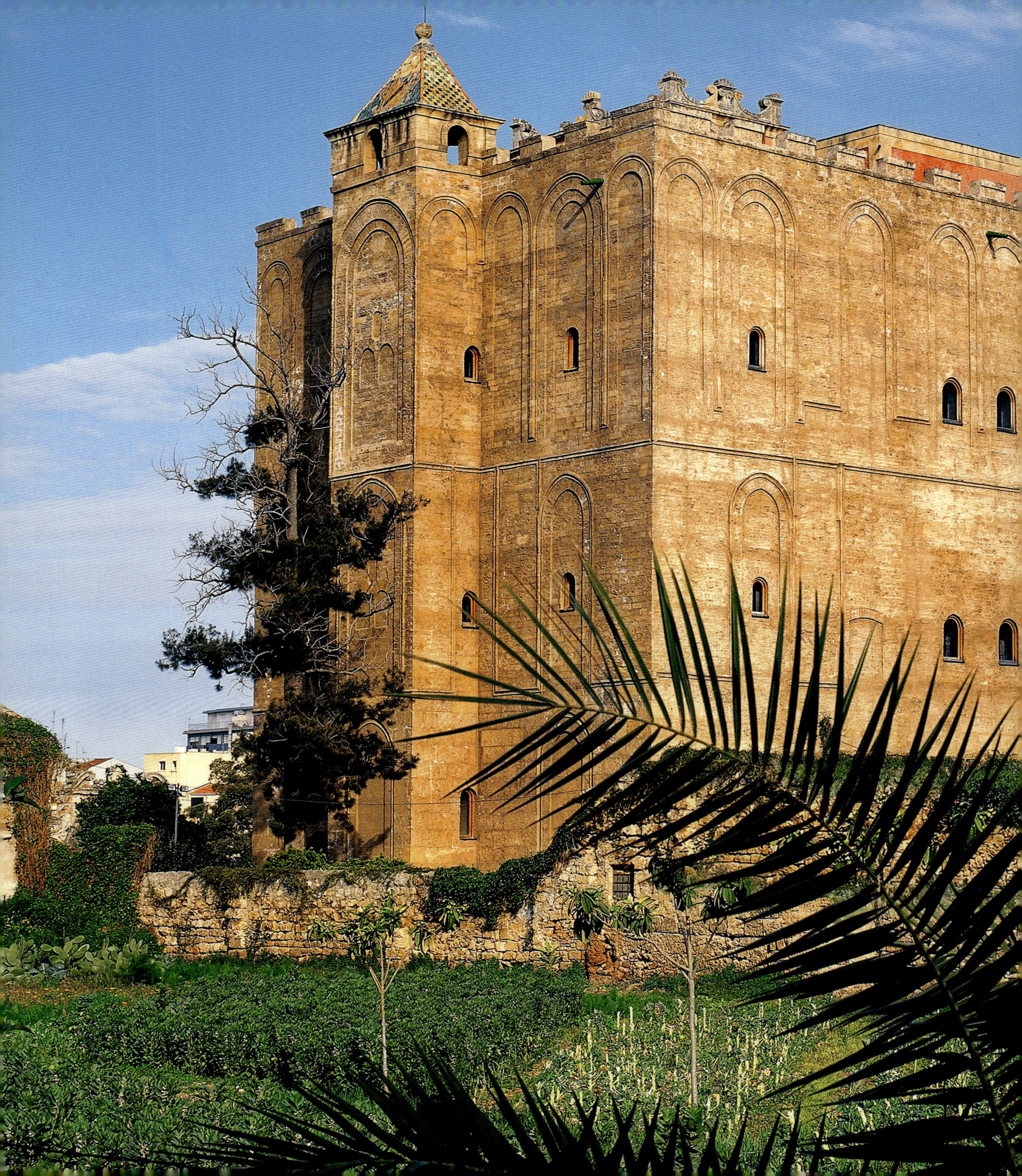

The palace of La Zisa, known in Arabic as al-Azīza, *perhaps from* al-azīz, *meaning "the resplendent one." At the time of its construction, it was outside the walls of Palermo, in the luxuriant royal park built by the Normans known as the Genoard. Construction was begun by William I and finished between 1165 and 1180 by William II. It was the summer residence of the Norman kings.*

"A voyage of twenty days takes one from Egypt to Messina, which rises at the extreme tip of Sicily. Situated on an arm of the Sea of Lipari, which separates it from Calabria, it is inhabited by some two hundred Jews. The area abounds in all types of riches, with orchards and gardens. This is the gathering place for most of the pilgrims who are on their way to Jerusalem, as it is the best place to ferry across. Some two days from Messina is the great city of Palermo. Here is the palace of King William, and the home of some one thousand five hundred Jews, besides a great number of Muslims and Christians. The region is rich with rivers and streams, wheat and barley, gardens and orchards, all without equal in all of Sicily."

Just a few words which display a relatively new geography, a map of Judaism that offered itself as a useful tool for those who might travel in the author's footsteps, and a map, above all, that confirms Sicily's role in the Mediterranean at the center of a strong network of social, religious, and intellectual contacts.

above:
La Zisa: Hall of the Fountain

opposite page:
La Zisa: exterior view

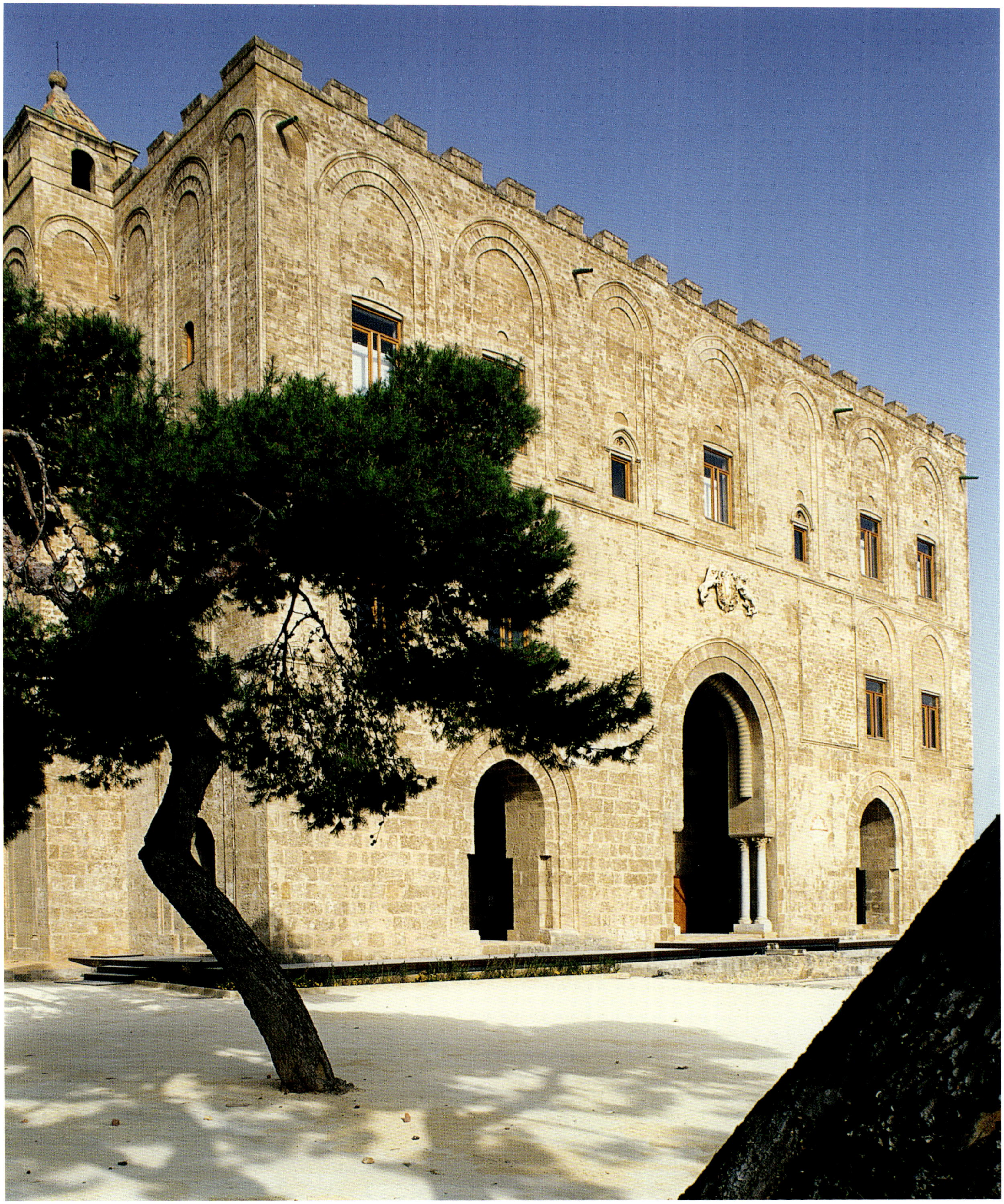

Mechanism of a water pump for a fountain, from a Seljuk manuscript by al-Jazari (1206). The Muslims who arrived in Sicily in the ninth century brought their hydraulic technology, which was of Iranian origin, with them. They created very complex water systems that produced abundant crops and luxurious gardens. Topkapi Museum, Istanbul.

ARAB CULTURE AND SCIENCE IN SICILY

Knowledge of Islamic Sicily is intimately and inevitably tied to the spread of the Arabic language. It is a language that, all things considered, at that time could still boast a certain youthfulness. Apart from a few early inscriptions, the first genuine text in Arabic is the Koran, which contains the preaching of Muhammad and was written down sometime after his death in 632. For this reason, if for a linguist Arabic is simply a southern-Semitic language, for the faithful it is the word of God that, in the Koran, has become scripture. It is a transformation that occurs in a more profound sense than the one shared by the Hebrew Bible and the Gospel: God, or *Allah*, physically becomes a word, and is embodied in writing, becoming scripture, book, and ink all at once. It is useless to warn that such a line of thought has consequences. In this way the Koran is understood as the repository of a definitive Arabic grammar and of a perfect language that is incomparable in its beauty.

Along with the Islamic conquest, the Arabic of the Koran and of the new community of believers spread rapidly, although it did so in fits and starts, as in each region it came up against the languages already spoken there. To the west, it came in contact with Coptic, a later form of ancient Egyptian, and in the rest of North Africa with the many variants of that native language which the Arabs called *barbariyya*, or Berber. The spread of Arabic proceeded, therefore, in stages, following the new military outposts and developing new hybrid dialects. As the encampments such as Fustât/Cairo in Egypt and Kairouan in Tunisia later became cities, they acquired mosques, schools, and administrative centers, all of which helped to

A boat transporting musicians, *from the* Book of the Knowledge of Mechanical Works *by al-Jazari. Topkapi Museum, Istanbul.*

preserve the Arabic language and which allowed it to exercise a parallel and at the same time unifying influence on the evolution of each separate group of local dialects. So on the one hand there was an everyday spoken language, derived from a continual hybridization among local dialects and the influence of classical Arabic. On the other was an official language used in public addresses and for writing that always remained the same, with the perfection of the Koran as its model. The same thing occurred, naturally, in Sicily. Little by little, classical Arabic inevitably became the language of institutions, here also following the establishment of mosques, schools, and new centers of government power. We do not know much about the spoken language of the Arabs of Sicily, but many authors indicate that it had diverged quite a bit from classical Arabic. Among them was the previously mentioned Ibn Makki, in his book on the linguistic errors of the Sicilians, and also the geographer Ibn Hawqal who, with truly not a little arrogance, did not miss any chance to criticize the ignorance of the teachers in Sicily and the provincial pronunciation of the Sicilians.

In any case, Arab-Islamic culture in Sicily remained substantially under the influence of the Maghreb, continuing to depend above all on Ifrîqiya and Muslim Spain. We have previously seen this, for example, in the law. The Malikite school, along with the Hanafite, was widespread. It was known above all for its prestigious school in Mazara, of which the greatest member was the eleventh-century imam al-Mâzarî (d. 1141). In addition to law, other disciplines connected to the Koran were cultivated, such as exegesis, the knowledge of the different interpretations of the Koran, and the traditions regarding the Prophet Muhammad. Besides the study of religion, although, at least at the beginning, subordinate to it, the study of philology

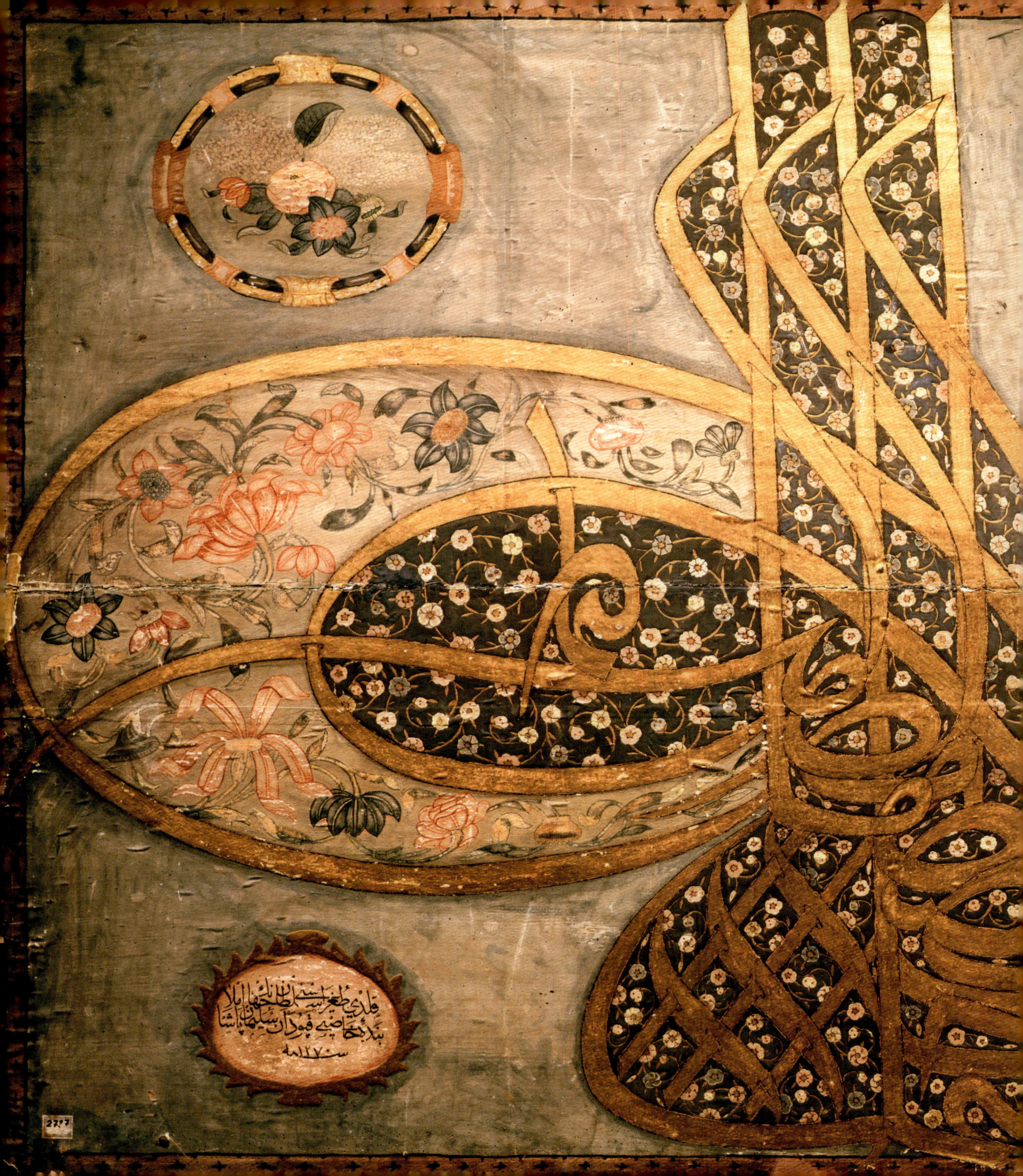
قلدی طغراسنی سلطان جهانك املا
بنده خاصی قپودان سلیمان پاشا

MUSLIM SICILY . 95

The precious Koran of Sultan Osman III, painted on wood in the ninth century. Museum of Islamic and Turkish Art, Istanbul. Islam's laws regarding the depiction of images, which were strictly applied in the religious context and less so in secular life, pushed artists in the direction of elaborate decorative forms based on the alphabet and on vegetal and floral motifs. These forms presented a wide range of choices and would be used lavishly in the varied and high-quality textiles produced in Sicily.

The prince, bitten by a serpent, is healed thanks to an antidote. From the Book of Antidotes *by the Pseudo Galen, twelfth century. Bibliotheque Nationale de France, Paris. Arab medicine, which both derived from and built on the medical knowledge and practices of the ancient Greeks, first arrived in Italy, in Salerno specifically, during the second half of the eleventh century. The pages of this treatise provide examples of the revisions and modifications made to the medical knowledge of the Greeks.*

opposite page:
Two musicians, a Moor and a Christian, play for the entertainment of the court. An illustration from Las Cantigas de Santa Maria *by Alfonso X el Sabio, in the Library of the Monastery of San Lorenzo, the Escorial, Madrid*

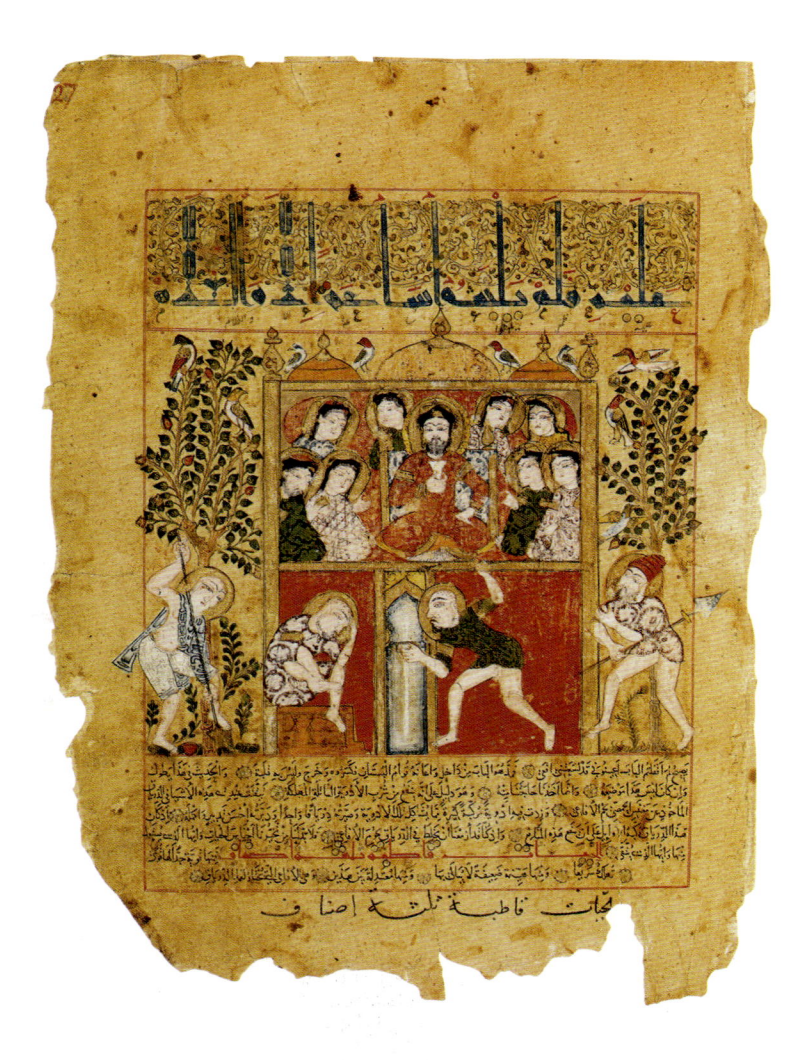

was also prevalent in Sicily. Ibn al-Birr al-Siqillî, who remained in Sicily until 1068, was the first to study pure grammar, while Ibn Makki was the most interesting exponent of dictionaries and word analysis.

The criticism and study of literature was dominated by Ibn Rashîq (d. 1070) and Ibn al-Qattâ (d. 1121). The second of these was perhaps the most learned of all the Sicilian men of letters. He was the author of a sadly lost "History of Sicily" and the editor of an anthology titled *al-Durra al-Khatira fî shu'arâ' al-jazîra*, or "The Precious Pearl about the Poets of the Island," which contained information on one hundred seventy Sicilian poets and twenty thousand lines of verse, but which has come down to us only in two brief abridgements. We do have two collections of poems, one by al-Billanûbi (d. early twelfth century) and one with more than six thousand lines by Ibn Hamdîs, the greatest of the Arab-Sicilian poets (d. 1132).

Even in its poetry, Sicily remained an offshoot of al-Andalus. The Sicilian poets known to us followed the more classic poetic tradition, in both language and meter, of their Spanish contemporaries, using their work almost as a template. The only note of particular interest comes from Ibn Hamdîs, the author of the lines which opened our brief history:

" My homeland does not wish to return to her people; I think badly of her, and have given up hope.
I lament it with all my heart, as I have seen her suffer a deadly, evil sickness.

MUSLIM SICILY

this page and opposite: *Arab astrolabe (front and back) built in 1102 by Muhammad Ibn Qasim Ibn Bakran. Museo delle Scienze, Florence. Due to their passion for observation and the description of natural phenomena, the Arabs were master builders of precision instruments, including flat astrolabes.*

And how could it be otherwise when she has been dishonored, when by the
 hands of the Christians the mosques are turned into churches?
The monks now ring their bells from morning till evening.
Fate has betrayed Sicily, which was once a fortress against its blows.
I see my land humiliated by the *Rûm*, while before, under my people, its honor
 was great.
The infidels once lived in fear of her, while today she lives in dread of them.
In those brave men, you have lost the Arab lions, in whose claws the barbarians
 were prey.
Was it not by them that Calabria was overrun, where they killed lords and
 bold warriors?
With their swords they opened the gates and left behind a light made of
 darkness, and took as captives unveiled girls whose long hair
 covered them like a cloak.
To reach the enemy, they went endlessly to the sea, and themselves
 became a sea, with waves of knights, and warships which flung
 their flaming oil that goes up the nostrils.
These galleys, with red and green felt hangings on their sides,
 seemed like black-skinned girls taken as brides.
When the furnaces of burning liquid sent up their smoke,
 it seemed as if the vents of a volcano had been
 blown open..."

But Arab culture, at least in its widest sense, did not show its influence only in the few manuscripts that have come down to us. It still echoes in the names of places and people, and it is found in their habits, customs, songs, music, and beliefs.

It is also there in the objects, architecture, and tools that in large part would pass to the new Norman conquerors, enriching their culture considerably. Even in this case, that which survives of the art and architecture of Arab Sicily is only a small part of what was extant at the time. The reason for this is the unusual circumstance of slow settlement by the Arabs and rapid reconquest by the Christians (although, perhaps, our lack of understanding may be due to a lack of sufficient archaeological research).

It is difficult, for example, to find any traces of the almost three hundred mosques that, according to Ibn Hawqal, existed in Palermo at the time. There is little evidence, and most of it vague, for the so-called "hypostyle hall of the Aglabids" in today's chapel of Santa Maria

following pages:
The constellations of Pegasus and Canis Minor. Illustrations from the Liber De Locis Stellarum, *a Latin translation of a work by the astronomer Umar al-Sufi (903-986) that was based on the* Almagest of Ptolemy *and compiled at the court of William II in Palermo. Its illustrations are now held by various institutions. Bibliothèque de l'Arsenal, Paris; private collection.*

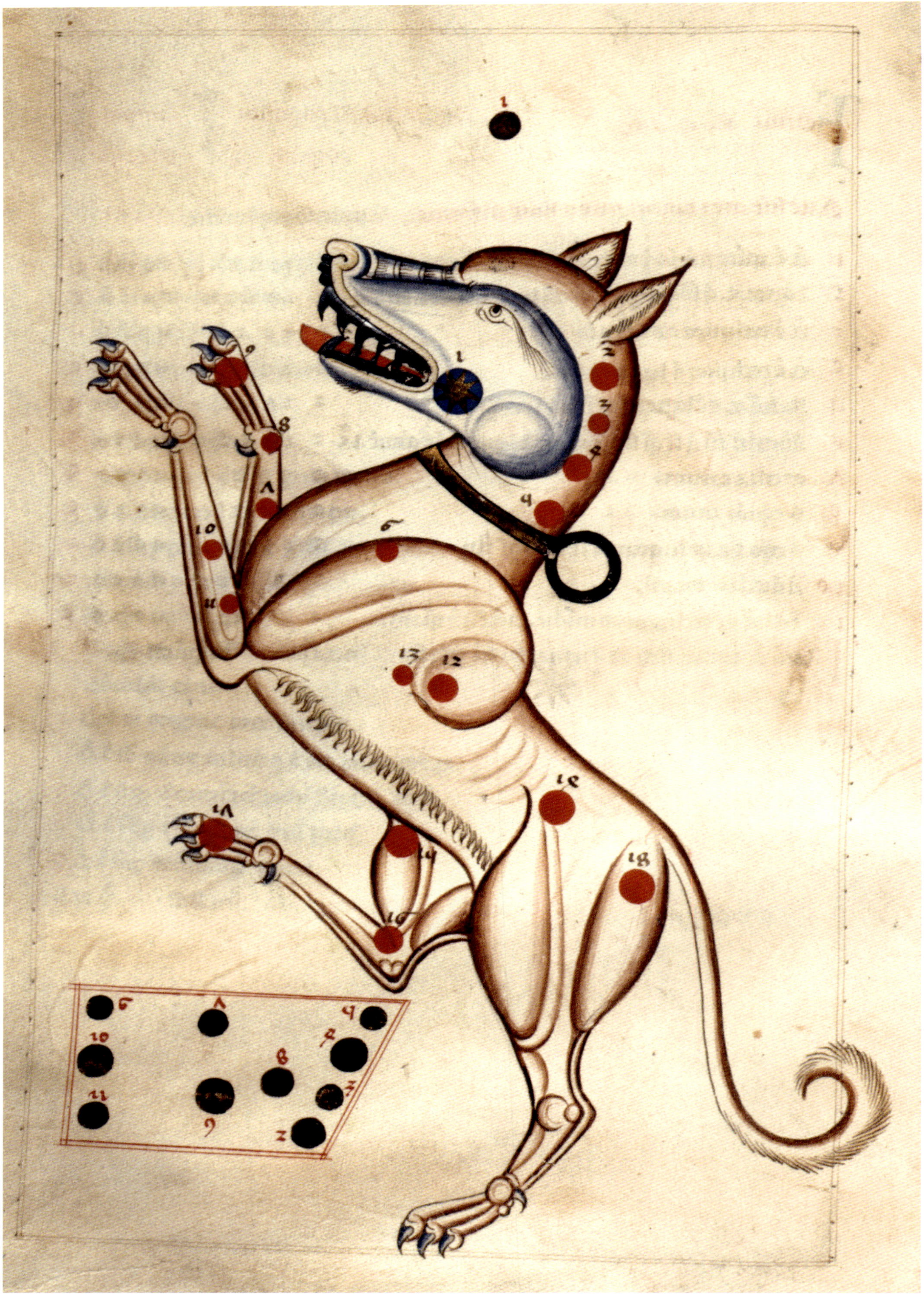

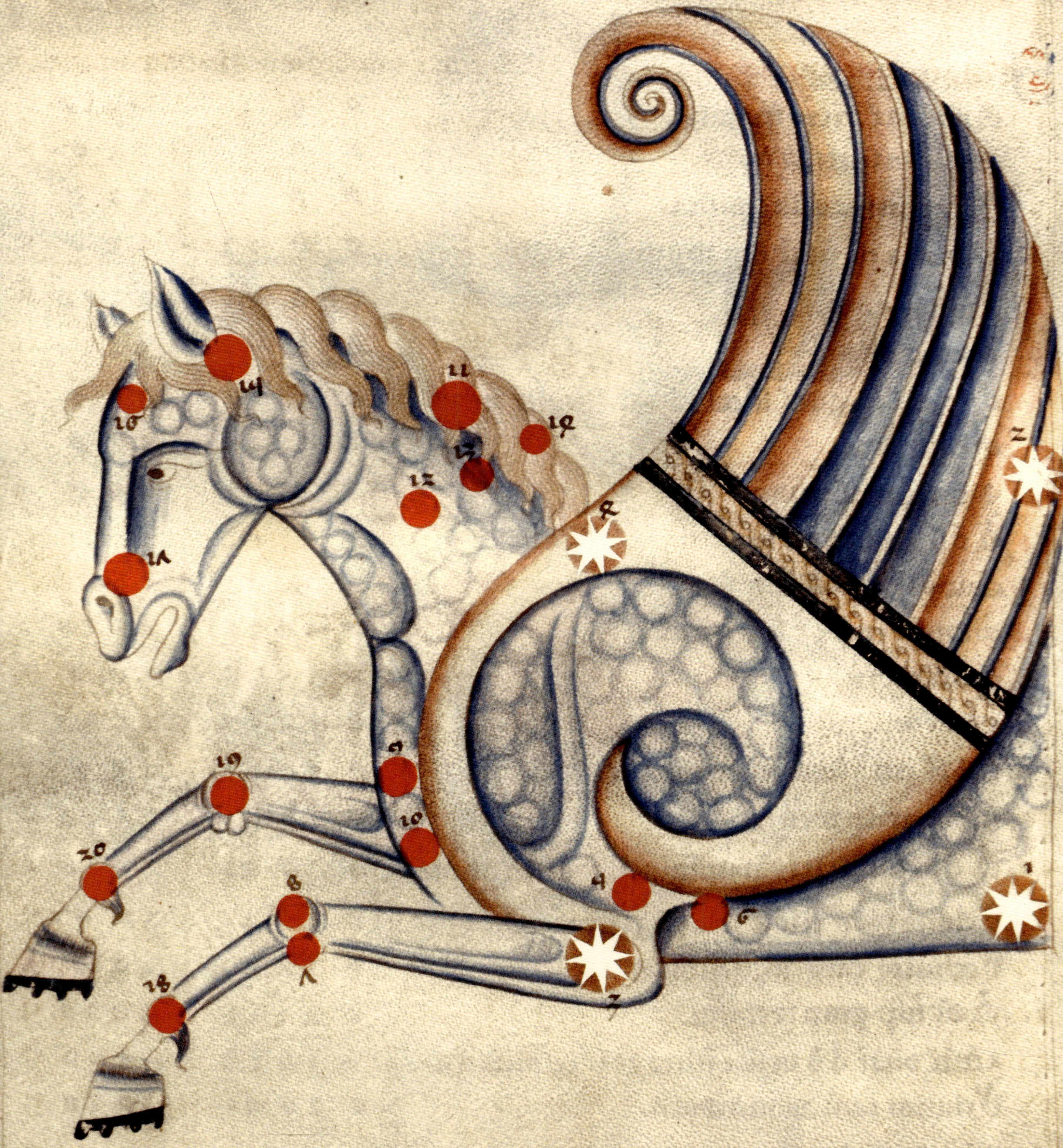

l'Incoronata, near the cathedral, or for the hall with two aisles on the southeast side of the courtyard of the church of San Giovanni degli Eremiti. In both cases, the hypostyle (with a roof resting on rows of columns) type of the hall and its ample width suggest a likely resemblance to the prayer hall of a mosque. There is also the mosque presumably identified at Segesta, based on the presence of a niche suitable for a *mihrab* on the one excavated wall. But in reality, perhaps, the most solid evidence for all these mosques is the great number of columns ornamented with epigraphic scrolls and Kufic script that can today be seen in the churches of the Magione and the Martorana, on the east door of the Duomo, and in the Pepoli Museum in Trani. All of them, and not by chance, are close in style to those of the great mosques of Kairouan and Tunis.

As concerns civil architecture, Arab influence may be seen in a small bathhouse in the town of Cefala Diana. Now somewhat reduced in size, it is next to a thermal spring and includes two basins of different sizes which are separated by three arches over a pair of columns. There is a simple decoration in Kufic script that probably dates to the eleventh century.

Inscriptions are often the only evidence for other buildings of the period. For example, there is one from the tenth century in Palermo and another in Termini Imerese whose text, even though it is brief and fragmentary, is in Kufic script in a Maghreb style. Similar ornamental writing is found on contemporary funerary markers. These indicate a society that was relatively prosperous, at least in its upper classes, and able to commission works of considerable cost, perhaps importing them from nearby Africa.

The production of ceramics was also important, and there is evidence of it in two kilns discovered at Agrigento which would have been active during the period of

Marble plaque with inscriptions in three languages marking the installation of a water-clock in 1142. Cappella Palatina, Palermo. It was an example of the various complex automata, mechanical devices constructed according to technical manuals such as the previously mentioned treatise of al-Jazari. The inscription is clear evidence of the multiculturalism and modernity of the Sicilian court.

opposite page:
The cathedral of Palermo, detail.

MUSLIM SICILY . 103

Bowl painted with brown manganese, green copper, and yellow iron, glazed with lead. Sicilian-Muslim production, late eleventh century. Museo Archeologico, Reggio Calabria. In Muslim Palermo a section of the city was set aside for the production of ceramics, and one neighborhood was occupied exclusively by potters.

opposite page:
Basin with colorless lead glaze. Made in Africa, eleventh century. Removed from the church of San Zeno, now in the Museo Nazionale San Matteo, Pisa.

Arab rule. The material found there indicates that the kilns produced non-colored (mostly black, grey, or white) pottery used for closed containers such as amphorae and jars, and also the leaded-glass pottery used above all for bowls and basins, which could be monochrome (usually green) or polychrome. The first type would have an impressed decoration, while the second would be painted with brown manganese and green copper. Besides vegetal ornamentation, it would include spindle-shaped elements, vine-shoots, lobed palmettes, and typical Arabic script. It is likely that several basins discovered in Pisa were produced in Sicily in the tenth or eleventh centuries.

This is little enough information, but it does not exhaust our knowledge of Islamic Sicily. Especially as concerns artistic activity, we can turn to that which came shortly after, in particular to the architectural evidence and luxury goods of the Norman period.

MUSLIM SICILY . 105

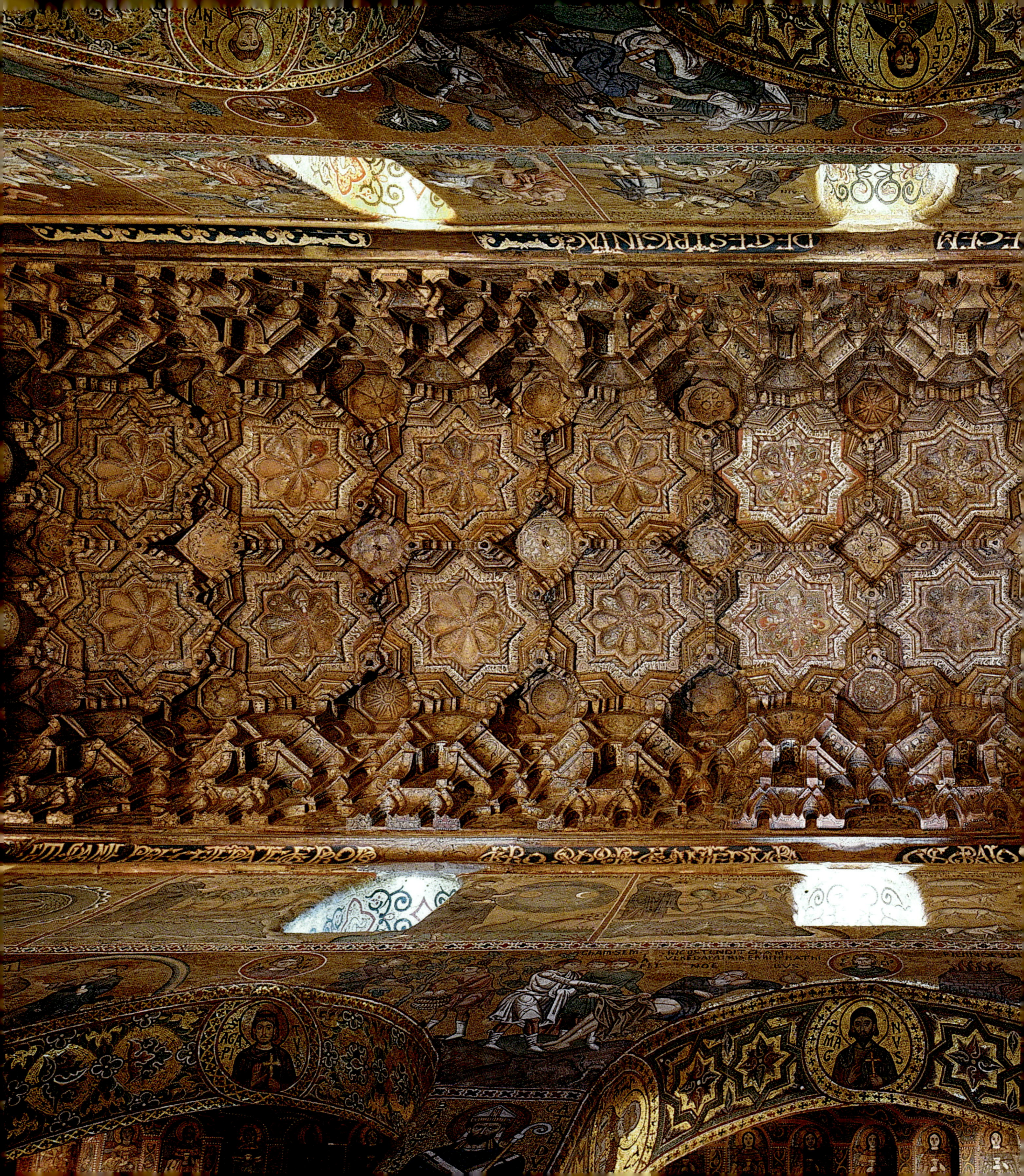

THE MEMORY OF MUSLIM SICILY

THE MEMORY OF MUSLIM SICILY

The fact that most of the traces of the Arab presence in Sicily are from the Norman period says a great deal about the close connection between those two cultures. It is well-known and not explained by the simple and slightly anachronistic notion of Norman tolerance. In any case, the influences were not in one direction only. If in one sense a process was begun by which the culture of Sicily became more Christian and Latin, in another we are well aware of the extent to which the culture and way of life of the Islamic world were welcomed by the Norman court and even, in general, by the higher levels of the social hierarchy. Above all, as some recent studies show, it is not maintained that the Arab influences absorbed by the Normans were all of Sicilian origin. They often came from outside, from the larger Mediterranean area that was linked to the Islamic world by geographic, commercial, and political ties. In fact, many of the customs connected to Norman kingship were inspired by the Fatimids of Cairo.

On an administrative level, well after the Norman victory, there was an institution in Sicily in charge of fiscal and tax matters that had the significant name of *dohana*, evidently from the Arabic word *diwân*, or counsel. In the same way, at least until the time of William I, the highest official of the royal bureaucracy would retain the Arab title of *amîr*. Islamic influence would also be seen in the army, where for a long time Arab and Berber soldiers fought alongside Norman troops, and in coinage, which would continue to indicate the year according to the Islamic calendar. But above all, the connection to the Islamic world would continue to be felt in things: in the objects of daily life, in the arts, and in architecture.

If it were necessary to settle everything with just two examples, the choice would be almost inevitable: the

above left:
Detail from a wheel on an ecclesiastical robe made of jasper or purple samite on which two backward-glancing parrots are shown. The parrot is an auspicious bird, a symbol of heavenly bliss and a decorative motif very common in Islamic iconography. From the Byzantine hexàmitos *(a textile produced on a loom with six heddles,* héx *meaning six, and* mìtos *meaning thread), samite was a silk cloth made from two warps and between two and four woofs that was very resistant and without a reverse side. Thirteenth century. Treasury of the Cathedral of Anagni.*

The "rooster-hawk," a rare Iranian bronze from 897, used as an incense burner. Bronze, delicately engraved with ornamentation and Kufic inscriptions. Church of San Frediano, Lucca.

preceding pages:
The inlaid ceiling of the Cappella Palatina.

ceiling of the Cappella Palatina in the Palazzo dei Normanni in Palermo, and the "Book of King Roger," which was compiled under the direction of the Muslim scholar Idrîsi with Roger's patronage. The fact that both date to the time of Roger II (1130-1154), founder of the kingdom, says a great deal about the importance that this cultural effect had for the new rulers of Sicily.

There are other later traces which are likewise justifiably famous. The pavilion of La Cuba, constructed on the order of William II around 1180, was one of these. It was

Detail from the Box of the Falconers. Sicilian-Islamic. Treasury of the Cathedral of Veroli. The figures are painted and show a favorite activity in both Arab and Norman culture.

110 . ALESSANDRO VANOLI

Among the folds in the ceiling of the Cappella Palatina, one can still make out some of the gold highlights that once enriched it. In the words of Teofane Cerameo, a Byzantine intellectual and official orator at the Norman court, "from every side the vault of the nighttime sky seems to glitter with gold when the chorus of the stars shines in the pure air."

MUSLIM SICILY . 111

The honeycombed ceiling of the Cappella Palatina. Seen from below, it is difficult to make out the small painted figures which nevertheless create the effect of a sumptuous web.

this page and opposite: *The* muqarnas *that are interlaced like embroidery on the ceiling of the middle nave of the Cappella Palatina are of Fatimid workmanship and constitute the most extensive Islamic pictorial cycle that has come down to us.*

MUSLIM SICILY . 113

used for ceremonial functions, and also for occasional relaxation, as can be understood from its reduced size and extreme simplicity of structure. The arrangement of the interior, with two large halls that open on one central hall that was originally domed (the name *Cuba* comes from the Arabic word *qubba*, or cupola), betrays Sicily's deep ties to other areas of the Mediterranean: the architectural traces recall Egypt as much as the Maghreb of the eleventh century.

Another monument deeply influenced by Islam is naturally the palace of La Zisa, in Palermo. It dates to the second half of the twelfth century and was built by William I and William II. It is an architecturally complex structure, with a rectangular antechamber that leads to a large cruciform hall with niches surmounted by small honeycomb-shaped spaces, or *muqarnas*. At the end, in an alcove on an axis with the entrance, is a fountain with water that flows into channels that cross the room.

In general, there are many churches from the Norman period in which the arches, pavements, and decorative elements (cornices, panels, and crenellations in the shape of stylized palms) echo important Islamic themes. Speaking of churches, it

La Cuba, a splendid example of Fatimid architecture, built by William II in 1180.

The stalactitic tapers known as muqarnas *on the ceiling of the Hall of the Fountain, a room in La Zisa in which diplomatic delegations were received.*

opposite page:
The church of San Cataldo, built on the order of Maio of Bari, the prime minister of William I, around 1155. Later known as "the Emir of Emirs," he was the most powerful man after the king. Hated by the clergy, he was assassinated in public on the streets of Palermo by Matteo Bonello in 1160.

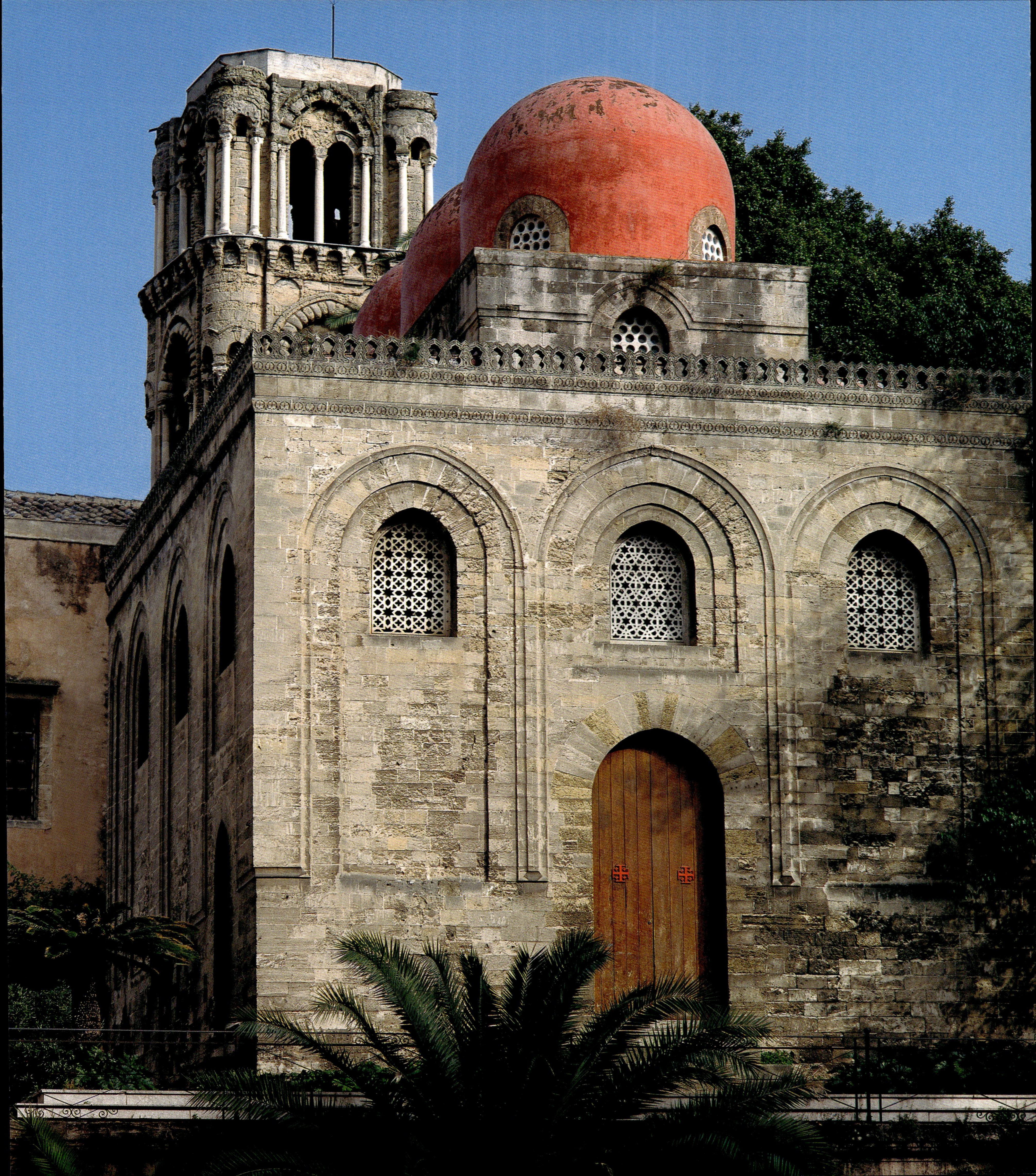

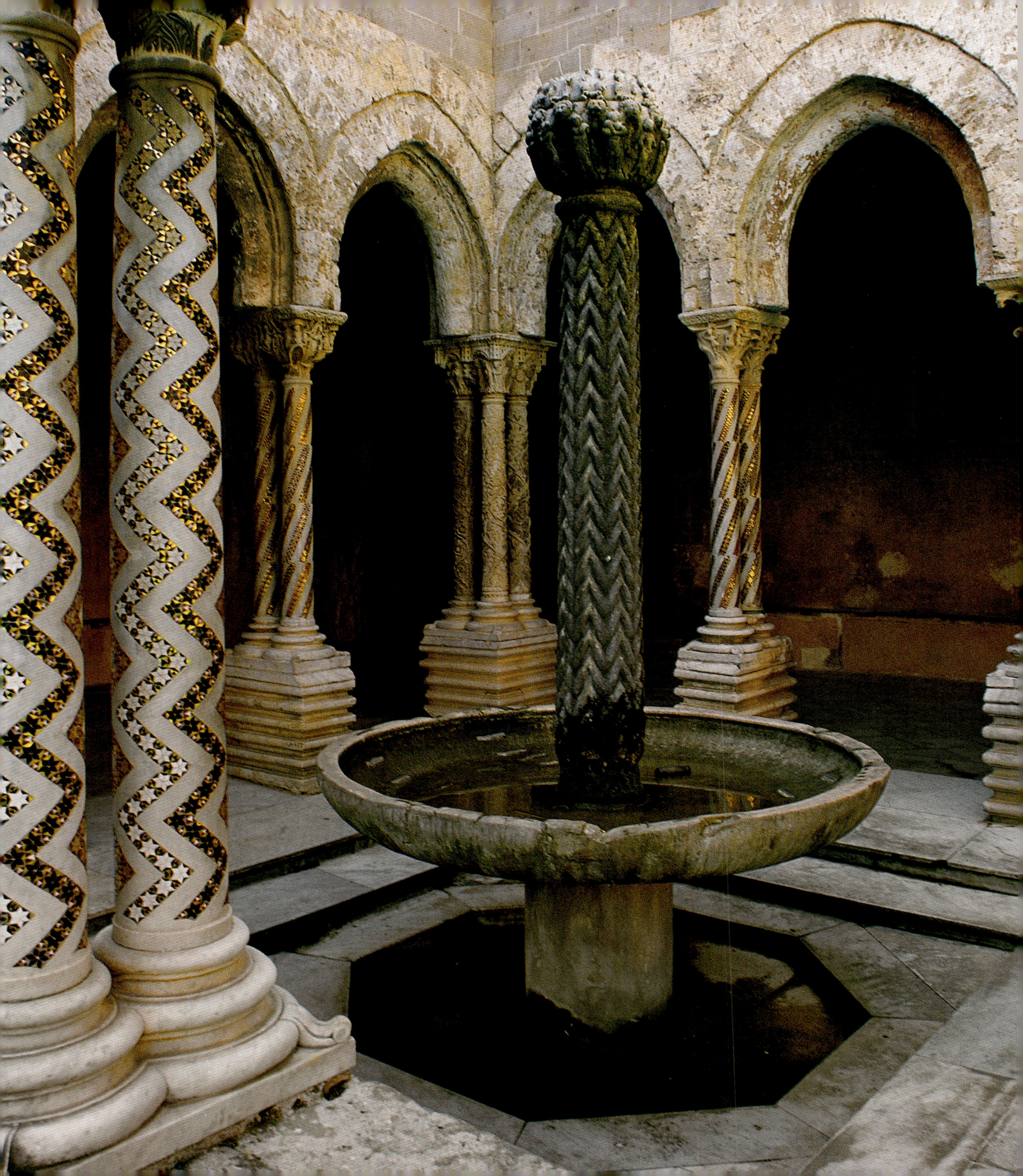

View of the small dome over the connecting niches on the ceiling of the chapel in the castle of La Favara (from fawara, *Arabic for "spring"), a suburban villa built on an artificial lake known as Maredolce ("sweet sea"). Both Ugo Falcando, a twelfth-century historian, and Romuald, the archbishop of Salerno, attribute its construction to Roger II, but it may have made use of an earlier building erected by the Kalbid emir Giafar (997-1019).*

opposite page:
Fountain in the Muslim style in the cloister of the cathedral of Monreale. Architectural elements such as gardens, fountains, and artificial lakes made Palermo "a city of marvels, built like Cordoba," according to Ibn Jubair.

is worthwhile to refer again to the ceiling of the Cappella Palatina. Located within the Palazzo dei Normanni (constructed on the orders of Roger II, begun in 1132, and completed around 1140), it provides in fact absolutely the most important pictorial record in all of Muslim art. It is a complex structure in wood, with recessed panels that enclose small lobed cupolas and which connect to the surrounding walls by means of *muqarnas* that are covered with a thin layer of plaster on which the decoration is painted in tempera. This unique work contains a kaleidoscopic repertory of figures, both human and animal. The main figure is the prince, pictured on his throne and surrounded by a court consisting of dignitaries who are drinking, listening intently to music, and admiring veiled dancers. There are also chess players, jugglers, and wrestlers, as well as scenes of the hunt, the favorite pastime of the prince, with its typical animals, birds, and plants.

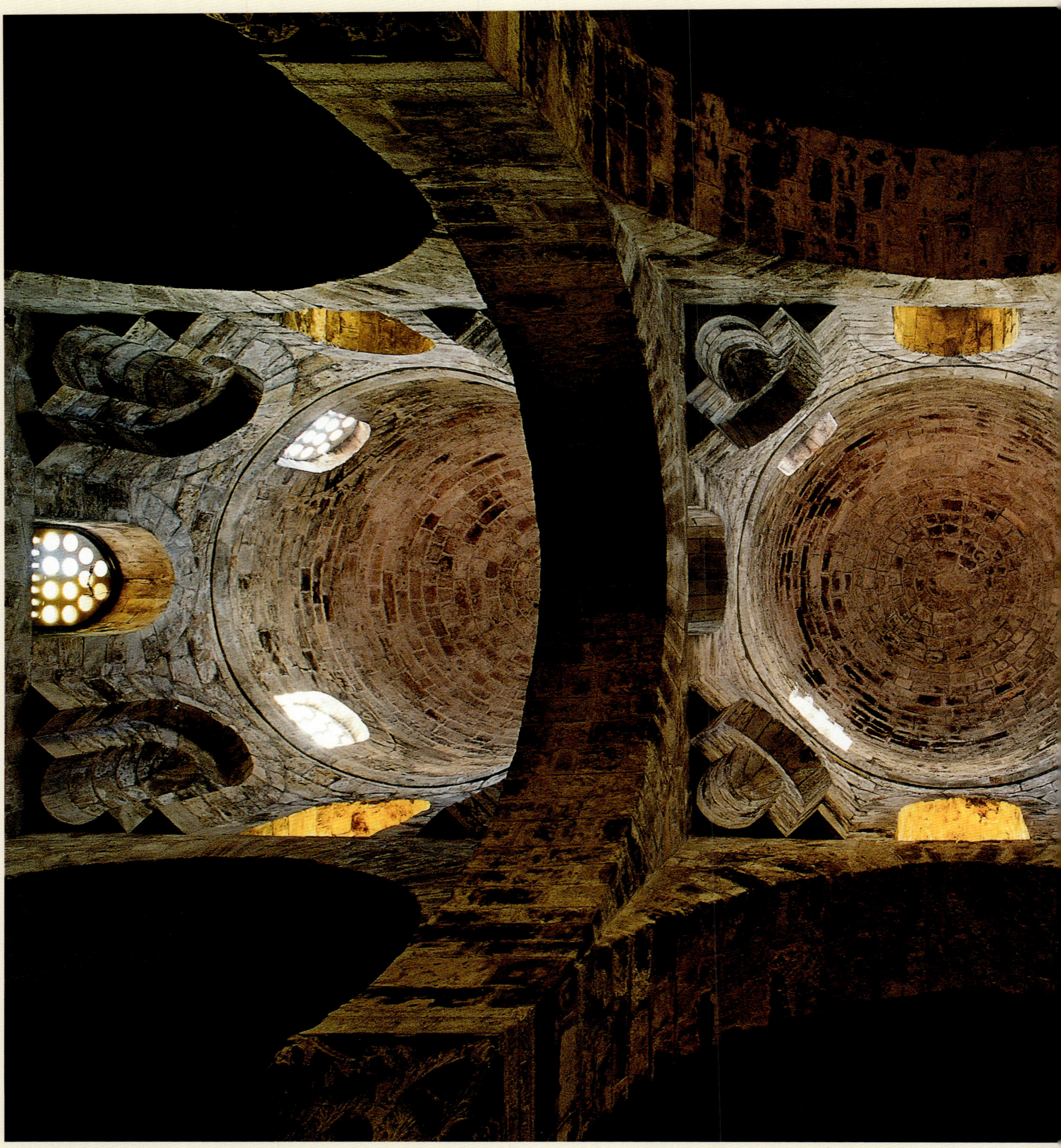

MUSLIM SICILY . **119**

Interior view of the three domes of the church of San Cataldo in Palermo. Built during the reign of William I, the church displays a sense of volume and ornament that is typically Arab.

following pages:
The bell tower of the church of Santa Maria dell'Ammiraglio (also known as La Martorana). Compared to the church itself, the construction of which was begun in 1143 by George of Antioch, the bell tower was built later, near the end of the twelfth century, after George had already died. In 1282, some one hundred forty years after the construction of the church, barons and representatives of the various Sicilian cities met there in order to offer the crown of Sicily to Peter of Aragon.

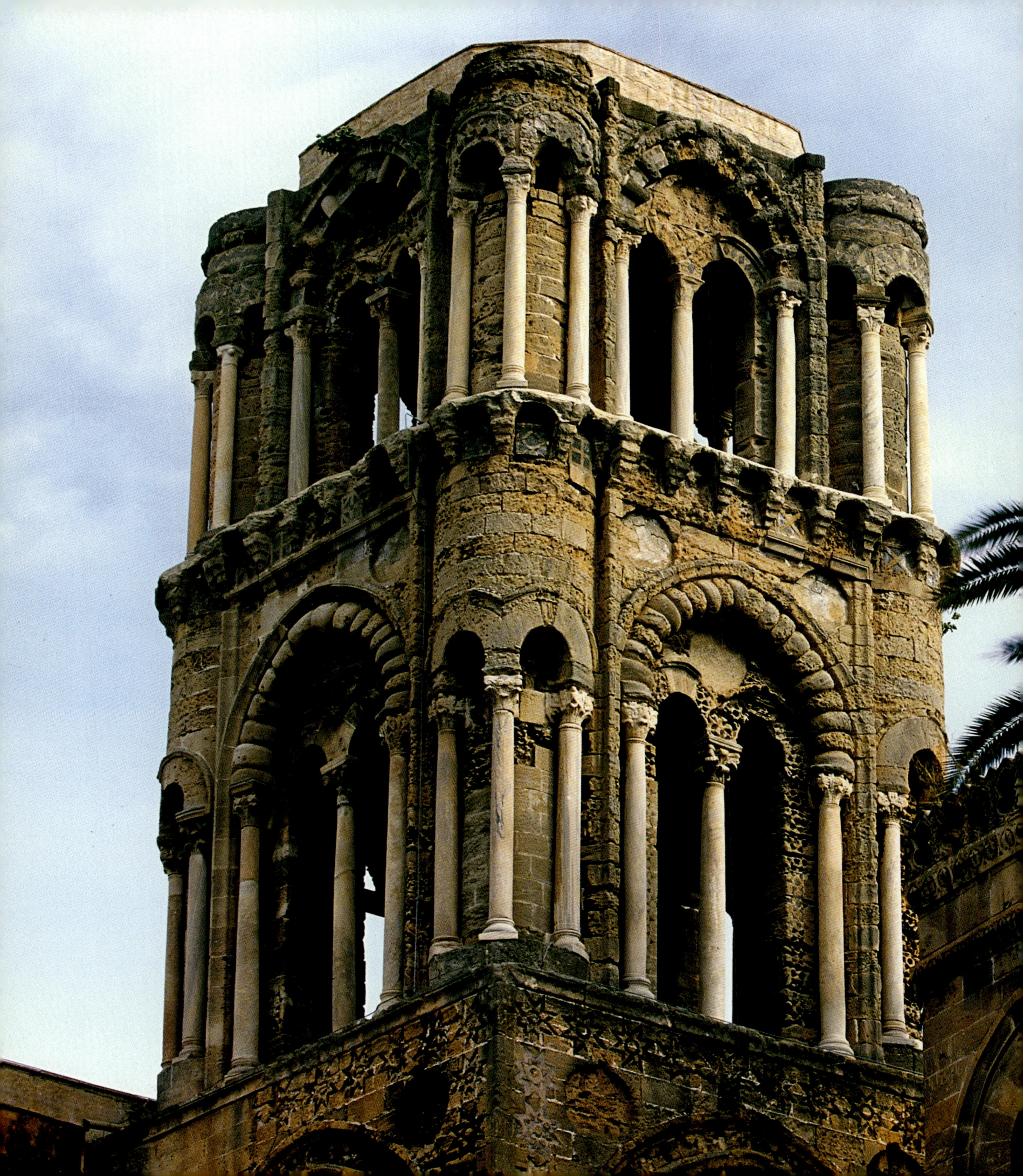

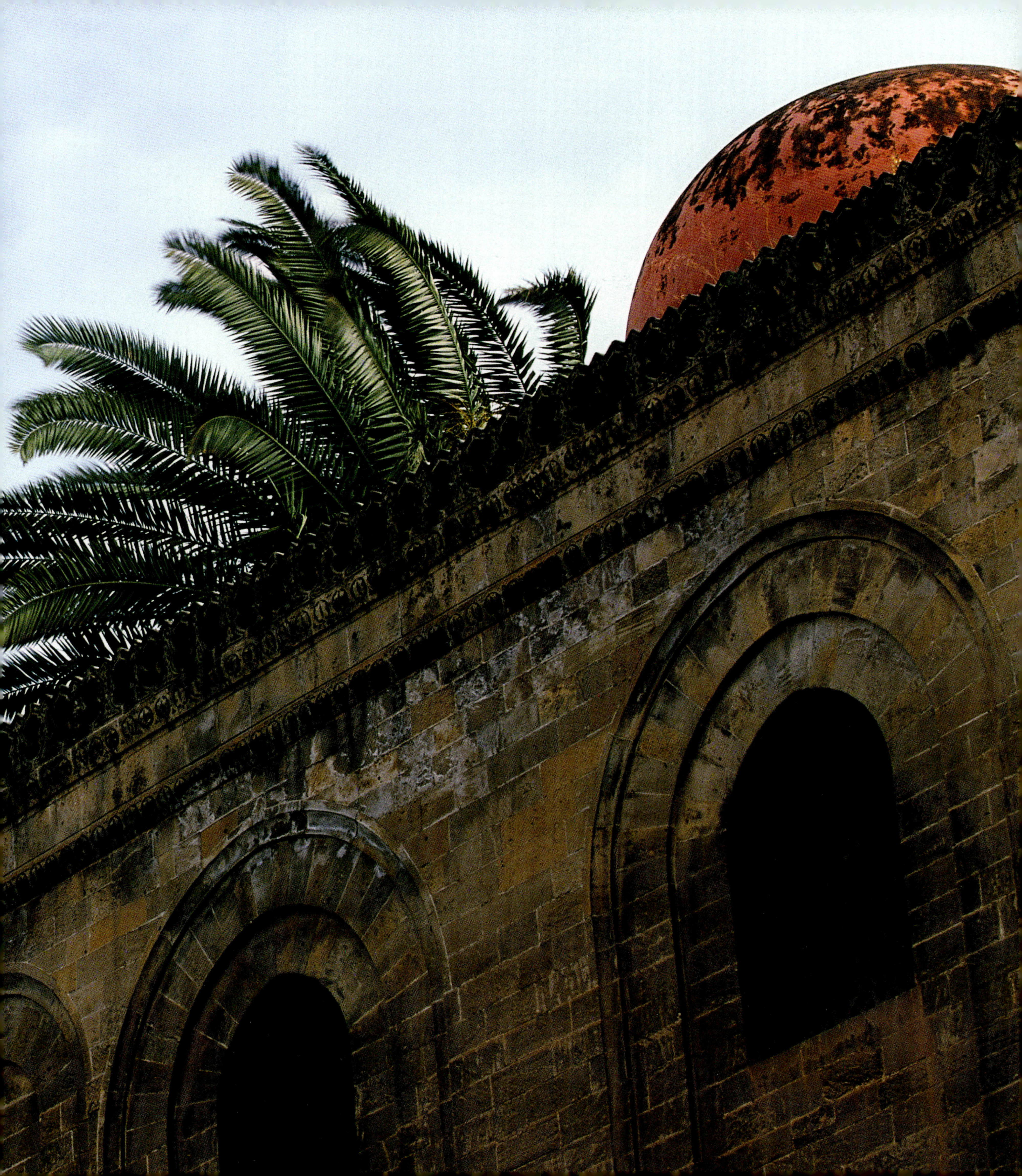

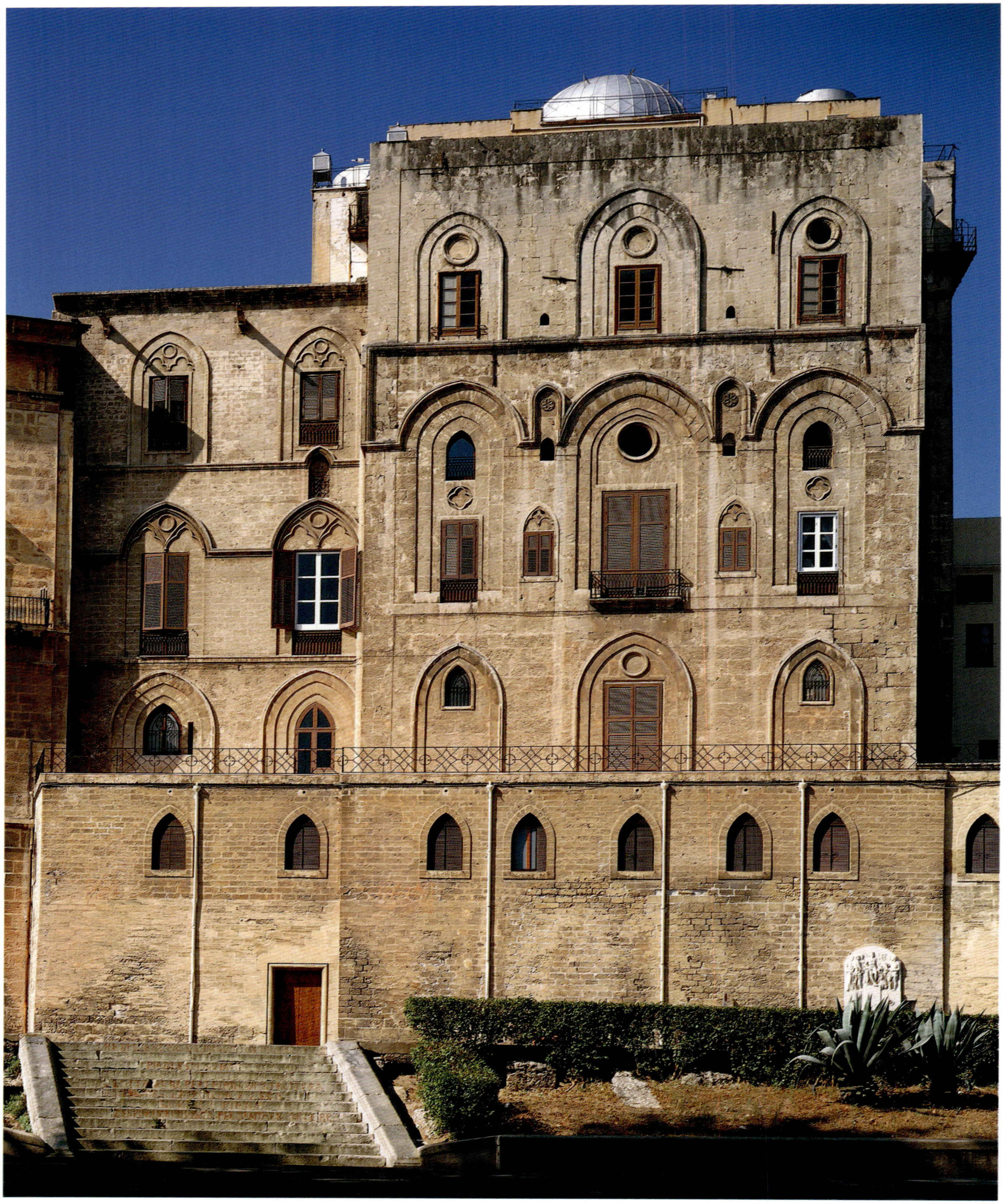

One can continue, recalling other domes, such as those of San Giovanni degli Eremiti and San Giovanni dei Lebbrosi. There were also ivories, precious boxes, stained glass, and jewels. All were the result of refined craftsmanship of great antiquity, as were the fabrics, the most famous of which is the robe of King Roger, now in Vienna, with an embroidered inscription that dates it to 1133–1134. This is the evidence of a world that for a long time continued to look east and south for its inspiration. And it is what can be understood from a famous work of geography by Idrîsi, the *Nuzhat al-mushtâq fî ikhtirâq al-âfâq*, or "An entertainment for those who love to travel the world," better known as the "Book of King Roger," who was its

The Church of the Magione, an elegant example of Arab style, founded in 1191 by the bishop Matteo d'Aiello for Cistercian monks.

opposite page:
The Palazzo dei Normanni, or Palazzo Reale, was built on the site of the Qasr, a ninth-century Arab castle that was renovated and enlarged by the Normans. Strengthened and reinforced by four towers, it became the principal fortress of the city.

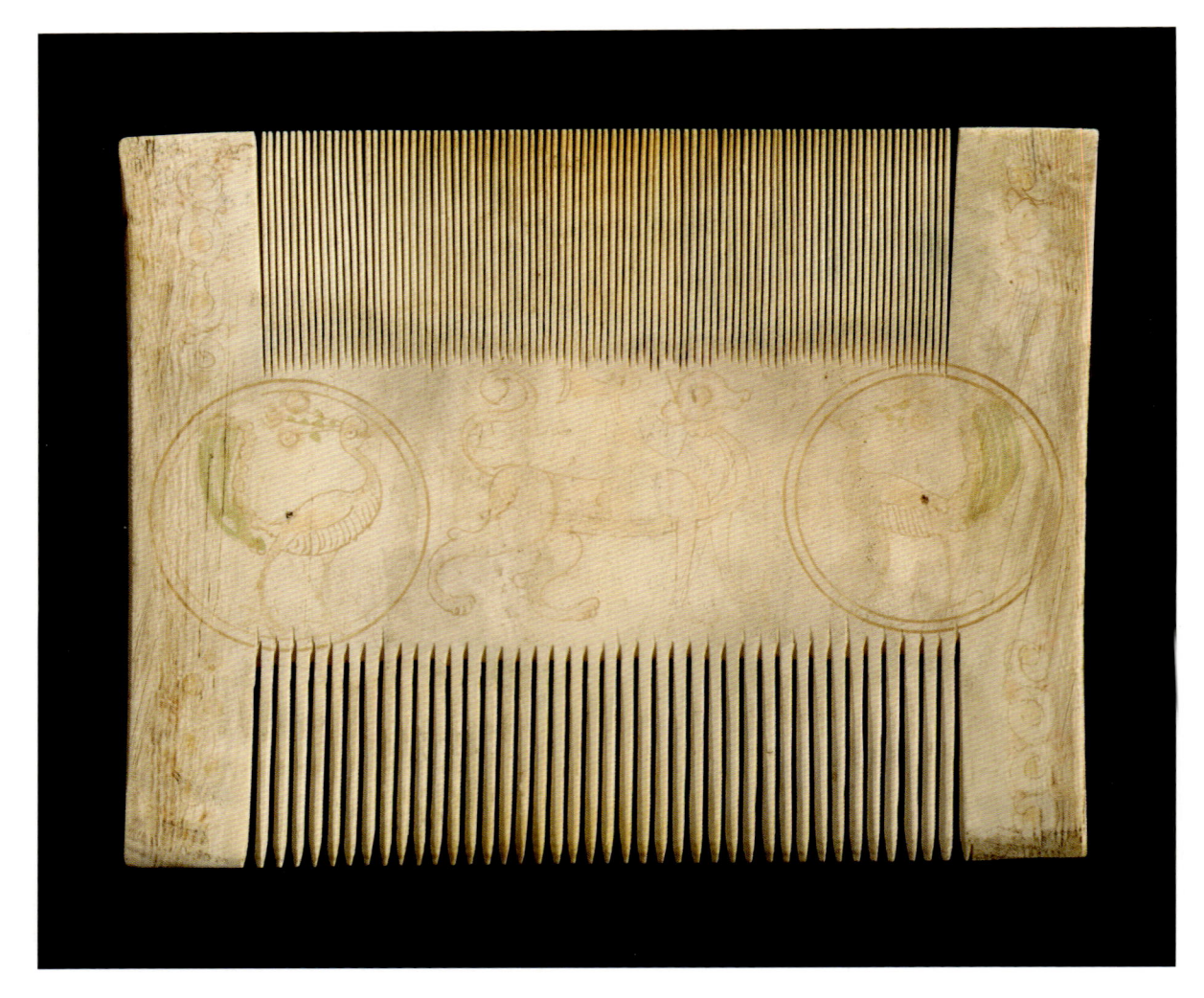

Ivory comb. Muslim workshops in Norman Sicily produced a considerable number of objects made from ivory, with decoration that was usually painted but sometimes incised. Pieces with carved, engraved, and perforated decoration are highly valued. This example is a comb made from a thin sheet of ivory with painted decoration. Twelfth century, Islamic-Sicilian. Chiesa di Santa Trinità, Florence.

opposite page:
Bottle made from carved rock crystal. Tenth century Fatimid, from Egypt.

patron. It divided the world into seventy sections, and there was a map for each. Here it will be sufficient to mention only Sicily and the still-living memory of its Muslim past:

> We say immediately that Sicily is the jewel of the century for its great value and beauty; the splendors of nature, its many buildings, and its remote past make it a truly unique country.... In the 453rd year of the Hegira [1061], the august ruler, illustrious champion, most powerful and glorious Roger, son of Tancred, chosen heir of the kings of the Franks, conquered the principal cities of Sicily and with his companions in arms crushed the rebellion of the usurping prefects and the army.... And when he became absolute master and strengthened the throne of his royal power, he made himself an apostle of justice among the people of Sicily, who were able to keep their respective faiths and laws, and were guaranteed their lives and possessions for themselves and their kinsmen.

After the required praise of the ruler, Idrîsi continued with a lengthy description of the cities on the coast, as they appeared in the twelfth century:

> The buildings of Palermo are so splendid that travellers extol the beauties of the architecture, the refinements of the construction, and their blazing originality. The city is divided in two parts: the Cassero and the Borgo.... In the Cassero is the majestic mosque, which at one time was a Christian church

MUSLIM SICILY . 125

Small box made of carved ivory with mountings of silver filigree and stones made of glass paste. Spanish workshop, late ninth century. Museo Nazionale del Bargello, Florence.

opposite page:
Small jewel box in ivory and wood. Likely Egyptian, late twelfth century. Treasury of the Cappella Palatina, Palermo.

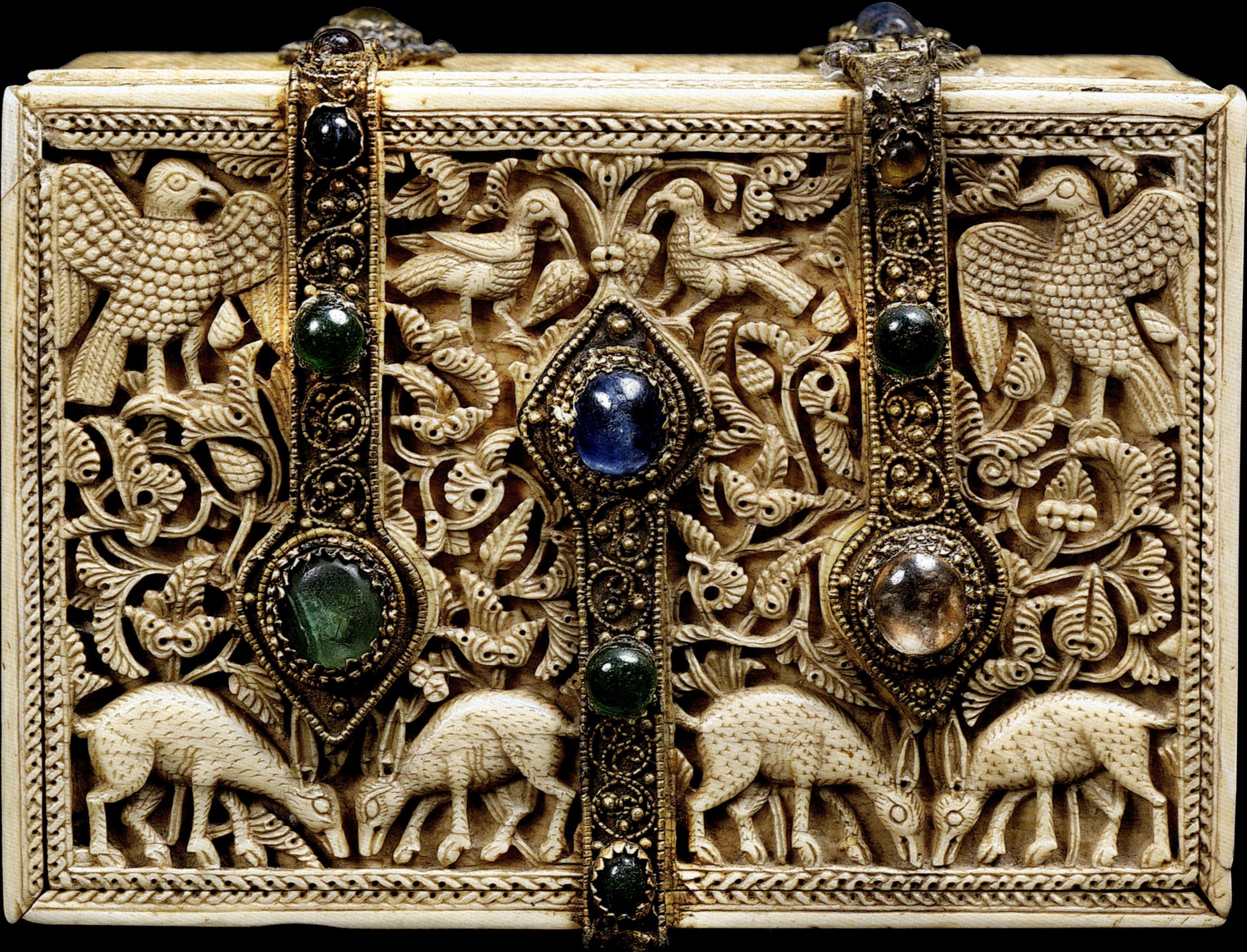

Cylindrical box in painted ivory. Sicilian-Islamic, thirteenth century. Museo del Duomo, Palermo.

opposite page:
Bronzes. Among the dictates of hadith *was a prohibition against the use of precious materials, because of which the working of bronze and ceramics and the engraving of wood and ivory predominate in the Muslim decorative arts.*

Bowl in cast bronze with incised decoration and encrusted with silver, clearly based on a ceramic prototype. On the outside are scenes of the hunt alternating with inscriptions in Kufic and naskhi *characters. On the inside bottom of the bowl is an equestrian tournament. From northwest Iran, first half of the thirteenth century. Museo Civico, Bologna.*

Incense burner made of brass, incised and encrusted in silver. The decoration is typical and shows the subject set within medallions, in this case a ruler in hunting clothes, alternating with geometric ornamentation and incriptions containing good wishes. Syrian or Egyptian, late thirteenth century. Museo Civico, Bologna.

MUSLIM SICILY . 129

Textiles. Workshops that produced textiles of high quality were found all over the Muslim world, including one in Palermo. During the Muslim period, fabric from Palermo could be found in the markets of Naples, Amalfi, Salerno, and Alexandria. The royal workshop in Palermo, known in Arabic as the Tiraz, in Greek as the Ergasterion, and in Latin as the Nobiles Officinae, produced silks, carpets, and precious objects. These were meant for the royal family, for use as gifts to foreign notables, and for export.

above:
Textile with inscriptions from the Koran. Baghdad, eleventh century. The decorative motif of a lion standing on top of an elephant is echoed in the mantle of King Roger, on which a lion standing on top of a camel is a symbol of Norman supremacy over the Arabs.

opposite:
Silk fabric with lions facing each other inside medallions. The stylized shapes are reminiscent of eastern Iran. Eighth to ninth century.

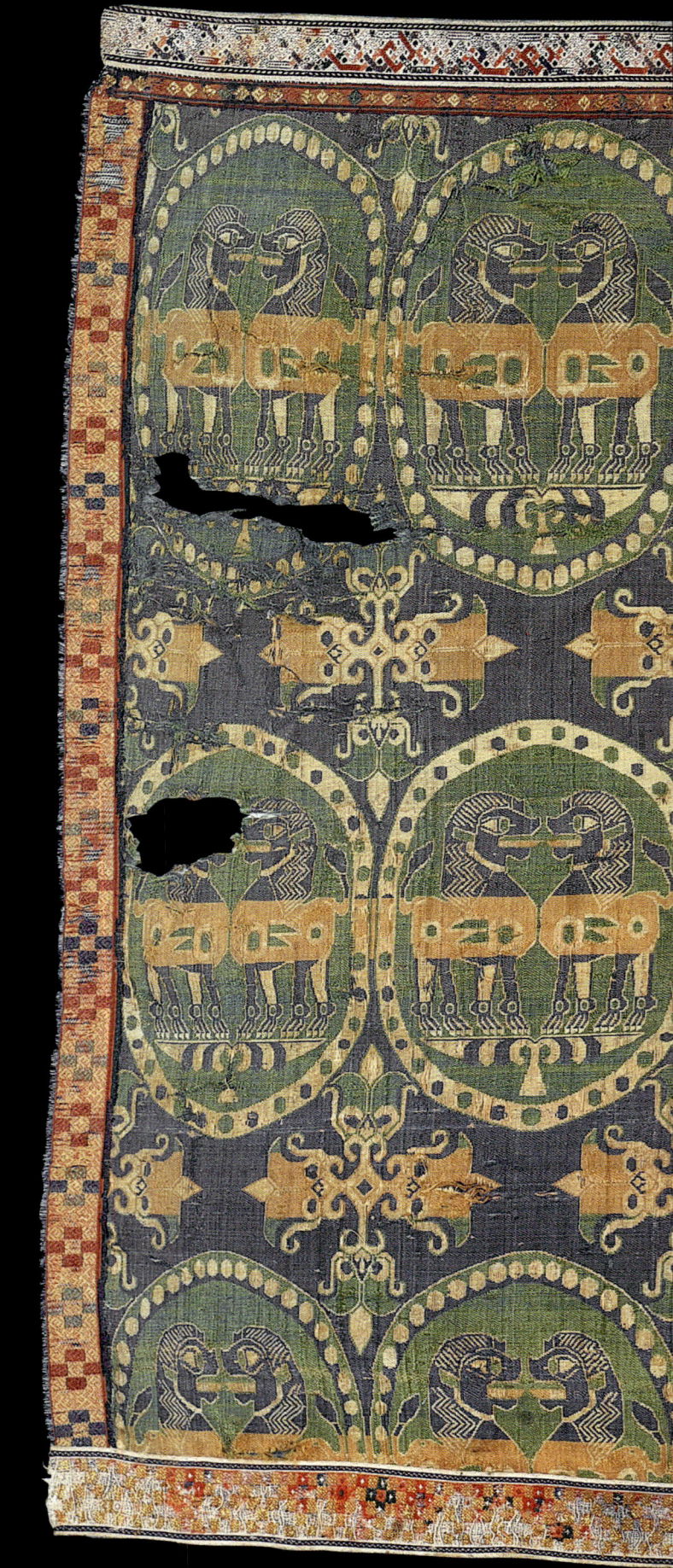

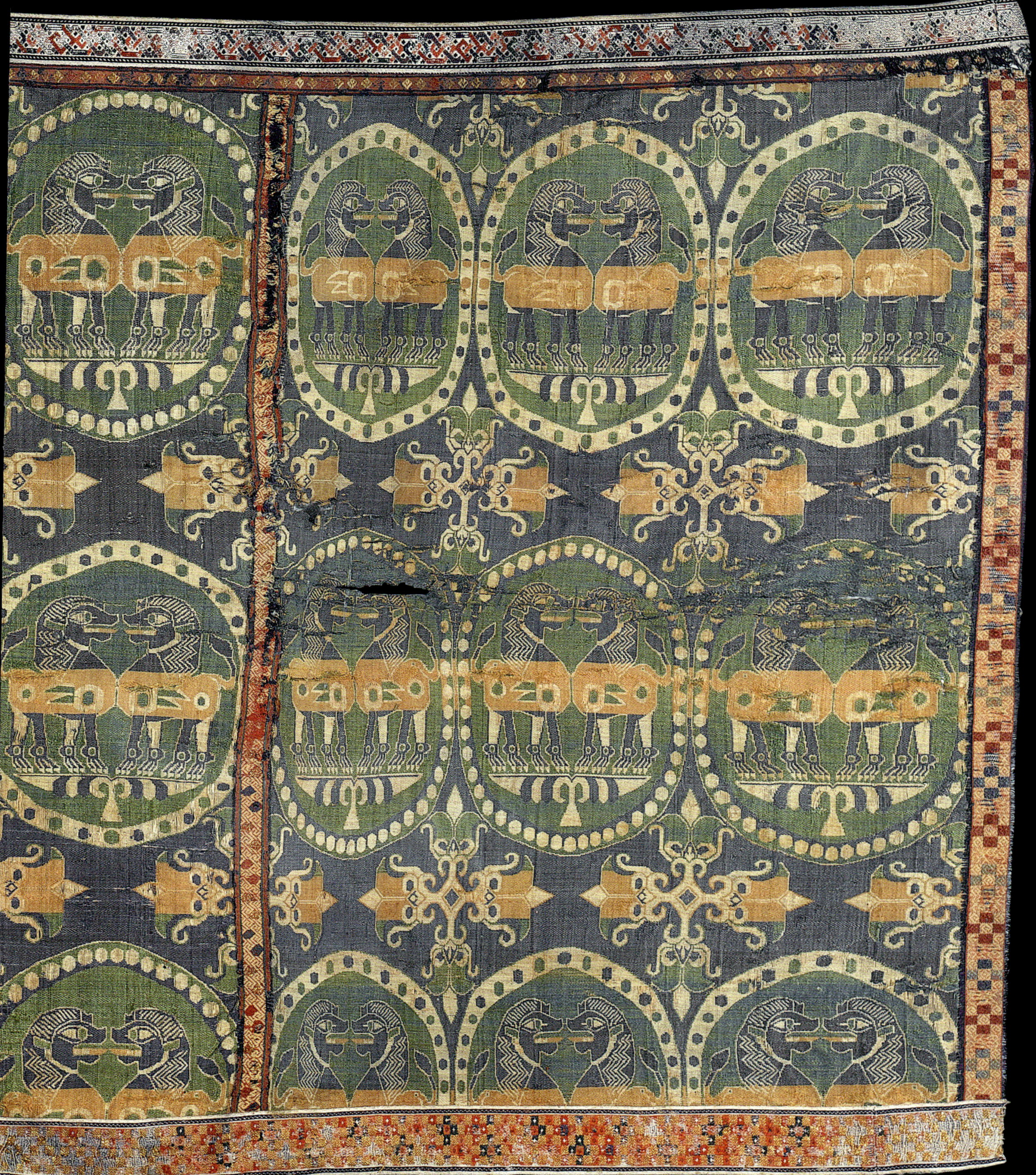

Two Muslims playing chess. From the Book of Games *(folio 62v) written by Alfonso X el Sabio in 1182. Real Biblioteca del Escorial, Madrid.*

opposite page:
An illustration from a treatise on falconry, the sixteenth-century manuscript Intikhab-i Hadiq *by Farid al-Din Attar. Bodleian Library, Oxford. The earliest treatises on falconry date to the seventh and eighth centuries and were written in Arabic at the court in Baghdad on the order of Caliph al-Mahdi. One famous work on the subject is the* Treatise on the flight of birds. *A culture that combined Byzantine, Persian, Turkish, and Indian elements appeared in Sicily during the Arab-Norman period, to the delight of those devoted to falconry.*

and today has been restored to its former function. It is difficult for the human mind to imagine the appearance of its sublime workmanship, the strange motifs rich with inspiration and fantasy, the varied images, the gilded friezes, and the calligraphic interlacings. As for the Borgo, it is a city in itself that encircles every part of the Cassero. It contains the old town center known as al-Khalîsa, which was the residence of the sultan and his court during the time of Muslim rule, the Porta Marina, and the shipyards. Water runs throughout the capital of Sicily, where perennial springs rise up. Palermo abounds in fruit trees and is blessed with buildings and places of delight so sumptuous as to bewilder anyone who sets himself to describe them and to dazzle the minds of experts: to try to express it in just one word would be a true temptation for anyone who admires them."

The voyage continues to the east, to Messina:

"At Messina, where great ships gather, along with travellers from all the different Latin and Muslim countries, the markets are flourishing, the merchandise sells, and the regular customers gather round in large numbers. The mountains near Messina have iron mines, and iron is sent to neighboring countries. The port is a true marvel, spoken about all over the world, as there is

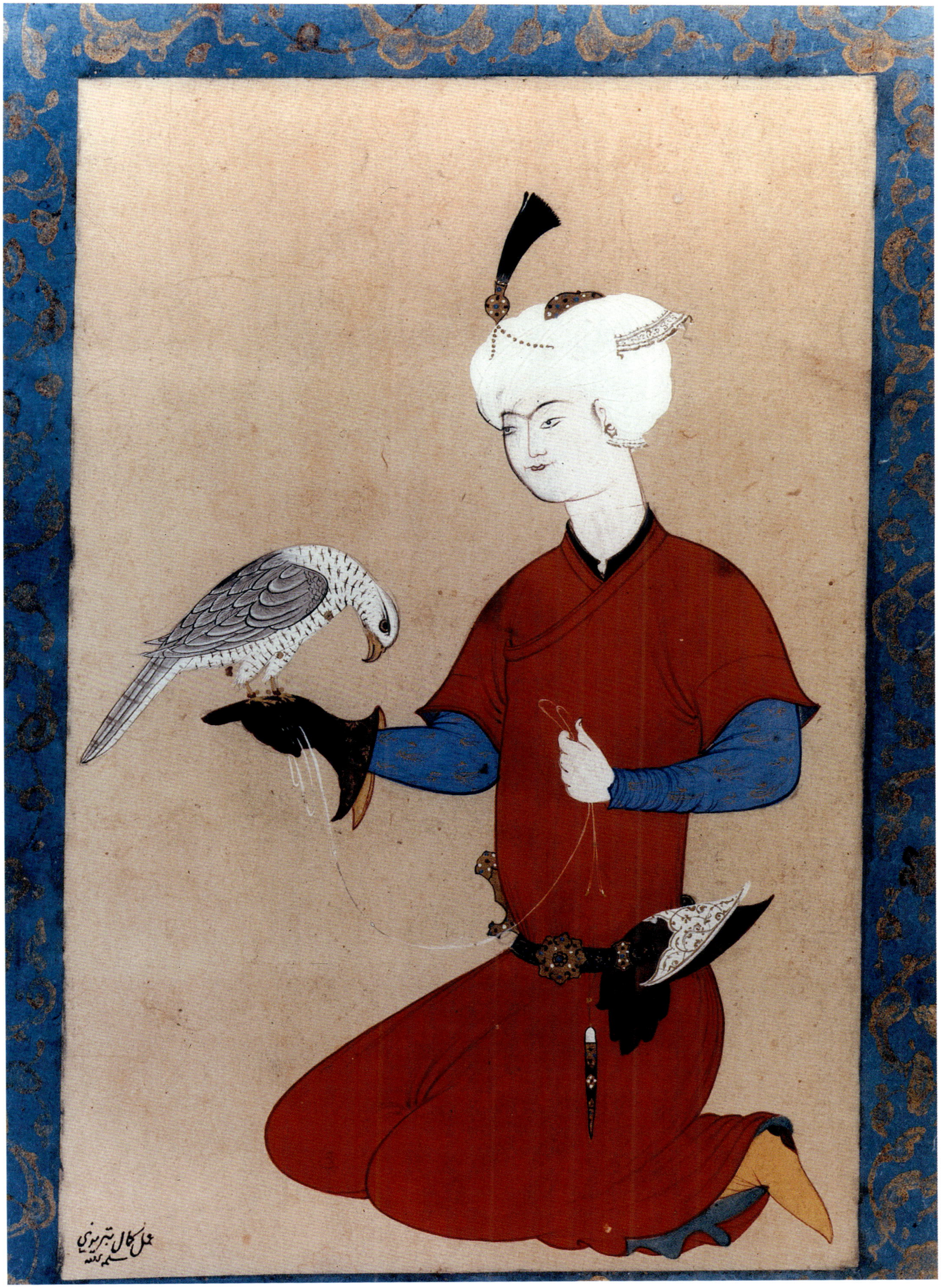
عمل کمال تبریزی

The rearing and shearing of sheep in the Middle Ages. Detail from Las Cantigas de Santa Maria *by Alfonso X el Sabio. Library of the Monastery of San Lorenzo, the Escorial, Madrid.*

C. a uella se começou a q́ŕxar a sca ōr. τ a ouella dis aq́ī mca.

C. chegou a uella a ŕxamador τ pos o uelloçino ant o altar.

> no ship, of whatever tonnage, which cannot drop anchor near the shore and proceed to unload its merchandise passing it from hand to hand until it reaches dry land."

A few days to the south, after Taormina, comes Catania, which at that time still maintained its Islamic character:

> "A great and beautiful city, Catania was known as the City of the Elephant, and enjoyed great prestige and fame. It is on the coast, has well-attended markets, splendid houses, large mosques and small ones, public baths, caravanserai, and a well-organized port. Travellers from every district come to Catania in order to load themselves with large quantities of merchandise of every kind.... Large amounts of land are cultivated in Catania, the countryside is rich and fertile, the walls of the city are strong, and it rules over a wide territory. The elephant for which it is known is a talisman made of stone in the shape of that animal, which in ancient times was at the top of a tall building, and has now been moved and placed in the church of the monastery."

In the descriptions of Sicily by Idrîsi, the island appears almost suspended between a political destiny that seemed to lead it northward and a strong connection to the world of Islam that made it look east and south to the markets and ports of Africa and Asia Minor. In that sense, we cannot deny the cultural openness of the Norman dynasty. There are too many indications for us to think that it happened by chance, or to believe that in those years something happened in Sicily that was the extraordinary and unrepeatable result of some rare harmony or some astonishingly strange tolerance for another culture. In fact, one must look over the entire Mediterranean of the period and discover, yet again, that that world continued to be intimately linked: by an ancient history, by recent and strong commercial links, and by a shared destiny resulting from geography and social ties. One would thus see that Spain experienced something very similar to the fate of Sicily. In 1212, a victory in the battle of Las Navas de Tolosa allowed Christianity to spread in the valley of the Guadalquivir in Andalusia. Around the middle of that century, in the reconquered cities in the north of Spain, the last great period of mutual influence and meeting between Judaism, Islam, and Christianity flourished under the leadership of Alfonso X, a king who not by accident is known to history as El Sabio, the wise. This was almost the period of Federick II and his court in Sicily. Each learned the same lesson: those rulers who welcomed the strong cultural influence of the East, and of earlier centuries of Muslim rule, were the same ones who both wished for and were able to lead the final great effort aimed at eliminating Islam's political and military influence. In this there was no great contradiction: the Sicily of Federick II of Hohenstaufen inevitably resembled the France of Louis IX and the Castile of Alfonse X. In that strengthening of royal authority and that development

opposite page:
The rearing and shearing of sheep in the Middle Ages. From Las Cantigas de Santa Maria *by Alfonso X el Sabio. Library of the Monastery of San Lorenzo, the Escorial, Madrid.*

MUSLIM SICILY . 137

of new administrative, legal, and political tools was the origin, if still vague and far off, of the modern state. Perhaps one must ask whether at that time the idea of the Mediterranean, of which we have followed the brief and partial history of one island, did not find itself giving way to a new focus on continental Europe. And also to ask with which of those worlds Sicily would from that time forward most strongly identify, while knowing that the island would always preserve the memory and influences of the East of which it is a part.

this page and opposite:
Gold coin known as an augustale *with a depiction of Federick II. Museo Archeologico Nazionale, Naples.*

MUSLIM SICILY . 139

NORMAN SICILY
Adele Cilento

DVX:

THE PEOPLES
OF THE NORTH IN
THE NINTH AND
TENTH CENTURIES:
FROM SCANDINAVIA
TO ITALY

THE MEN OF THE BAYS AND FJORDS

The term *Viking* usually refers to the ancient inhabitants of Denmark Norway, southern Sweden, and a large part of Finland. The presence of these people, who were of Indo-European origin, is documented in written sources starting only in the eighth century A.D., although according to the archeological evidence their first settlements are much earlier. About the precise origin of the term there are only theories, none of which have so far been proven, partly because since the first appearance of the Vikings in north-central Europe the written sources have referred to them by many different names. The Anglo-Saxon term *wic* and the French *wik* indicate a marketplace and would therefore refer to their main activity. But *Vik* is also the name of a province in Norway and in ancient Norse it indicates "a bay, an inlet, or a fjord." A Viking would therefore be someone "who goes out from a bay or fjord," with an obvious connection to sailing, at which the ancient Scandinavians were very expert.

As a result of their many raids and extensive migrations between the ninth and eleventh centuries, the Vikings came in contact with many different peoples, each of which gave them a particular name, often based on their most prominent characteristics. In relation to their origin, for example, the plundering Scandinavians were described by the Irish chronicles as "Ostmen," or "Men from the East." According to the German chronicles, they were "Ascomanni," or "Men of the Ash Tree," which to the Vikings was sacred. The Anglo-Saxons called them "Dani," and Danelaw was the name given to the eastern part of England in which the Vikings settled at the end of the ninth century. Less clear are the roots of the words used by the Byzantines, who called them "Rus" and "Varangians" (from *varingr*, a word of Slavic origin). The Muslims of Spain, very impressed by the destruction that the Vikings caused in the Bay of Biscay, called them *al-Magius*, or "Magus," from the word for magician and sorcerer, because they worshipped fire and other strange idols that were incomprehensible to them. The Frankish chroniclers, who came to know them around the middle of the ninth century, called them *Nord-männer*, or "Men of the North," and it was as *Normans* that they were known in the Latin chronicles of the ninth century and later.

Detail of the splendid mosaic pavement in the church of Sant'Adriano in San Demetrio Corone, Cosenza. Late eleventh century. The depiction of animals in this opus sectile *type of mosaic is unusual, as geometric forms are more common.*

preceding pages:
Detail of the opus sectile *mosaic pavement in the church of Sant'Adriano in San Demetrio Corone, Cosenza. Late eleventh century. The lion was the symbol of the de Hautevilles who left Normandy and within less than forty years became the rulers of Sicily and a large part of southern Italy.*

The Bayeux Tapestry, some two hundred twenty-eight feet long, illustrates the conquest of England by William, Duke of Normandy, between 1064 and 1066. It is an extremely important document that clarifies numerous aspects of the culture of the Normans and of the Vikings of whom they were direct descendants. Archaeological finds confirm a perfect correspondence between the illustrations on the tapestry and the tools actually used. In this scene, the shields positioned on the sides of ships in order to protect the oarsmen and the fighters are clearly visible. Musée de la Tapisserie de Bayeux, Calvados, Normandy, France.

SEAMEN AND MERCHANTS, FARMERS AND WARRIORS

Vikings first appear in historical documents in 795, when they sacked a monastery on the island of Lindisfarne off the north-east coast of Great Britain. Even though there is a good deal of evidence of Viking activity in the North Sea and the Baltic quite a bit earlier, it is only at the time of their first raids on the English and French coasts that they are mentioned in written records. This was the first mention of the warlike nature usually attributed to the Vikings, who with their earliest settlements would also display other characteristics. For sure, the Scandinavians were masters of the art of war, and for centuries they were invincible and feared throughout Europe. This was based, to a greater extent than with land armies, on attack by sea, as over the course of centuries they were able to perfect their navigation skills, even in the difficult natural environment of the North Sea, with its deep fjords, many deserted islands, and land that was frozen for much of each year.

Lindisfarne, on the east coast of England, where the Vikings landed in June 793 and brutally sacked the monastery. This bloody incursion marked the start of the Viking era.

From their first appearance in northwest Europe, the Vikings had powerful, maneuverable ships that allowed them to sail throughout the Baltic and into the Atlantic off the coast of Europe. Their level of technical skill in ship construction is remarkable, considering that they did not use a saw (which came into use only in the eleventh century) and that the planks were carved with axe and hatchet only. The same techniques were used for merchant ships, known as *knorr*, and for warships, known as *drakkar*. The planks were laid one on top of another like tiles and fastened to the hull with iron rivets. This gave the ships great maneuverabiliy and resilience during storms as the boards absorbed the stress caused by the waves and transferred it to the entire structure of the hull. During raiding expeditions, long rows of shields were hung along the sides of the ships in order to protect the oarsmen. Viking ships were also easily recognizable by their bows, on which were placed the carved heads of animals, often dragons, or *drakkar*, from which the ship itself took its name. The function of this particular figurehead was not just to ward off evil spirits during the night, but also to strike fear in the crew of an enemy ship. Regarding their design, the warships had hulls that were long and narrow, while the merchant ships had hulls that were wider and not as long, which enabled them to carry more cargo. From the many depictions of ships incised in stone during the Viking period we have a good idea of the sails, which were square in shape with a checkered pattern. Often found in Viking burial sites and often represented in their art, the equipment of a Viking warrior was rich and costly. It included a long two-edged iron sword with a strong, flexible blade and a powerful hilt. The axe, no longer used in Europe, was a Viking's second weapon and, like his sword, was decorated with beautiful engraved designs on the blade and the hilt. There was also a metal-tipped lance and a long wooden bow

For the Vikings, the hatchet and the two-handed axe were used as both weapons and tools, as shown in various scenes on the Bayeux Tapestry.

opposite page:
The Oseberg boat, an important archaeological find recovered intact because it was used as the tomb of a queen, is the most beautiful Viking ship that has come down to us. It was constructed in the ninth century and, like other Viking and Norman ships, has overlapping planks and a narrow hull. It was steered from the stern by an oar used as a rudder and propelled by oarsmen or by wind. These ships were very maneuverable, could easily go up rivers, and were able to land on almost any beach. Bygdoy Museum, Oslo.

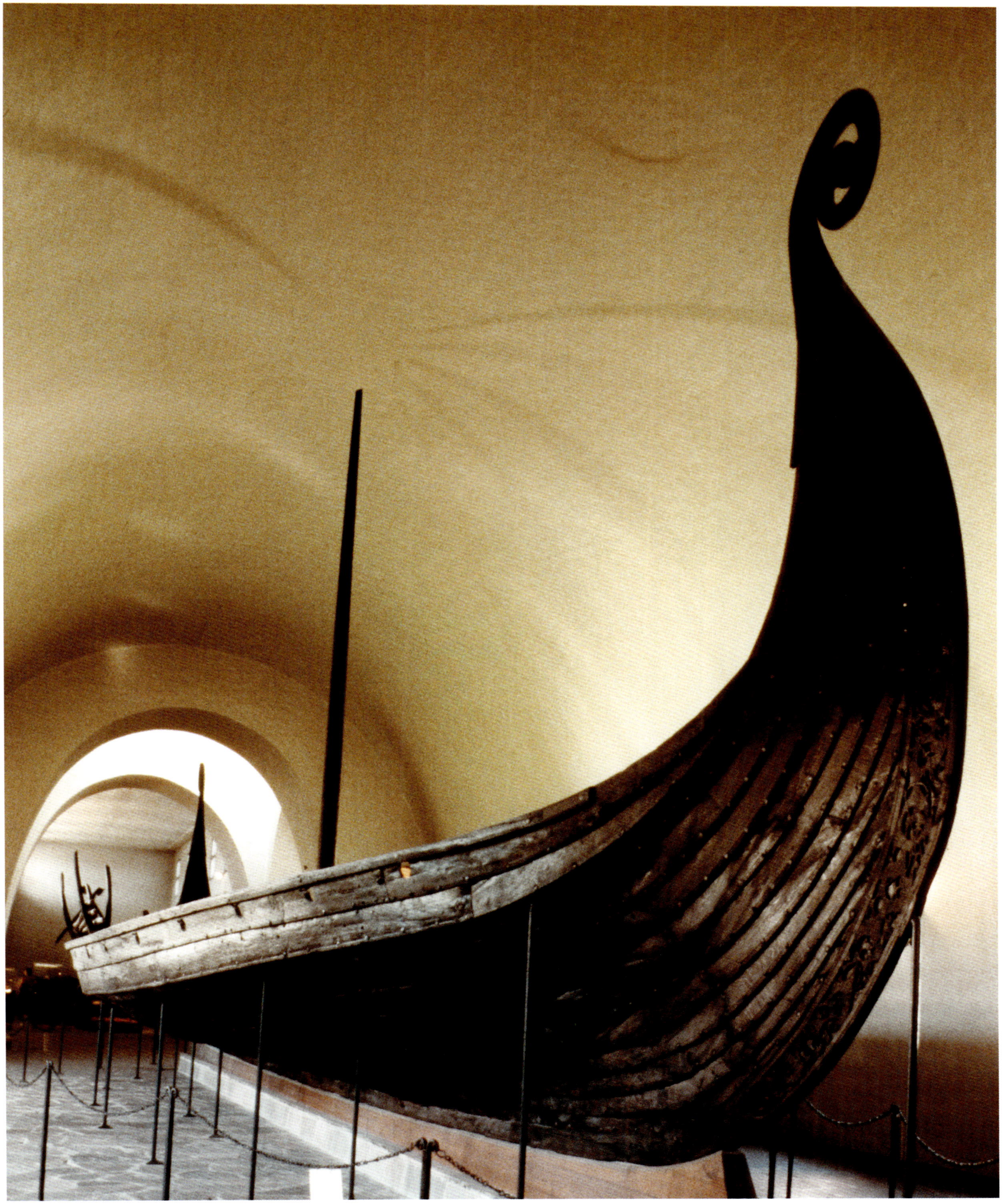

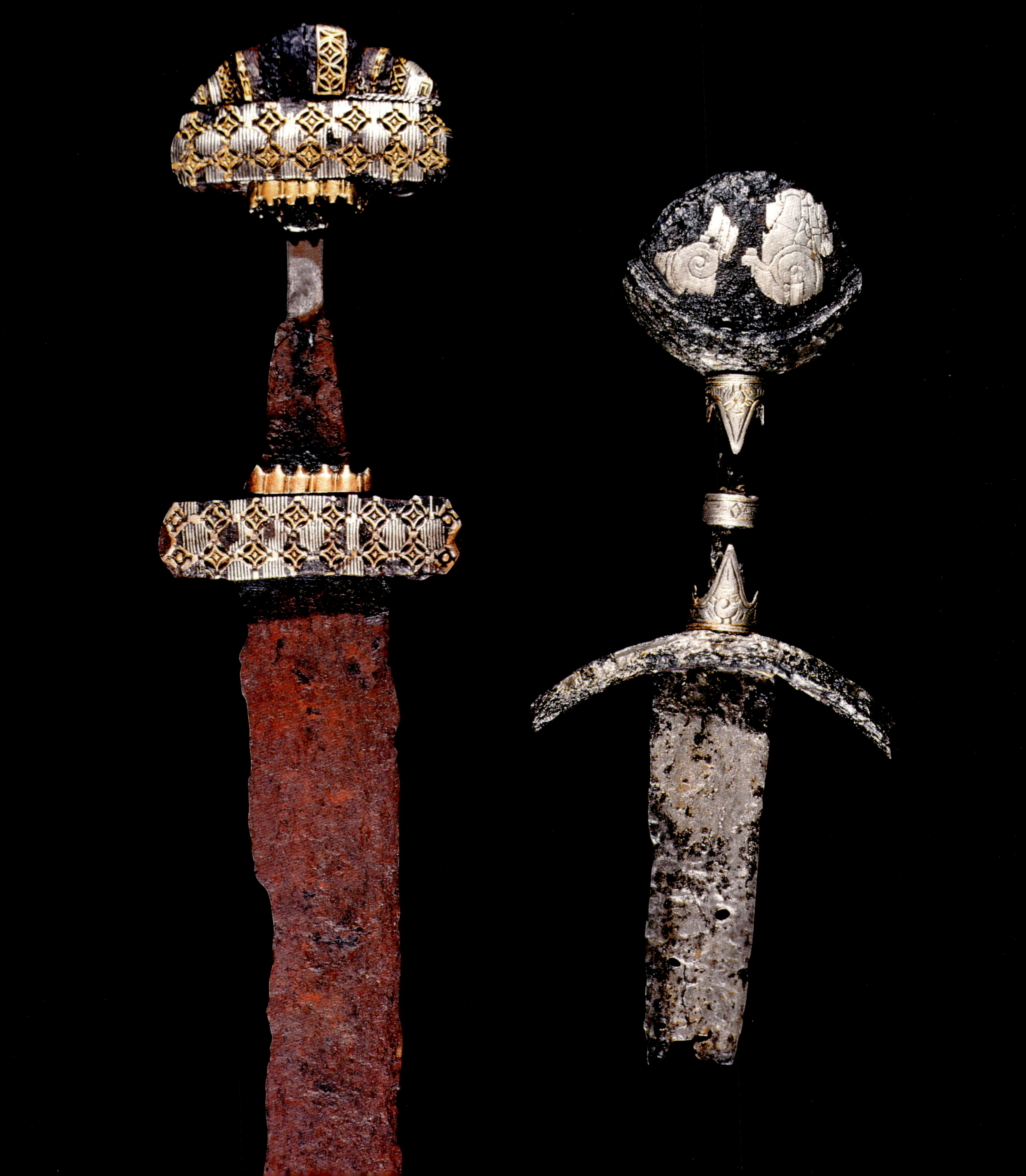

opposite page:
Viking swords made of iron, tenth century. Prehistoric Museum Meesgard Hojbjerg, Denmark. The Viking sword had a wide, straight, two-edged blade and was almost three feet long with a concave ridge in the middle and a pointed tip. It was fitted with a short hilt that could be either curved or straight and a pommel that was either round or lobed.

Viking helmet, eighth century. It has the typical features present from the pre-Viking Vendel period up until Norman times, including a headpiece reinforced with bronze strips fastened by rivets, metal ornaments protecting the eyebrows and cheekbones, and a metal nose-piece. Historiska Muséet, Stockholm.

that shot lethal iron-tipped arrows. Another much-used weapon was an iron dagger with a bone handle carried by both men and women. Defensive equipment consisted of shields, body armor, and helmets that were often decorated with motifs inspired by nature. There were many zoomorphic images, both realistic and stylized, that were meant to give courage and strength to a soldier in battle. The helmet in particular was often decorated with the head of an animal, with the cheeks and nose protected by long plates.

As evidence that there was more to Viking society than its warlike character, various objects that relate to the peaceful activities of daily life have been found even in tombs and burial mounds that hold a truly striking number of weapons. These include sickles of different shapes as well as the farmer's hoes that accompanied the happy sleep of the deceased, placed next to other tools that were

The Bayeux Tapestry is an extraordinary epic-narrative document and presents exceptional iconographic evidence regarding the technology and military practices of an entire people. In this scene it shows the "parade" of a group of Norman soldiers, with their swords, lances, and axes.

opposite page:
Large Viking shield, in block-worked steel, painted. Eighth century. Heavy, with a rectangular shape, this shield is quite distinct from the more tapered almond-shaped shield of the Normans. Historiska Muséet, Stockholm.

NORMAN SICILY . 151

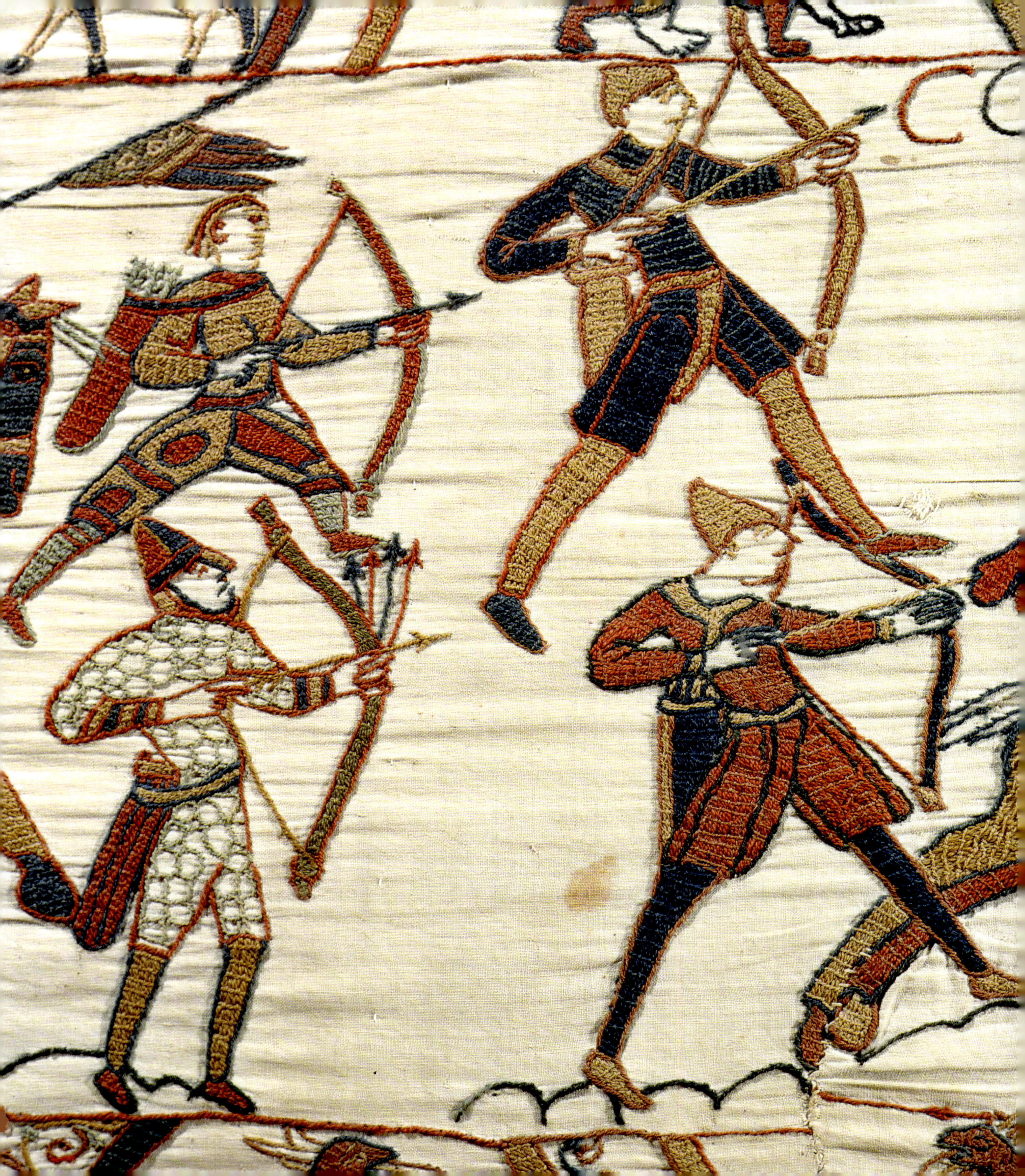

used for much more dreadful purposes. The blacksmith would be buried with his hammer, tongs, anvil, and file, and the peasant who lived near water with his fisherman's tools. Sometimes the tomb was a ship, as we are told by Ibn Fadlan, the ambassador of the caliph of Baghdad, after he saw the cremation of a Viking chieftan with his own eyes.

THE DISCOVERY OF NEW LANDS

The basis of Viking society was a system of land ownership connected to the nuclear family. According to Viking law, all ancestral goods were held in common by the entire family. When a father died, the eldest son would inherit, and he was obliged to pay the other brothers for their part of the inheritance. This system naturally encouraged all the younger sons to seek their fortune through trade or from plunder, and to attempt the conquest of new lands.

The original social structure of the Vikings was based mainly on a tripartite system that was common in the Middle Ages. At the apex were the local lords (*jarls*), then the free peasants (*karls*) and artisans (*bondi*), and finally the slaves (*traells*). The connection between the social groups and the land was secured by a system of *centena*, or "hundreds," a measure on which the ownership of land was based. The lords, or *jarls*, who governed different centena were representatives of the primitive aristocracies that ruled the various small kingdoms. In the ninth and tenth centuries these local lords and landowners became the vassals of more powerful kings who over time gained control over what would gradually become the countries of modern-day Scandinavia: in 872 Harald I Fairhair brought Norway under his rule; in 950 Gom the Elder consolidated power in Denmark; and in 970 Sweden was unified by the house of Ynglinge. It is not by chance that this achievement of national unity coincided with the moment when the Viking conquest of other lands reached its greatest extent. As the Vikings slowly achieved political and social stability in their homelands, they also improved their military organization and navigational skills. This allowed them to undertake ever larger expeditions in the North Sea. It also helped them maintain alliances and relationships with their homelands, a system that would lead to their colonization of the lands of North Europe.

The territorial expansion of the Vikings beyond their lands of origin in Scandinavia began in the last decades of the eighth century and gave rise to the so-called Viking Era. It began with seasonal raids on the northern and western British Isles by the Vikings of Norway, who first invaded the Shetland and Orkney Islands and then used them as bases from which to launch plundering raids on Scotland, Ireland, and the west coast of England. The Vikings of Denmark sacked and plundered the east coast of England and the coasts of western Europe. Raiding activity was followed by trade and demands for tribute, although raids did continue in the British Isles and

opposite page:
Archers on foot, in one of the fifty-eight scenes of the Bayeux Tapestry. The small bow seen here is Norman, a direct descendant of the bow used by the Vikings. Solid, rigid, and heavy, it shot arrows that were short and thick, with tips that were likewise especially thick and heavy, and was used to penetrate body armor. It was quite different from the flexible English longbow, with its enormous range, that was used to distract the enemy, more for defense than attack.

Small box made of whale bone with runic inscriptions and splendid reliefs. The runic alphabet consists of twenty-four symbols known as runes, *from the Old Icelandic word* runar, *for "secret," and from the Saxon word* rna, *for "whisper." These ancient and fascinating symbols, carved in stone or wood, narrated the lives and exploits of men and often served a ritual function. Already in use during the third century by the Germanic people who invented them, runes were adopted by the Vikings in a simplified form with sixteen symbols. Originally from the Treasury of Saint Julien du Briand, Northumbria, and now in the Museo del Bargello, Florence.*

opposite page:
Detail of a precious Viking gold necklace from the sixth century. The use of dragons as an ornamental motif was widespread, found even on helmets and the figureheads of ships. It most likely referred to the dragon Fafner, the guardian of treasure in Scandinavian myth, and entered the decorative arts of medieval Europe through the Normans. Historiska Muséet, Stockholm.

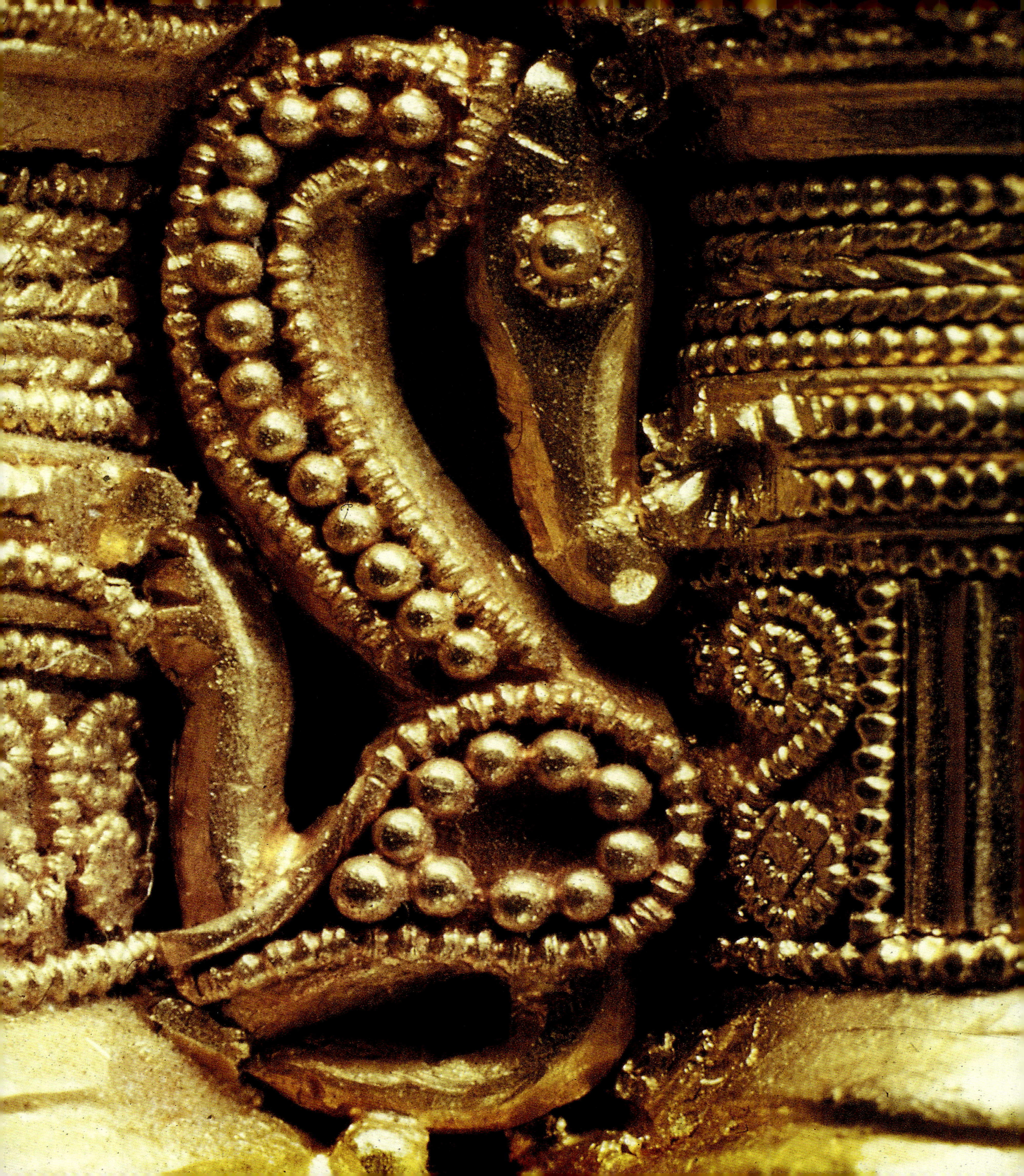

western Europe on a sporadic basis for another two hundred years, reaching even the Mediterranean coasts of Spain, North Africa, and Italy.

By the end of the ninth century, the first stages of the conquest had become apparent. While the Vikings of Denmark and Norway established themselves in lands such as England, Scotland, and northern France—where the duchy of Normandy would soon be founded—which they had formerly visited as plunderers, the Vikings of Sweden went further east, following the course of the great rivers Dniepr and Volga, reaching the Black Sea and the Caspian, and then Constantinople. In these places they engaged in intense commercial activity along an axis that connected the Russian steppes with the population centers of the Black Sea and the cities of the Byzantine empire. Thus the Vikings of the east—known to the Byzantines as Varangians and Varyags—were appreciated for their mercantile abilities as well as their physical strength, and many of them were soon enlisted in the personal guard of the Byzantine emperor, the so-called Varangian Guard. As a result of their permanent settlements in Novgorod and Kiev, and their assimilation with the ethnic Slavs, the nucleus of modern Russia was formed. This was the principality of Kiev, which in the tenth and eleventh centuries would become the dominant power in eastern Europe.

The Vikings who ventured further west came mostly from the southwest coast of Norway and from the already colonized areas of the British Isles. From there they went on a completely different course, aimed at the uninhabited islands of the North Atlantic, to which they brought the agriculture and economy of their homeland. They arrived in the Faeroe Islands around 800 and in Iceland around 870. All the inhabitable parts of Iceland were settled by 930, the same year that saw the establishment of an Icelandic parliament, the *Althingi*, which was the first parliament in European history.

Detail from the Bayeux Tapestry.

opposite page:
The Flabellum *(a fan with its case) of Tournus, made of carved bone and ivory, engraved metal, and painted and gilded parchment. Second half of the ninth century. Various figures are depicted on the fan, some of them fanciful, others realistic, including St. Philibert, to whom the inscription is dedicated. It refers to the monks of his abbey who, attacked by Vikings, had to abandon the island of Noirmoutier in 836 and take his relics with them. After various stops they came to Tournus, in the Burgundy region of France, in 875. Museo del Bargello, Florence.*

FROM NORMANDY TO THE SOUTH OF ITALY

Viking raiders plagued the coasts of England and France for almost three centuries. At the end of the eighth century, Danish fleets began to attack the villages on the coasts of England, Friesland, Saxony, and eastern France and, by the middle of the ninth century, of Spain. The arrival of the Vikings in western Europe is generally marked by the sack of Portland, England, in 787 and the previously mentioned attack on Lindisfarne of June 8, 793. A series of very destructive raids that began in 841 forced Charles the Bald of France to make heavy payments to the Vikings as a way to secure peace. That brought with it the creation, by the middle of the ninth century, of a series of encampments on some of the islands of the Seine and the Loire. These then became launching points for new military operations in the heart of France as new contingents of troops arrived to reinforce the earlier settlements. By the beginning of the tenth century the Viking presence in the north of France had become too well-established to ignore. In 911 the king of France, Charles the Simple (from the Latin *simplex*, meaning straightforward, or uncomplicated),

Aelfgyva, the daughter of William the Conqueror, with Harold II, in front of William's palace in Rouen, in a scene from the Bayeux Tapestry.

opposite page:
Ivory plaque used to bind a psalter, encrusted with gold. It depicts King David, identified by an inscription above his head, enthroned, and was made for the court of Charles the Bald, king of France. Second half of the ninth century. Museo del Bargello, Florence.

granted the entire territory of ancient Neustria in modern-day northwest France to the Viking chief Hrolf—known in the Latin sources as Rollo—hoping thereby to limit the expansion of the Vikings in his kingdom. A treaty was signed at Saint-Clair-sur-Epte by which Rollo agreed to restrain his own warriors and to help Charles defend against other Viking hordes in France.

This grant of territory to the Vikings in 911 marks the birth of Normandy and anticipates Rollo's control of a large swath of territory centered on the mouth of the Seine with Rouen as its capital. When Rollo and his subjects converted to Christianity in 912 he was made a duke and to all intents and purposes became a vassal of the French king. The consequences of this act became evident in the feudal relationship between them. Rollo became lord of a territory, the duchy of Normandy, which constituted a genuine fief, and its inhabitants, both natives and Viking newcomers, followed the same religion, Christianity, and spoke the same language, an early version of French. Between 911 and 933, Rollo and his son William Long-sword extended their power over most of the ancient ecclesiastical province of Rouen so that under Rollo's successors the duchy of Normandy became one of the most stable and powerful dominions in the kingdom of France.

Despite internal struggles with other feudal lords over the consolidation of ducal power, under the regency of Richard I and later of Richard II (966-1026) the duchy

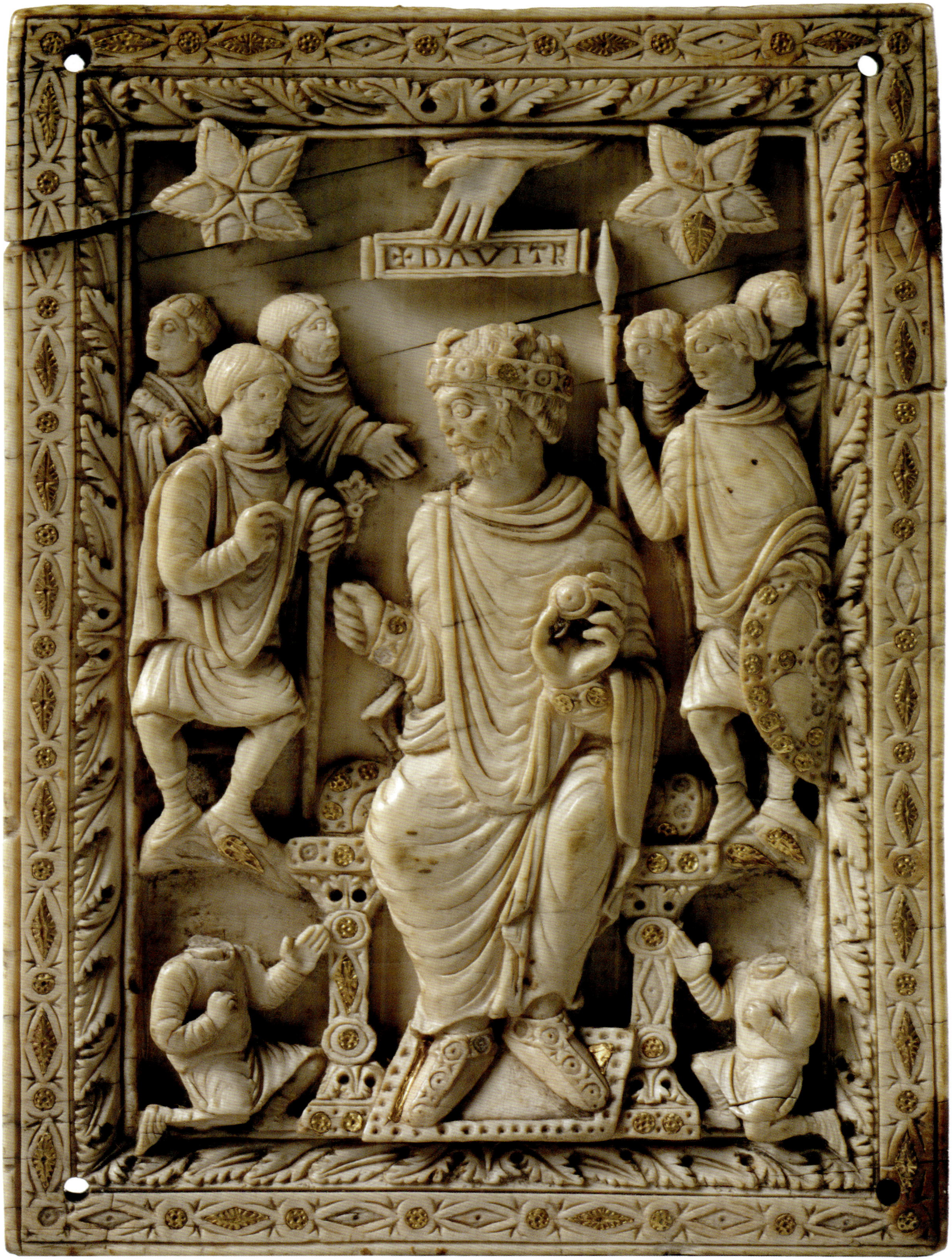
DAVITR

of Normandy experienced a period of peace and prosperity. On the death of Richard II power passed, not without conflict and difficulty, to his son Robert, who had to contend with many opponents both lay and ecclesiastical. Among these were his own uncles, Robert, the archbishop of Rouen, and Hugo, the bishop of Bayeux, who were supported in the conflict by the French king. Robert, who was called "the Magnificent" due to his love of finery, was eventually able to re-assert his power to the fullest. Not only did he protect the borders of Normandy against encroachment, but he enlarged them further, taking control of other territories in the Vexin region between Mantes and Pontoise. In addition, he continued the traditional policies of the dukes of Normandy and made donations to certain grand abbeys such as Saint-Wandrille, Jumiège, Fécamp, and Mont-Saint-Michel. The political considerations involved in this important ecclesiastical act did not preclude other actions that may have been motivated by sincere religious feelings, and at a certain point these caused the king to make a pilgrimage to Jerusalem. It was during this journey that he died at the age of twenty-five, leaving a young son, William, and a province that was rich and well-governed in which commerce flourished thanks to preexisting connections with the Anglo-Saxon world. This very same William was the famous Norman who laid claim to the throne of England, taking advantage of the death of the previous king who was the son of his aunt, Emma of Normandy. William launched an invasion fleet and defeated his rival, the Anglo-Saxon king Harold, at the famous Battle of Hastings on October 14, 1066. He thereby inaugurated a new and long-lived period for the English monarchy which combined the Anglo-Saxon tradition with the Norman feudal system.

The end of the Viking era in England thus coincided with the arrival of a new race of conquerors who were also of Viking descent, the Normans. But the victors, although of Nordic origin, were in fact a new nation, one which spoke French and had severed its connection to the primitive culture and ancient traditions of Scandinavia. Opening themselves to the West, the Normans succeeded in asserting

above left:
The ruins of the abbey church of Saint-Wandrille, in Seine Maritime, Normandy, built during the twelfth century.

above right:
The Benedictine abbey church of Notre Dame a Jumièges in Normandy, built between 1040 and 1067 on the model of the main building of Mont Saint-Michel.

opposite page:
King Harold with a falcon, on a powerful horse and preceded by a pack of dogs, in a detail from the Bayeux Tapestry. The hunting scene with a falcon is a recurring motif in medieval iconography. As first among warriors, the victorious king also had to be first among hunters.

NORMAN SICILY . **161**

an identity of their own. It was no longer only that of their Viking ancestors, and was also different from that of their Frankish neighbors. They were a new people, able to bring elements of change to the regions they conquered, yet at the same time maintaining legal, social, and ecclesiastical continuity. This involved the social hierarchy, local taxation, the law as it applied to freeholders (the *vavassores*), as well as the administration of government. The Normans were thus able to achieve an ethno-cultural fusion of their own traditions with those of the people they conquered. This was a process that recent historians prefer to define not as assimilation but as the formation of a new identity that combined the character and customs of both Vikings and Franks. The conquest of England by Duke William can be seen in a general sense as a process that by the end of the eleventh century resulted in the difficult and not always peaceful birth of an Anglo-Norman society. This would also be the meaning of a conquest on which another group of Normans would embark in those same years in the south of Italy. There, too, as earlier in Normandy and in England, the process by which the Normans established themselves would have as one of its prominent elements the close ties that their leaders were able to create in the conquered areas, and in neighboring ones as well, through the contacts, friendships, and marriages that became stages in the progressive integration of the Vikings in Christian Europe.

The Battle of Hastings, in the year 1066. Harold II commands the Anglo Saxon army, and Duke William commands the Normans, in a scene from the Bayeux Tapestry.

opposite page:
Duke William of Normandy, known as William the Conqueror (1027-1087), with Bishop Odo and Robert de Mortain, immortalized in the embroidery of the Bayeux Tapestry.

ODO:EPS: ROTBER[T]

WILLELM:

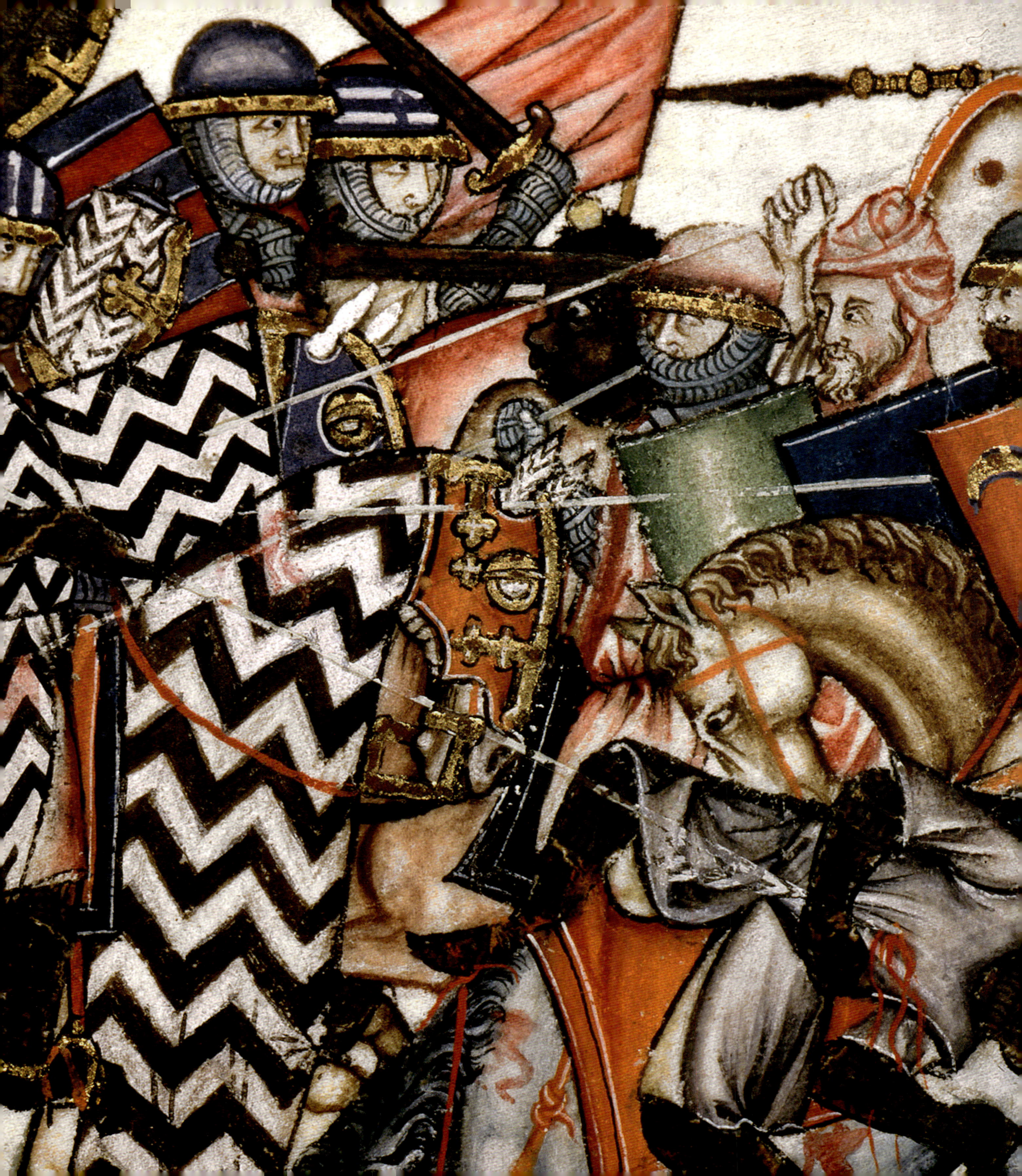

KNIGHTS IN CONQUEST OF THE SOUTH

FROM MERCENARIES TO PRINCES: THE BEGINNINGS

Information about the first appearance of adventurers from Normandy in southern Italy is scarce. The historical sources are incomplete and we are dependent on the limited evidence contained in contemporary chronicles that were written mostly in order to celebrate the conquest itself and which therefore tend to exaggerate its legendary and sensational aspects. But despite their numerous contradictions, the sources seem to agree on at least one point, which is a connection between the arrival of the Normans in Italy and the pilgrimage routes to the sanctuary of San Michele Arcangelo sul Gargano in Apulia. According to the chronicle written by Amatus of Montecassino, some Norman pilgrims met the Longobard prince Guaimar in Salerno, a city which at that moment was besieged by Arabs. But according to a chronicle by William of Apulia, the Normans met Melus, a rebel from Bari who was fighting the Byzantines in that part of Italy.

In order to understand the validity of these accounts, it is necessary to keep in mind that by the middle of the eleventh century, while a large part of Apulia and the Salento peninsula, along with Calabria and certain parts of Campania and Lucania, remained under the direct control of Byzantium, the Longobards in the duchy of Benevento and the principalities of Salerno and Capua had extended their power to the interior of Campania and Lucania, including parts of Molise and Apulia. Besides this, the Muslims of Sicily continued their coastal raids, often pushing to the interior, as in their siege of Salerno as mentioned by Amatus of Montecassino.

And so, without having to consider the veracity of accounts written at least fifty years after the fact, we can say that the arrival in southern Italy of the first contingents of Normans was not accidental, but the result of their enlistment in the ranks of various rulers in the area who were in perennial conflict with each other. Moreover, as confirmed by later evidence, the information contained in both chronicles proves to be true, because the Normans who came to help Melus of Bari, beaten in October 1018 on the Ofanto River near Canne, entered the service of Guaimar of Salerno and of other local lords such as Pandulf of Benevento, the count of Ariano, the abbot of Montecassino, and the duke of Naples, Sergius IV.

As a reward for the help that the Norman knights gave him against the Longobards of Capua, Sergius granted Rainulf Drengot and his men the town of Aversa, with its

Detail from a refined twelfth-century mosaic pavement in the cathedral of Sant'Agata dei Goti in Benevento.

preceding pages:
Battle scene between Moors and Christians in a detail from Las Cantigas de Santa Maria *(folio 92r) by Alfonso X el Sabio (1221-1284), in the Library of the Monastery of San Lorenzo, the Escorial, Madrid.*

castles and rich lands. The connection between them was later reinforced by Rainulf's marriage to one of Sergius' sisters. Although the Normans received many grants of land for their military service, Aversa would remain the earliest permanent center of Norman rule in the south of Italy. All the more so because once Rainulf was named count of Aversa he quickly set about bringing other Normans to Italy. He also began to insert himself with unscrupulous skill in the fluid political scene and in the struggles of the Byzantine and Longobard dukes, as well as those of the German emperor Conrad II, who had renewed his interest in southern Italy and his policy of interference in local affairs.

The ability of the Normans to open a gap in the southern Italian territories held by the Byzantines later became clear in the adventures of Argyrus, the son of the same Melus of Bari who some decades earlier had played a principal part in the insurrection in Apulia. During the revolt led by Argyrus, the Normans gave help to

Longobard gold cross, decorated with embossed stylized figures of animals. Mid seventh century, found in the necropolis of Benevento. Museo del Sannio.

the rebel, but when he, after some early successes, decided to go over to the side of the Byzantines, they also joined the imperial troops. In this way, while the revolt was put down by diplomatic means, the Normans became aware of their own possibilities, and the areas they conquered during the revolt remained solidly in their hands, creating a dangerous wedge in Byzantine territory. These areas contained important strongholds such as Lavello, Ascoli Satriano, and Melfi, to which they were able to add key fortresses up to Matera. These conquests were officially recognized in September 1042 through an act of homage by which the Norman knight William de Hauteville, known as "Iron Arm" because of his strength, acknowledged himself to be a vassal of Guaimar, the Longobard prince of Salerno.

With the formation of the county of Aversa and the duchy of Melfi, the Normans set out to change their way of life and to leave behind, even if in a different way for each of the two, the precarious life as mercenaries which had characterized their first contacts with southern Italy. In Aversa, a village in the countryside of Campania and a strategic center for the Longobards, Rainulf established a city that was open to settlement by all people, but in which the ruling class of landowners consisted of the Norman aristocracy. On the other hand, Melfi, a city founded for defensive reasons in 1018 by the Byzantine *catepan*, or provincial governor, Basil Boiannes, was set

Tomb slab of a Norman noble, end of the twelfth century, in the church of Santa Maria a Piazza in Aversa. The city of Aversa was founded in 1030 by Normans who received a grant of territory from Duke Sergio IV, count of Naples, in consideration of the help given him in 1027 against Pandulf IV, the Longobard prince of Capua. Aversa was the first Norman county in Italy, acknowledged by Emperor Corrado in 1038. This territorial dominion was the "homeland" of the Normans in southern Italy, the true cradle of their civilization.

on a volcanic hill from which one could control the road to Naples. After the conquest it became the center for all later Norman incursions. Reinforced by a castle and surrounded by walls, the city and all its territory would be divided, according to a tradition full of symbolism, among the twelve counts who took part in the expedition. They had shared command, according to a sworn agreement similar to those customary among the Germans.

A leading figure in this first phase was William de Hauteville, the firstborn of a family that for many decades would play a prominent role in the Norman conquest of southern Italy. Guaimar, the prince of Salerno, not only granted him the title "Count of the Normans" by which his own men already referred to him, but also gave him his niece in marriage. By acknowledging the strength and ability of the Norman chief, this powerful Longobard prince, who just at that time had extended his rule to Gaeta and Capua, hoped to find support for extending his authority even further. But his effort was destined to fail because of meddling on the part of the new German emperor Henry III who, having gained the throne in 1047, came to Italy and restored the principality of Capua to Pandulf, a Longobard prince opposed

The Castle of Melfi, a true medieval castle, was built by the Normans but altered greatly in the Swabian and Angevin periods. Its structure reveals its strategic importance as an administrative center and a stronghold. Robert Guiscard confined his first wife Abelarda there, after repudiating her in order to marry Sichelgaita, the sister of the prince of Salerno. Frederick II lived there as well.

A coin known as a follaro, *produced in Salerno during the time of Duke William (1111–1127). On the front, with a halo, is St. Peter (incription: BEATVS PETRVS). On the back is a knight with a Norman shield and a cone-shaped helmet (inscription: W DVX APULIE). Museo Archeologico Nazionale. Naples.*

to Guaimar. From this complex interplay of forces, the Norman knights did derive some benefit, which was their feudal investiture by the emperor, who wished to use them as a way to better control the movements of the Longobards. In this way Rainulf Drengot was confirmed as Count of Aversa, and Drogo de Hauteville, the brother of William (d. 1046), was made Duke of Apulia and Calabria.

THE STAGES OF THE CONQUEST: APULIA, CAMPANIA, AND CALABRIA

By the first phase of the conquest, the Normans had already shown an ability to become part of the local power structure, quickly seeking to legitimize their rule over territories that had been acquired by force, exactly as happened in France. In the case of southern Italy, the interests of these knights from the North crossed not only with those of the German emperor but also, as we shall see, with those of the church in Rome. This situation would reinforce a tendency toward pluralism and disintegration that was typical of southern Italy during this period. In fact, according to the chronicle of Leo Marsicanus, when Emperor Henry III left Italy he gave the Normans the task of conquering Benevento and making the Longobards submit to him once and for all. In 1048, faithful to their promise to do so, a group of Normans led by Drogo de Hauteville occupied Bovino and Troia and took control of all the roads between Benevento and Apulia. They later clashed with the Byzantines at Tricarico, on the banks of the Busento, and thus opened the way to Calabria.

To this region came Robert, the youngest of the de Hautevilles, who was known as *Guiscard*, from an archaic French word meaning shrewd, for his boldness and cunning. Said by the chronicles to be "more subtle than Cicero and more cunning than Odysseus," Robert was described in a Byzantine source as a man "with a large build such as to exceed all other men, ruddy, fair-haired, with broad shoulders, blue eyes, and nimble in his movements." This description appears even more lively and interesting for having been made by a woman, the Byzantine princess Anna, daughter of the emperor Alexius Comnenus. She ended by saying that Robert was on the whole "handsome from head to toe."

Robert arrived in Italy some time between 1046 and 1047 with just five knights and thirty foot soldiers, and he was received coldly by his brothers, who were obviously little inclined to share their recent conquests with him. According to the chronicles, at first he made his living as a mercenary in the service of the prince of Capua. Later, when his brother Drogo granted him the castle of Scribla in Calabria, Robert showed his zeal and from there embarked on a campaign of rapid conquest that in 1051 saw

Detail of the huge rose window with eleven spokes that ornaments the facade of the cathedral of Troia, a masterpiece of Romanesque architecture built in 1093. It combines echoes of Byzantium and the Orient with innovative and sometimes bizarre elements such as the zoomorphic sculptures in high relief on the archivolt and the brackets.

la valente cõtessa matelda laquale　　　　　　　　citta di toscana e di lombardia e qua
regnaua ĩ toscana e lombardia e i　　　　　　　si a tutto ilmõdo sicome piu umana

him take possession of several fortresses in the Val di Crati. Having succeeded his brother as ruler of Melfi, Robert would in 1059 complete the occupation of Calabria and conquer Reggio, the capital of the Byzantine territories in the region and a fortress which up to that moment had been impregnable. Robert's subjugation of the local population was forceful and at times very violent, as Dante recalls with mournful words in Canto XXVIII of *Inferno* when he describes all the wars visited on the people of southern Italy as more horrible than the hellish torments of the pit, including those wars of resistance to Guiscard.

Hailed on the battlefield as "Duke of Apulia and Calabria" by the soldiers and knights who accompanied him on his conquests, Robert thought it wise to strengthen his position by means of marriage. He divorced his Norman wife Alberada, who had given him a son, Bohemond, and married the Longobard princess Sichelgaita. She was the daughter of Guaimar V, the prince of Salerno, and she also gave Robert a son, Roger Borsa. This was a very significant choice in terms of political and family

The coronation of Robert Guiscard, Duke of Apulia. A miniature from the Codex Chigi of the Nuova Cronica *by Villani. Biblioteca Apostolica Vaticana, Vatican City.*

alliances because it legitimized the power acquired by this daring Norman knight and connected it to a long tradition of sovereignty and royalty that predated the Longobards. According to the chronicle of William of Apulia: "Because of his marriage to that noble family, the illustrious fame of Robert began to increase, and the people, having already yielded to him by force, submitted to him now with the deference that accompanies a duty to one's ancestors."

Robert succeeded in driving back a final Byzantine attempt to retake at least their principal cities that was organized by Emperor Constantine Ducas in 1060. The Byzantines gradually lost all their strongholds and headed to their final defeat, which took place on April 16, 1071 at Bari, after a long and difficult siege that lasted three years. The capture of Bari was one of Robert's greatest strategic achievements. He set up a naval blockade of this capital of the *catepanato* (the Italian provinces under Byzantine control, from the title of the officer, or *Catepan*, in overall charge of them) and forced the capitulation of one of the mostly strongly fortified cities in southern Italy. In this way the entire southern peninsula was taken from the Byzantines and reunified. This time the population was treated with a certain degree of magnanimity by the Norman prince, who showed wisdom and moderation in his dealings with the defeated, including the Byzantine officials. It was Robert's task to settle disagreements and opposition among the nobles who were in his service, and to them he distributed land according to the feudal system that had been customary among the Normans for some time.

Robert's last years were characterized by a continual struggle for the legitimization, even on a religious level, of his power, and by a political vision that was no longer content to rule over the Mediterranean areas of Italy but which also looked to the East. Not satisfied with having snatched all their territory in southern Italy away from the Byzantines, Robert planned to launch an expedition to the Balkans that would be a prelude to his final, most ambitious objective, the conquest of Byzantium. Taking advantage of a period of crisis and political upheaval in the empire, Robert and his son Bohemond embarked for Durazzo in 1081 and over the course of two long campaigns spread terror among the people and among those at court in Constantinople. At first victorious on the coast of Dalmatia and in Macedonia, Robert would nevertheless not live to see the realization of this last dream of conquest. Sick with typhus, he would die on July 17, 1085 on the island of Cephalonia.

this page and following: *Cross that once belonged, according to an old tradition, to Robert Guiscard. Gold and cloisonné enamels, reworked in the fourteenth century. Museo Diocesano, Salerno.*

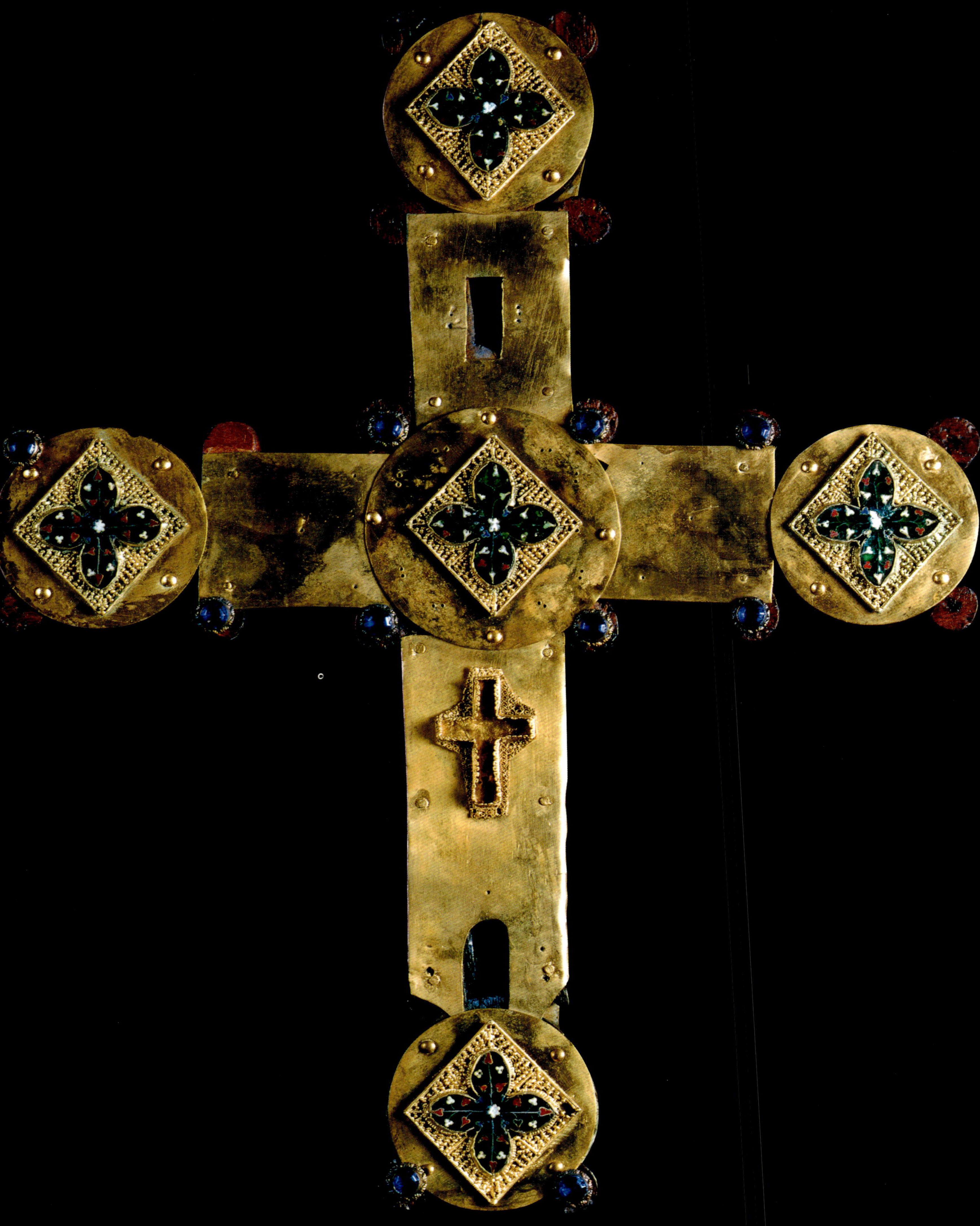

NORMAN SICILY . 175

RELATIONS WITH THE CHURCH AND THE ALLIANCE WITH THE POPE

The events of the Norman conquest of southern Italy cannot be understood without taking into account the Church of Rome. In 1050, with the election of Pope Leo IX, events in southern Italy were once again within its sphere of action. In fact, among the principal objectives of the new pope, who wished to affirm the superiority of the Roman church and to centralize its hierarchy, was that of restoring his complete authority in matters of patrimony, finance, and doctrine over the churches of Calabria, Apulia, and Sicily which since the eighth century had been placed by the Byzantine emperor under the jurisdiction of the patriarch in Constantinople. This was therefore a religious and cultural confrontation with the Byzantine church, and also a conflict over power. As a result the church in Rome began to look on the Norman knights first as new rivals and then as possible allies.

Initially, in fact, Pope Leo IX had assumed an attitude that was decidely hostile to the Normans, as he was worried that the new conquerors might be able to threaten his influence in the south. So at first he sought an alliance with the German emperor Henry III as a way of restoring papal authority in Benevento and other cities in Campania, and then he entered into negotiations with the Byzantine emperor in the hope of recovering control over the dioceses in the south. But the pope's plans were destined to fail on both fronts. It was precisely at this time that the churches in Rome and Constantinople experienced one of their

The town of Tursi, in Basilicata, suffered through many Muslim raids as well as an extended occupation, and recovered only in the tenth century when it became the seat of a bishopric. Signs of the Muslim presence are still visible, such as the church known as "the Rabàtana," from the Arab word rabad, *which referred to its location in a certain part of town and meant "village" or "suburb."*

opposite page:
A bishop's crosier made of ivory, tenth to eleventh century, with delicate floral ornaments and strange, imaginary creatures such as the dragon on the inside spiral of the handle. Originally in the Treasury of the Cathedral of Beauvais, now in the Museo del Bargello, Florence.

NORMAN SICILY . 177

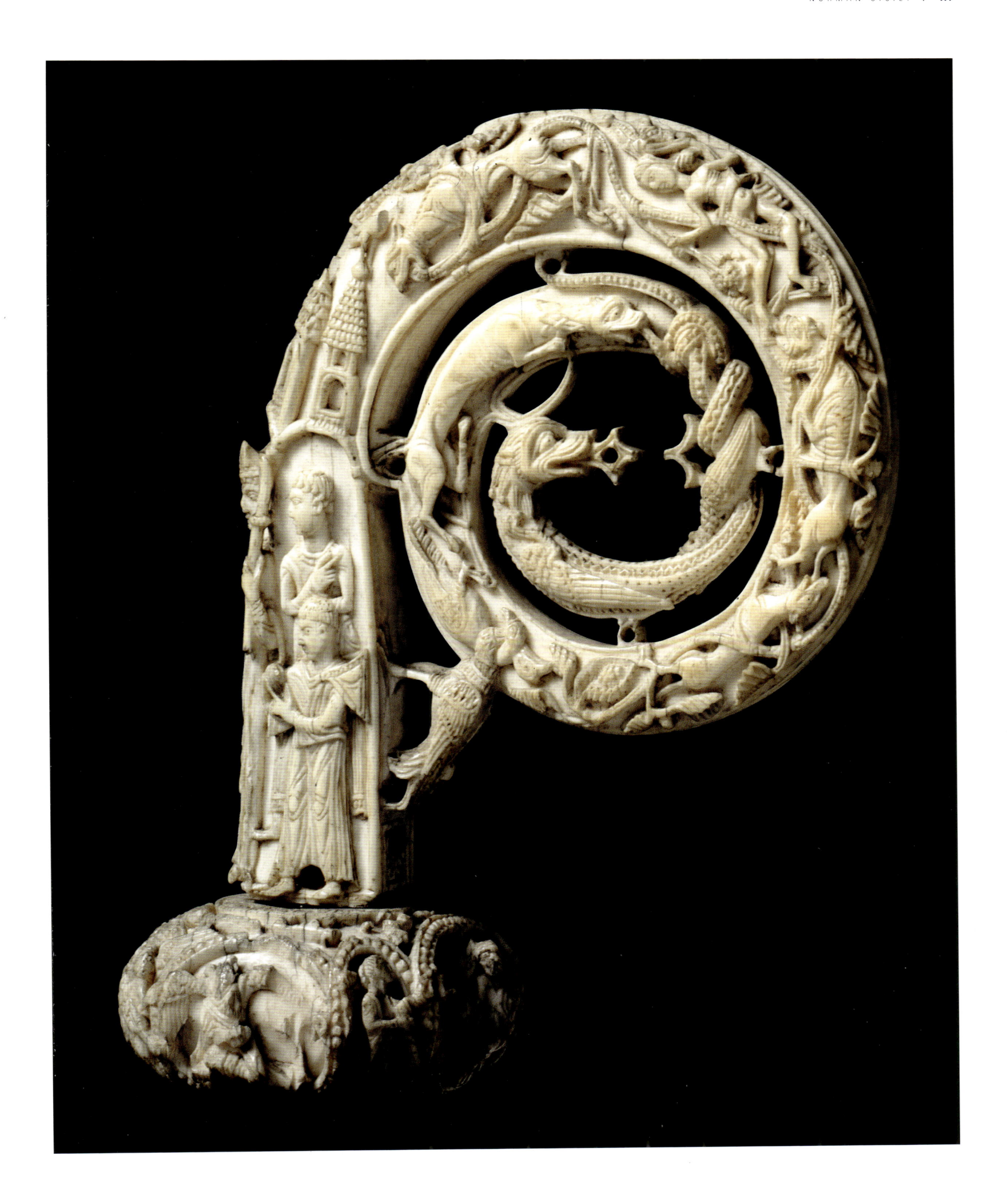

178 . ADELE CILENTO

The abbey of Santa Maria di Cerrate in the town of Squinzano, in Apulia, is an outstanding example of Romanesque architecture from the beginning of the twelfth century. It was built by Tancred, the Norman count of Lecce. The military victories achieved by the Normans had results in the religious sphere as well, with the reorganization and rebuilding throughout southern Italy of many ecclesiastical sees that had been suppressed by the Muslims.

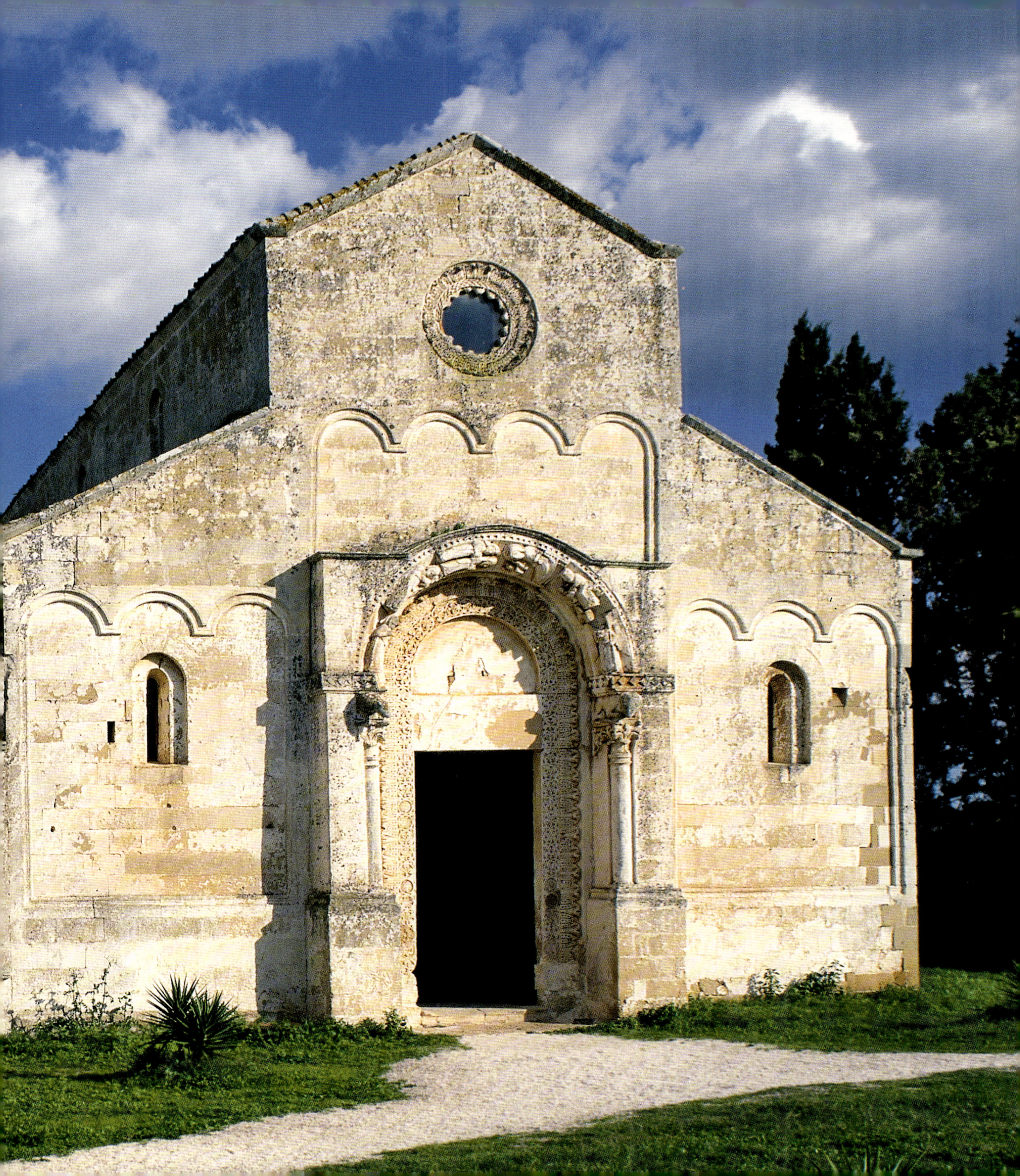

most heated and unresolved conflicts over doctrinal matters, and this problem, along with long-standing mutual misunderstandings of a political nature, resulted in the reciprocal excommunication of the two churches in 1054 and in what would become the most incurable of schisms.

There was nothing left for the pope but to negotiate with his new rivals, the warlike Normans. Their mutual interests brought them together, as both desired to play a role in the politics of southern Italy. Also supporting an alliance with the Normans was the most important spiritual center in all of south-central Italy, the monastery of Montecassino, in the person of its abbot, Desiderius, who was a leading figure in the political and cultural events of the time. This monk, who was related to the princes of Benevento, was a firm advocate of working with the Normans. He sought an accommodation with them that might also provide a convenient way to further general reforms in the church and purge it of the most corrupt elements of the clergy. He also sought to increase the church's freedom and independence, especially by reducing the influence of the emperor in Germany over the election of the pope and the investiture of bishops.

On June 24, 1059, Pope Nicholas II went to Montecassino and, after a stop in Benevento, convened a synod of all the Latin bishops of southern Italy in Melfi. The declared purpose was to depose certain bishops that were guilty of simony (the sale of church offices or favors), and to enforce the celibacy of the local clergy. But in fact everything seems to have been organized as a way to arrange a meeting with the Normans and to ratify the terms of a political alliance, as is shown by the presence at the synod of Richard of Aversa and Robert Guiscard. At this synod, Nicholas confirmed Robert's possessions and his title as duke of Calabria, Apulia, and Sicily—at such time as the island would be reconquered—, and he recognized Richard's sway over the principality of Capua. Finally, he granted both of them the territories belonging to the church that had previously been taken by the Byzantines. In exchange, the two knights swore fealty to the Church of Rome and acknowledged its ultimate authority over those lands, including the right to collect taxes on the church's estates, thus promising never to violate the *patrimonium* of St. Peter. At last, Robert obtained a legitimate title to lands that he had conquered by force, a title received thanks to investiture by one of the great universal powers, by means of which his superiority over the other Normans was confirmed. For their part, having become vassals of the pope, they recognized his supremacy in matters spiritual, but not in matters political, and this would later cause considerable problems.

In fact, Robert did not hesitate to further threaten the territories over which the pope had hoped to exercise direct control. In 1073 he occupied Amalfi, violating the agreement made at Melfi, and some years later he also occupied Salerno, Naples, and Benevento, virtually destroying Longobard power. The new pope, Gregory VII, excommunicated him repeatedly but was eventually forced to recognize, by means of an agreement signed at Ceprano in 1080, his authority over the territories of the

opposite page:
Desiderius, the Abbot of Montecassino, receives a gift from Prince Jordan, in an illustration from the Regesto di Sant'Angelo in Formis. Twelfth century. Archives of the Abbey of Montecassino.

Iordanus princeps
Desiderius abbas

Praeceptum sci Rufi cum omnibus pertinentiis suis

INNOMINE Dni salvatoris nri ihu xpi di eterni.

Campagna that he had taken by force. In exchange, the pope obtained a new promise of protection, which Robert did not fail to observe. When in 1084 the pope was taken prisoner by Emperor Henry IV, with whom he quarrelled over the investiture of bishops, Robert went to his aid with six thousand knights and several thousand foot soldiers, freeing him and taking him to Salerno.

Richard I, Prince of Aversa and Capua, makes a donation to the Abbey of Sant'Angeloin Formis, in an illustration from the Regesto di Sant'Angelo in Formis. *Twelfth century. Archives of the Abbey of Montecassino.*

opposite page:
Bishop's throne, of Pope Gregory VII. Marble, eleventh century. Cathedral of Salerno.

CONSEDIT + QVVM + IN CARDINALIVM CORONA + D. XI
TATIS VINDEX GREGORIVS + CVI IPSVM

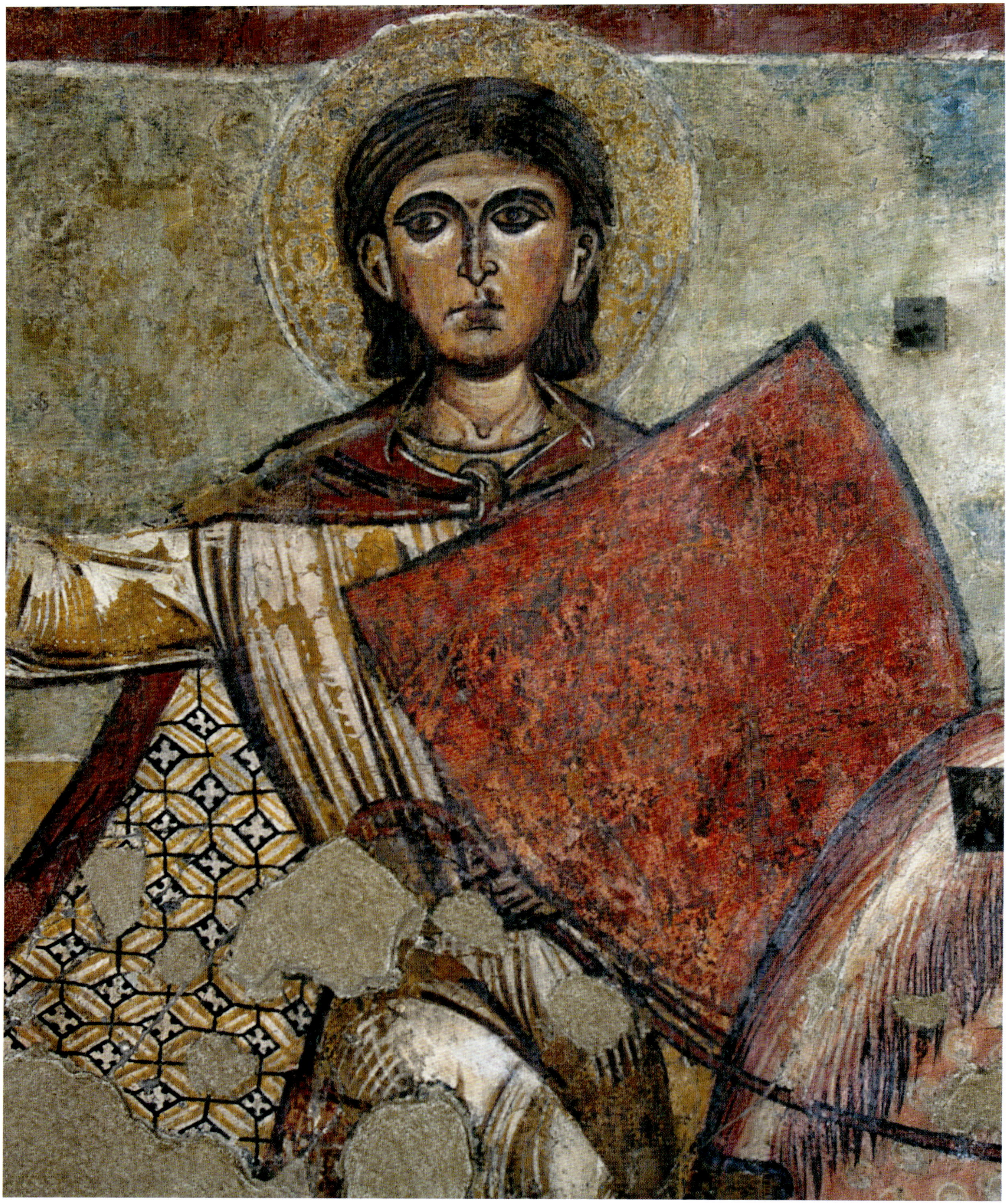

THE CONQUEST OF SICILY AND THE RULE OF THE GREAT COUNT

With the occupation of Reggio and the elimination of all the Byzantine garrisons in Calabria, it became necessary, in accord with his promise to Pope Nicholas II, for Robert Guiscard to land in Sicily. But compared to his fight against the Byzantines, a victory over the Muslims would carry much greater significance and have the character of a crusade. With the expulsion of the Muslims from Sicily the de Hautevilles would be able, in the words of Geoffrey Malaterra, "to earn both spiritual rewards and worldly goods." Moreover, the conquest of Sicily was without doubt one of the most legendary of the Norman exploits in Italy, and a de Hauteville was once again the leading figure. But this time that figure was Roger, Robert's younger brother.

The first military operations carried out in Sicily by the Normans were made easier by internal crises and factionalism among the Muslims. As previously happened in 827 when the turmarch Euphemios had called on the Aghlabids for help, this time it was the emir Ibn al-Thumanah who asked Roger de Hauteville for help. With a small fleet, Roger landed on Sicily's Ionian and Tyrrhenian coasts simultaneously. He was able to approach the city of Messina from its land side and in 1061 quickly forced its surrender. The subsequent stages of the conquest of the interior and eastern parts of the island are not well known, but one cannot accept the celebratory tone of the

opposite page:
Detail of a fresco in the chapel of San Giovanni in a Norman castle in the town of Paternò, near Catania, in Sicily.

this page:
A duel between a Norman and a Moor. Mosaic, twelfth century. Museo Camillo Leone, Vercelli. The characterization of the two subjects is remarkable, not only in their physical appearance but also in their clothing and weapons. The Arab shield is round and light, and the Norman one has a typical elongated shape.

Norman chronicles that speak of a rapid campaign among people who were oppressed by the infidels and wished to make Roger their ruler.

After the capture of Bari by Robert Guiscard in 1071, operations in Sicily were reinforced by new troops from peninsular Italy. In that same year Roger was able to occupy Catania and, on January 10, 1072, after several months of siege, Roger was able to force the capitulation of Palermo, the capital of the emirate. Once again, the victorious Normans showed themselves to be merciful, if we can believe William of Apulia, who tells how Roger "did not exile anyone and, in keeping with his promise, did not harm anyone, even though they were all pagans. He treated all those he conquered with fairness. And with glory to God he shattered the foundations of the impious temple: in place of the mosque he built a church to the Virgin Mary. And the temple of Mahomet and the devil, transformed into a sanctuary of God, became a portal to heaven for the righteous."

At first, both the occupied areas and those still to be conquered were divided between the two de Hauteville brothers. In accord with the agreement of Melfi, Robert had jurisdiction over the island in its entirety, and particularly over Palermo, the Val di Demone, and part of Messina. Roger had authority over the other half of Messina, Troina, Catania, and Mazara. The historical sources seem to indicate that sovereignty over the island initially belonged to Robert and that Roger was subject to his older brother. Between 1077 and 1086 the Normans, equipped with a more substantial fleet, renewed their conquest and overwhelmed first Trapani and then Taormina. Finally, with a rout of the last Arab resistance around Agrigento, they took Syracuse and Castrogiovanni. The last stronghold to fall was Noto. And thus, in 1091, after thirty years of hard fighting, all of Sicily, along with Malta, came under Norman rule. But it was a final victory that Robert Guiscard did not live to see, as he had died in 1086.

Now the sole master of Sicily, with the title "Great Count," Roger at first had to reward with land grants all those who had helped in the conquest, including Bretons, Frenchmen, Italians, and Longobards. The knights among them received very substantial benefits, including land and the privileges of lordship that went

Capital in the shape of a winged lion. Eleventh century. Originally from the cathedral of San Nicola in Bari, now in the municipal museum.

opposite page:
Muslims besiege a Christian fortress, from Las Cantigas de Santa Maria *by Alfonso X el Sabio, in the Library of the Monastery of San Lorenzo, the Escorial, Madrid.*

NORMAN SICILY . 187

188 . ADELE CILENTO

Fresco with St. Barbara and St. Simon, from the Grotta dei Santi, near the city of Caserta, in Campania. The fresco seems Byzantine, but is actually Norman, of the Benedictine school between the tenth and eleventh centuries. It clearly shows how the Normans were aware of the artistic styles that came before them and from which they learned extremely quickly.

BAR · BARBARA

Situated high above the outlet of the Alcàntara River, the majestic castle in the town of Calatabiano, northeast of Catania, together with the fortress of Taormina, protected an important access route to the interior of Sicily. It is certainly Arab in origin, as indicated by its place-name. The Norman elements are found only on the summit, while the defensive outbuildings and the residential areas date from the Swabian and Aragonese periods.

opposite and
following pages:
The Norman castle and the promontory of Erice, near Trapani. The city and the surrounding territory were occupied by the Arabs in 831. The geographer Idrisi called the site Gebel-Hamed, *"gebel" being the Arabic word for mountain, referring to the landscape, its strategic qualities, and a Byzantine fortress that was there. The citadel gained new importance under the Normans, who rebuilt the walls during the twelfth century.*

with it. Large amounts of land were placed within the feudal system, especially on the eastern side of the island, where even two large cities, Syracuse and Catania, were ruled by feudal lords. Remaining under Roger's direct authority were important fortified towns such as Termini, Trapani, Agrigento, Castrogiovanni, and Palermo. Roger tried in one way or another to prevent any bullying of the peasants by his vassals, partly just to protect them but also in hopes of increasing the production of grain, which would benefit him as ruler. It likewise seems that Roger avoided unnecessary violence in his dealings with the Muslim population, displaying instead a certain magnanimity towards those who had been part of the administration of the emirate.

Roger had to establish an administrative system for a region in which conditions differed markedly from those on the Italian mainland. Sicily was in a state of crisis and its civil administration had broken down. Moreover, the few men of learning who survived the invasion were Greek in both religion and culture, and Roger sought to maintain some connection with them. Not only were there many Greek churchmen and monks in Sicily at that time, but many of the more qualified officials

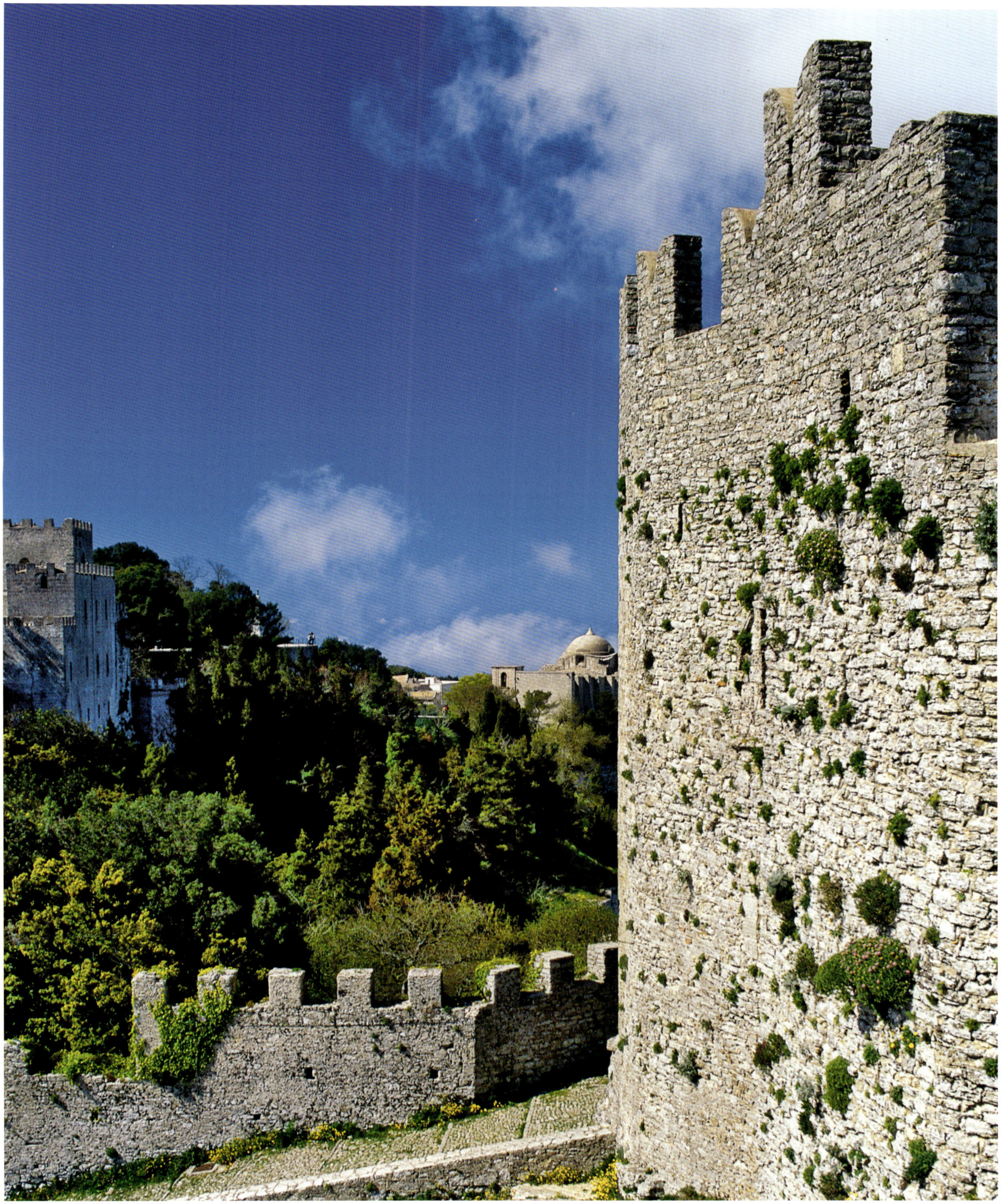

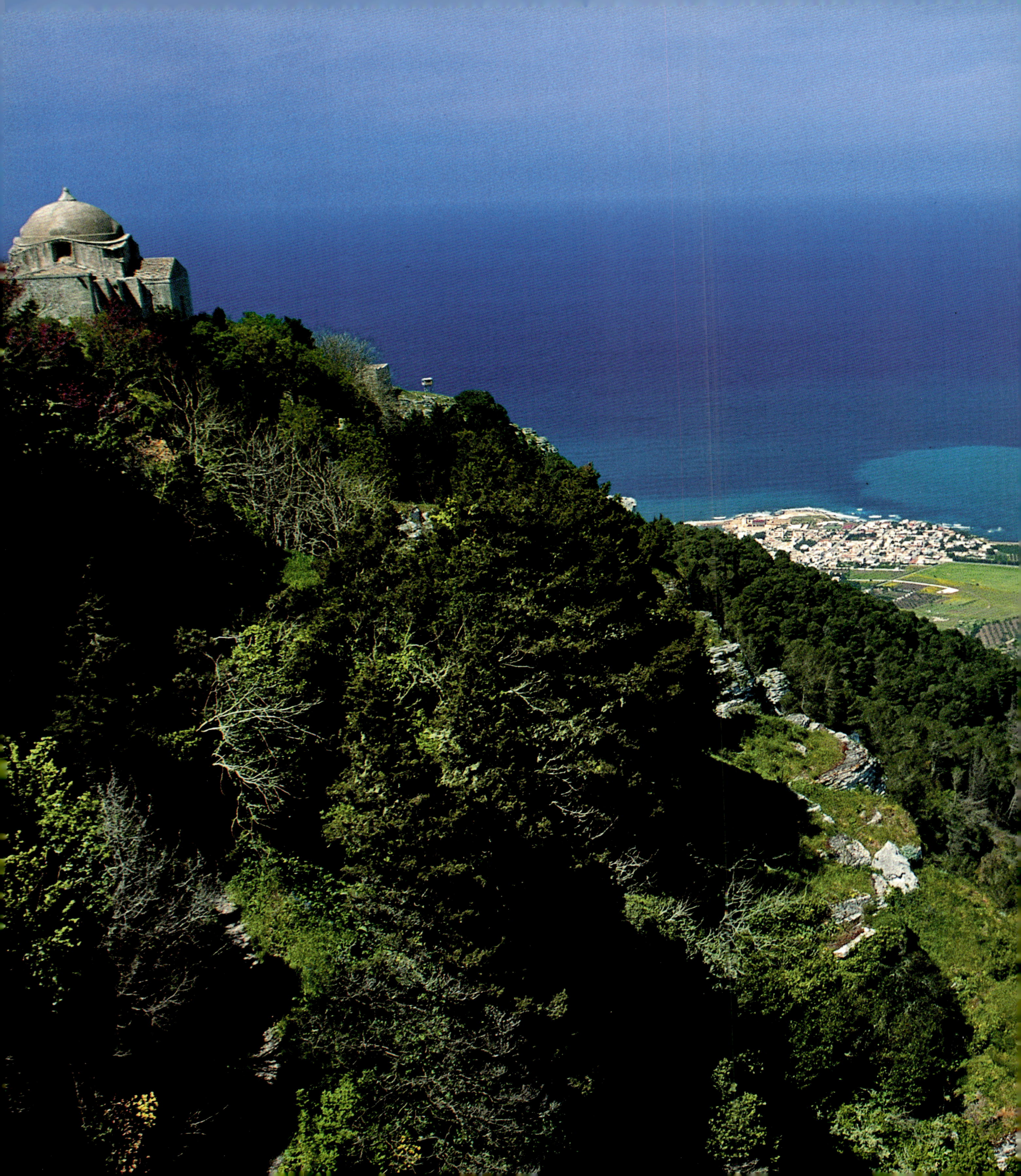

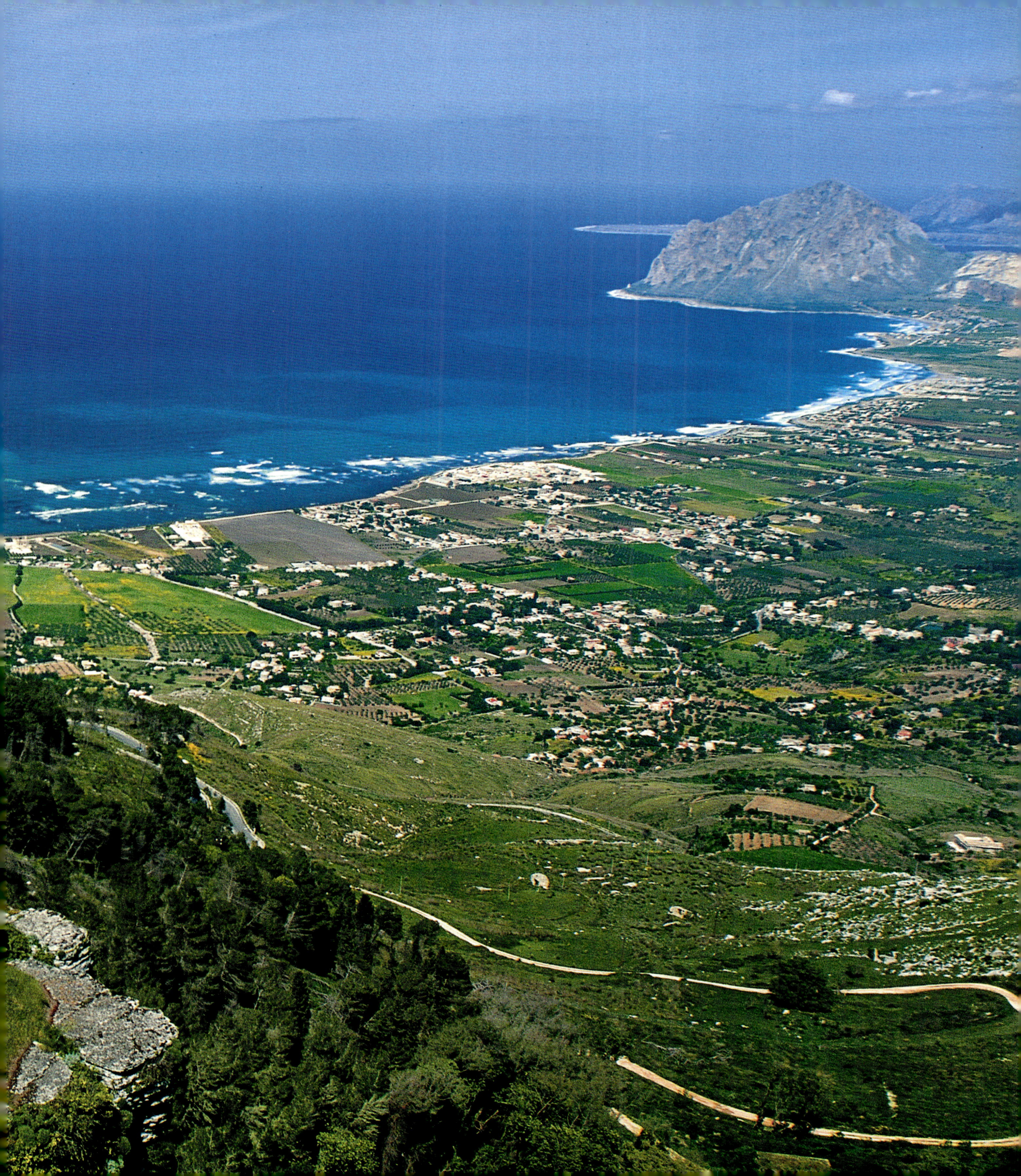

that Roger wished to have at his side in various administrative posts were of Greek extraction. The court protocol chosen by Roger was in the Byzantine style, as were some of the terms used by the Norman chancellery, which drafted documents in Latin, Greek, and Arabic. The finance department was structured according to Arab custom, and in fact the Muslims who remained in Sicily were given the task of drawing up the land registries and the records of goods owned by the monasteries and villages. The terms used to indicate the various positions in the finance office were of Arab derivation, and the Arab mint continued to coin money with Khufic letters on it.

But the most profound transformations took place in the structure of the church. In Sicily, compared to the other areas of southern Italy conquered by the Normans, the church had for some time been rather disorganized, even though various small Greek monasteries did manage to preserve the Christian faith throughout the Arab period. Roger gave these monasteries strong support by founding new ones and by means of large donations, with the aim of enhancing the very pure spiritual element which they had preserved. As did his successor, Roger understood the value of the tradition of eastern spirituality that existed in southern Italy, along with the deep attachment that its people felt for the Greek monasteries. Nevertheless, faithful to his pledge to the pope, Robert had to place limits on the activities of the Greek clergy. Between 1081 and 1088 he created new bishoprics in Troina, Agrigento, Catania, Mazara, and Syracuse, and these were entrusted to Latin prelates from northern Italy and France. The investiture of new bishops, a delicate problem that was much discussed in the church at that time, was the cause of a big quarrel between Pope Urban II and Roger. The pope, during a visit to Sicily, confirmed the bishops chosen by Roger but also nominated a new bishop for Troina. Roger, who did not like this interference by the pope, reacted by imprisoning the new bishop. Nevertheless, they eventually reached a compromise and a papal bull issued in 1098 set out the terms of their relationship: Roger promised to release the imprisoned bishop and not to violate the jurisdictional immunity of the church again while Urban recognized Roger's control over the ecclesiastical institutions on the island. By virtue of his new role as protector of Christianity in Sicily, Roger obtained the right to carry a shepherd's crook and to wear the ring and the dalmatic (a wide-sleeved overgarment worn by a prelate) that were the symbols of imperial majesty. He was also the first of the Norman lords to combine an explicit religious purpose with the notion of sovereignty, a concept that echoed the ideology of power current in Byzantium.

this page and opposite:
The most luxurious item of clothing of a prince or ruler was a silk tunic richly embellished at the hem and sleeves, as can be seen in this detail of a garment worn by Frederick II. Kunsthistorisches Museum, Vienna.

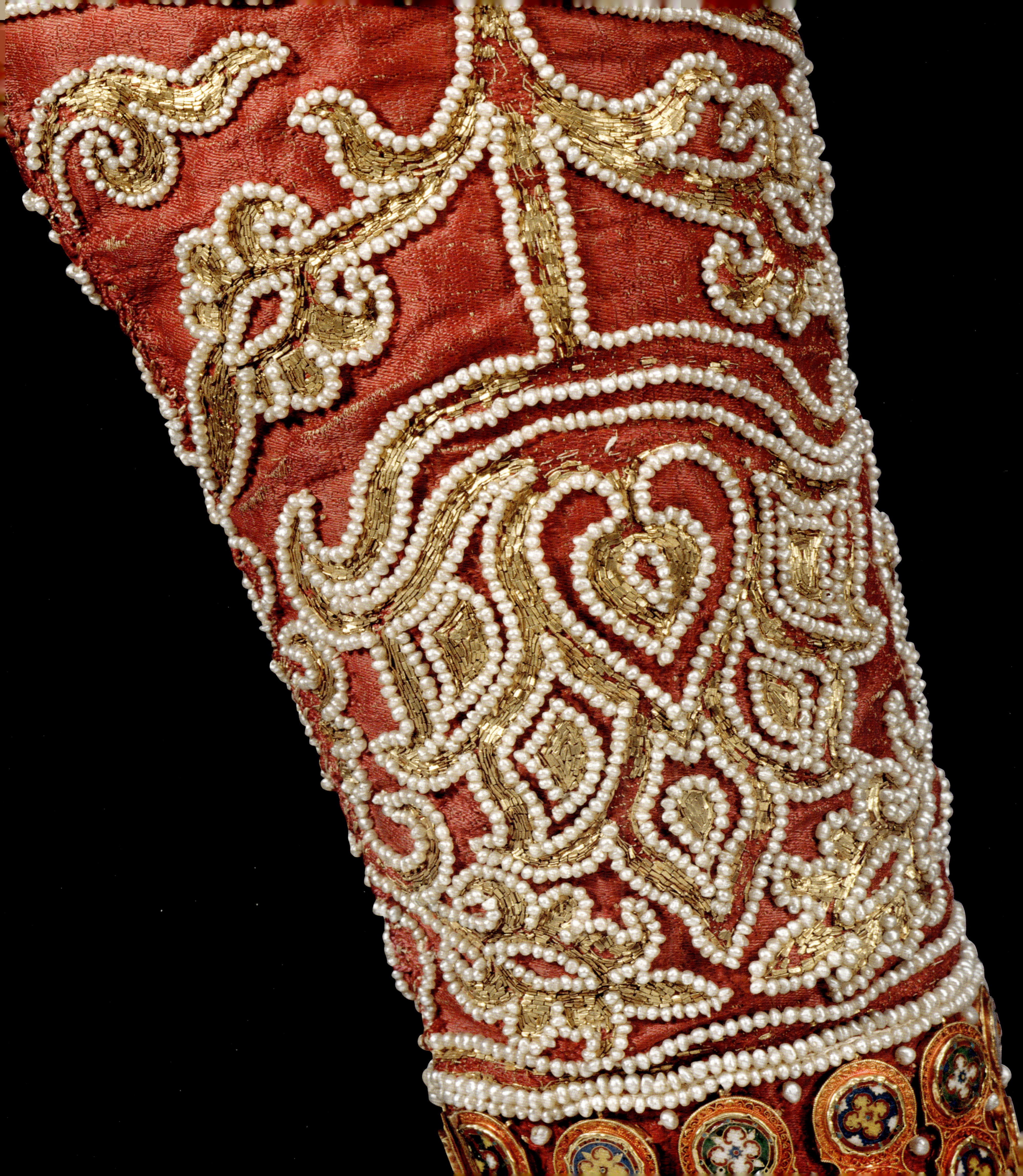

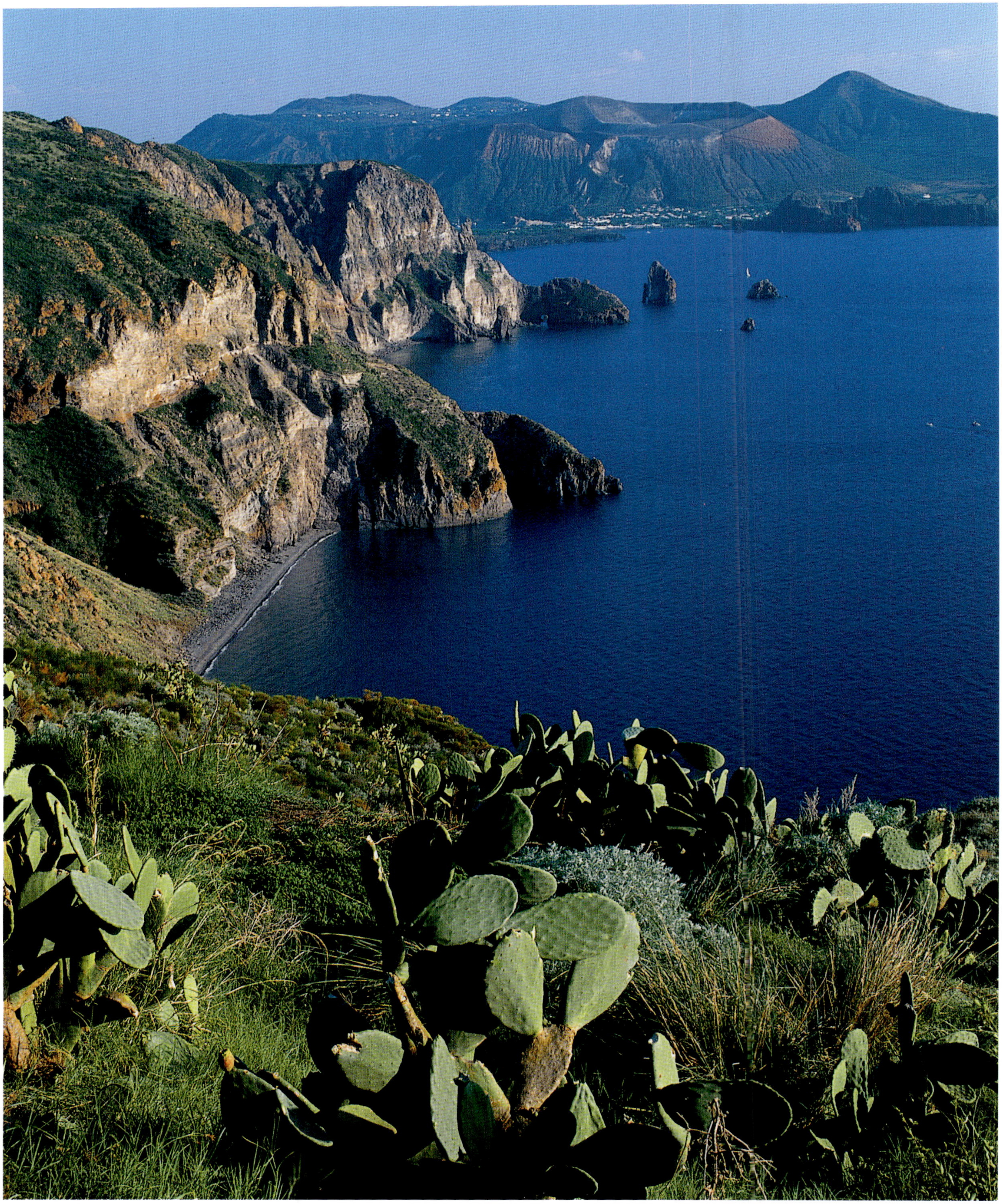

WOMEN AND POWER

Roger died in Mileto, a small town in Calabria that he had chosen as his residence, on June 22, 1101. He was buried in the small church of the Benedictine abbey of the Santissima Trinità di Mileto, which he himself had founded. The sarcophagus, rescued from the ruins of the earthquake of 1783, is today in the Archaeological Museum of Naples.

He had arrived in southern Italy at the age of twenty, in the full vigor of youth. The chronicler Geoffrey Malaterra describes him as a young man "quite handsome, tall, of elegant proportions, well-spoken, wise in counsel, farsighted in his affairs, always pleasing and cheerful in character, and gifted with great physical strength and courage in battle." Of his physical strength, courage, and farsightedness Roger did not fail to give evidence, as well as of the great charm with which he conquered the hearts of three women. In fact, Roger married three times: his first wife was Judith of Evreux, his second was Eremburga, the daughter of William of Mortain, and finally, when he was already sixty, he married Adelaide del Vasto, a woman from northern Italy. After Roger's death Adelaide was regent in Sicily until their young son Roger attained his majority and became Roger II.

Adelaide is described in the historical sources as a beautiful young woman with a strong personality who was capable of taking on great responsibility. She probably accompanied Roger during the years of his most intense activity in Sicily and perhaps thanks to the experience acquired at her husband's side the Norman nobility was willing, after his death, to accept her as regent. Moreover, the Normans were by that

opposite page:
The island of Lipari, off the coast of Sicily near the province of Messina, has seen various rulers succeed one another since antiquity. In 836 it was destroyed by the Arabs, who scattered the inhabitants. It remained abandoned for some two hundred years until Roger I established a community of Benedictine monks in 1083. His wife Adelaide spent a great deal of time there, often visiting the abbey of San Bartolomeo, to which she donated many jewels and precious objects.

this page:
Cloister of the abbey of San Bartolomeo in Lipari, founded by Robert Guiscard and Roger I in 1085.

time accustomed to seeing women in prominent positions. One example was Sichelgaita, the wife of Robert Guiscard and the daughter of Guaimar IV, the prince of Salerno. In a society in which women of noble birth had to accept arranged marriages that were made for strategic and diplomatic reasons, she had learned how to carry out the roles of Longobard princess, Norman countess, wife, and mother with great dignity and courage. This same Sichelgaita, on the death of her husband Robert, showed herself to be a woman capable of passing the kingdom on to her son Roger Borsa, the legitimate heir. This was not easy, as there was another claimant, Bohemond of Taranto, the son of Alberada, Robert's first wife. Sichelgaita asked her brother-in-law Roger I for help, as she was afraid that she would not with her own forces be able to defend her rights against the Norman lords who supported Bohemond. In the end, the departure of Bohemond and many other unruly knights on the First Crusade would, at least temporarily, strengthen the position of Sichelgaita's son.

Something similar happened in Sicily when, after the death of Roger, the Norman aristocracy did not look with pleasure on the idea of a woman as regent. Adelaide showed herself to be hard and inflexible, suppressing all opposition. She would govern for ten years, following the policies of her husband with regard to the transferability of feudal rights, strategic marriages, and legal issues. But it was above all in her dealings with religious institutions that Adelaide showed her diplomatic and organizational skills. She made rich donations to the Greek monasteries in Sicily and Calabria and also founded large abbeys, providing a way for all the Greek monastic institutions that were scattered throughout southern Italy to maintain contact with each other. In this way Adelaide won over her subjects who were of Greek descent and created support for her own rule and for her son's. Furthermore, while Roger had spent most of his time in Calabria, Adelaide transferred her court to Sicily. She held court first in Messina and then Palermo, cities that were by tradition and appearance markedly Mediterranean, in which the beauty and lavishness of their buildings and streets made it possible for them to rival the most famous urban centers of the time.

Some decades later, the fortunes of the kingdom of Sicily would be entrusted to yet another woman, Marguerite of Navarre. The wife of William I, she would rule Sicily as regent from 1166 to 1171 in place of her young son. This woman, the daughter of the king of Navarre and of Norman descent on her mother's side, would also show herself capable of governing during a very complicated period, restraining for at least a few years the dangerous intrigues of the nobles who tried, through various factions, to seize power. In this way the queen was able to secure peace for the kingdom and to preserve the power of the de Hautevilles until William II came of age.

opposite page:
Cloister of the abbey of San Bartolomeo. The eleventh and twelfth centuries saw a flowering of monastic institutions supported by the Normans throughout southern Italy.

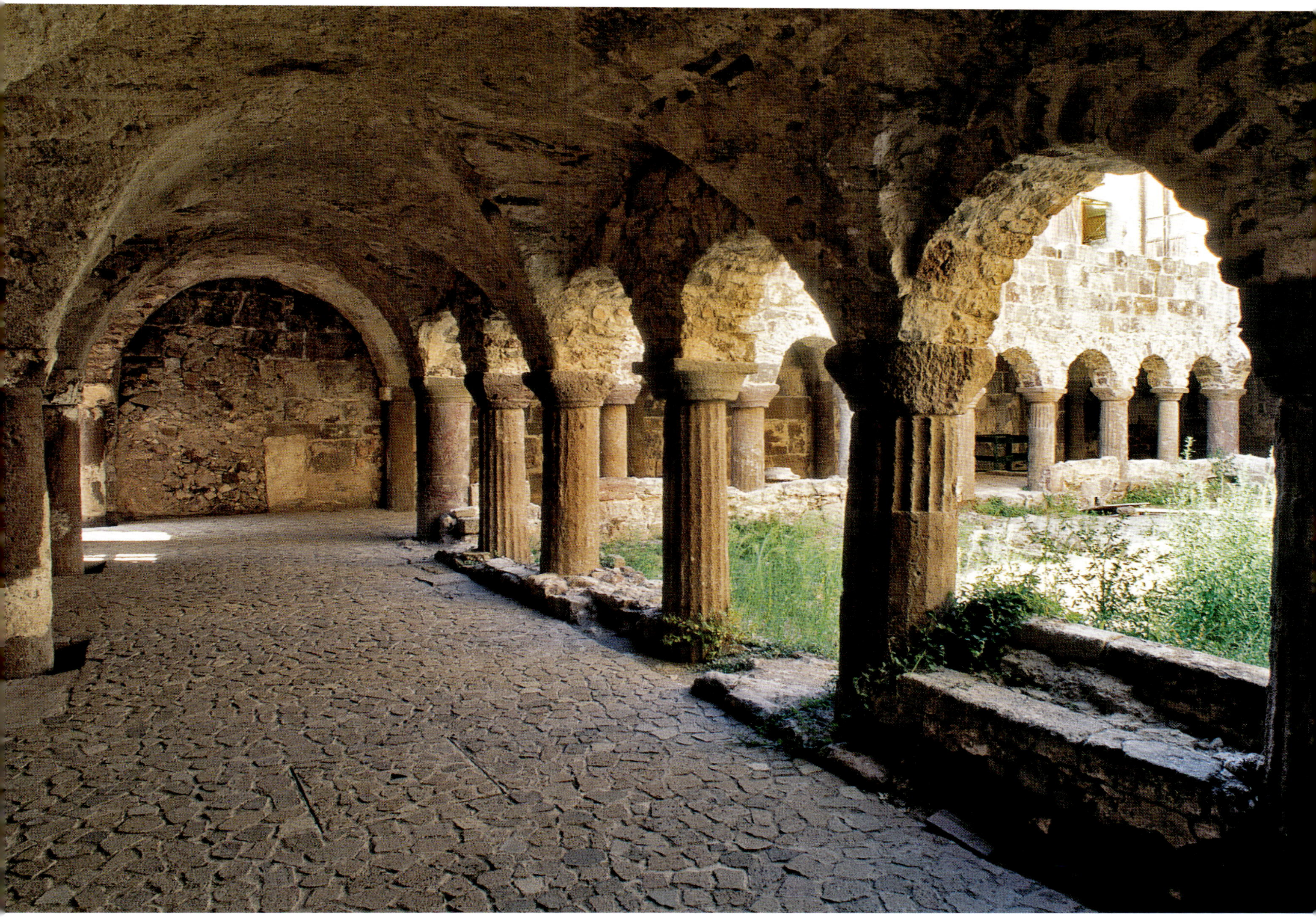

CATHEDRALS, CITIES, AND CASTLES

With the lands that they conquered, the Normans inherited a richness and variety of cultural tendencies that were sometimes in conflict with each other but which had an illustrious tradition. To this variety they learned to add new stimuli, especially in the first decades after the conquest. The cultural panorama was thus notably enriched and the results were at times surprising. Furthermore, as is well known, the first years of Norman rule correspond, in the artistic field, to the spread in southern Italy of the figurative culture that is usually referred to as Romanesque. Scholars are often asked at length about the connection between the arrival of the Normans and the first appearance of this style in Italy, a problem that is not easily solved given that Romanesque appears in many parts of Europe. But there was an undeniable deepening of the ties between southern Italy and the artistic culture of Europe north of the Alps, where Romanesque originated, and this occurred during the Norman period. In fact, the religious policy followed by the Normans that called for a renewal of various ecclesiastical and monastic practices favored contact with northern Europe, thanks to the arrival in Italy, especially from France, of prominent members of the Benedictine monastic order. This would explain, at least in part, the sudden appearance in southern Italy of Romanesque features that have clear roots north of the Alps. Norman monks and churchmen were in fact sent to many dioceses that would later see the construction of very innovative churches, cathedrals, and abbeys. The most well-known case is that of Robert de Grandmesnil, the Norman abbot to whom Robert Guiscard entrusted the founding of several important churches in Calabria. A new wave of cultural borrowings from beyond the Alps arrived as a result of the First Crusade, which began in 1099 and caused many soldiers and pilgrims to gather in Apulia while waiting to embark for the Holy Land. Among these armies, even if they were more interested in war than in cultural exchange, were noblemen, knights, and churchmen who on the whole belonged to an elite that was accustomed to artistic patronage, while among the pilgrims and soldiers there certainly were artists and artisans.

The close connection that characterized the relationship between the Normans and the church, starting with their first involvement in Italian politics, resulted above all in the construction of cathedrals, which in the Norman cities was inextricably linked to the investiture of bishops. This was the case in Aversa, of which Richard Drengot demanded the right to appoint the bishop as soon as he became count in 1053. The cathedral in Aversa, the construction of which was begun by Richard and continued by his son Jordan, was placed right in the center of the city, as was customary with the Normans. The urban layout chosen for their settlement developed in the shape of a circular double ring of which the cathedral occupied the center, without necessarily indicating that this religious building was

A copper coin known as a folloro, *showing Roger I with the date 1098 and an incription on the back: ROG E RIV S COME + S. Museo Archeologico Nazionale, Naples.*

opposite page:
Detail of a fresco showing a Crusader. Twelfth century. Chapel of Saint Gilles, Montoire.

following pages:
The figurative art of the Romanesque style spread throughout southern Italy along with the Normans, achieving its most complete and mature expression during the first half of the thirteenth century. Among its many wonderful masterpieces are the elegant open gallery in the cathedral of Bitonto and the portal of the abbey church of San Leonardo a Siponto, both in Apulia.

CASTITAS

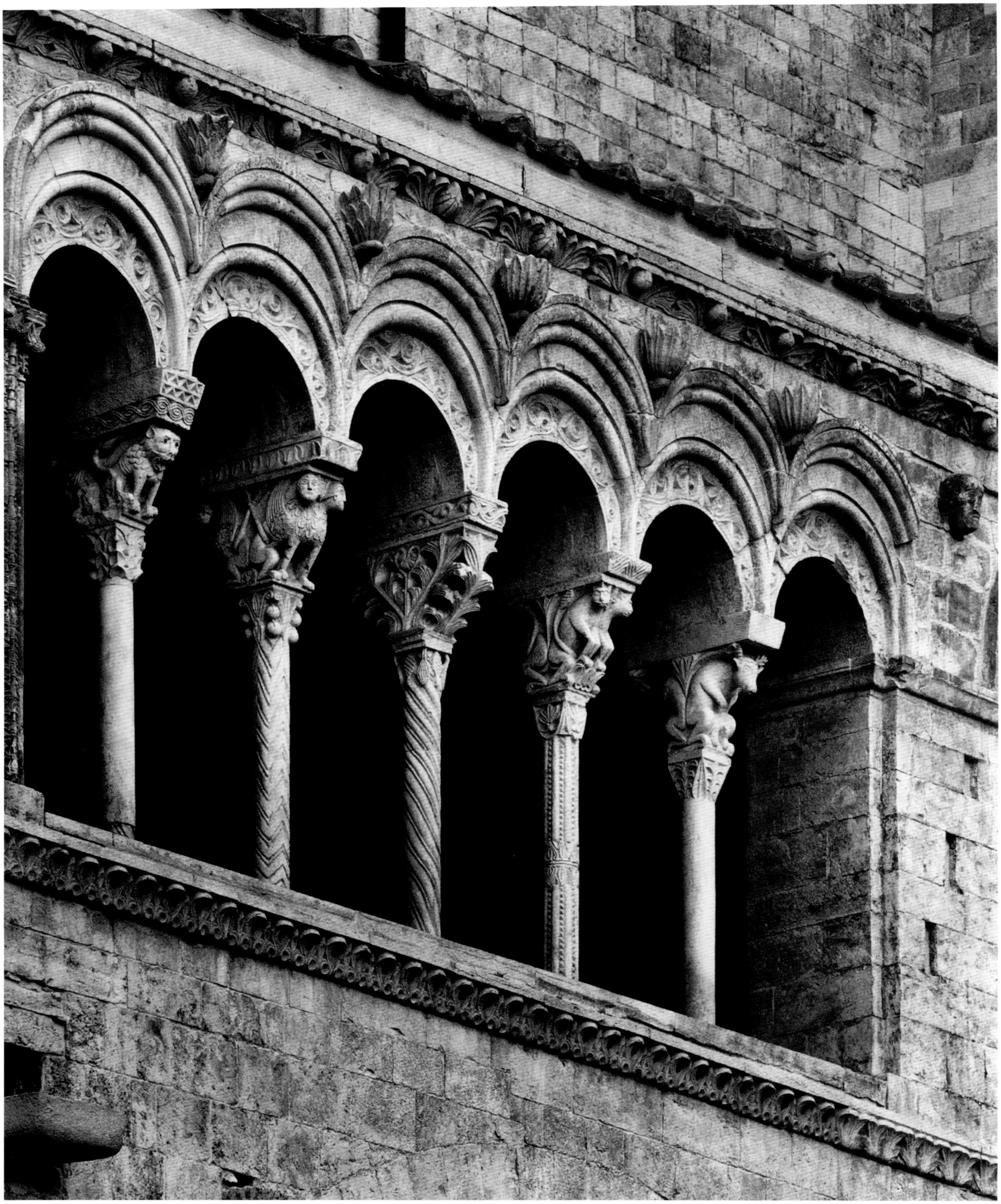

NORMAN SICILY . 203

The cathedral of Aversa, construction of which began in 1053 under Count Richard I and was completed in 1090 by his son Jordan. It was devastated by a fire in 1145 and later damaged by the earthquake of 1456. The only elements of its early construction that remain are the apse and connecting ambulatory and the dome in a mixed Arab-Norman style.

The monastery of Santa Sofia in Benevento was founded by the Longobard prince Arechis II in the second half of the eighth century. It was placed under the authority of the abbot of Montecassino, from which it broke away in 1159. This interior view shows the large number of capitals and columns salvaged from ancient buildings and re-used in ways that differed from their original purpose, such as the cut-down columns with their capitals made into basins for holy water.

the most important in town. An innovative feature of the cathedral is its large absidal ambulatory, an architectural structure that was unknown in the south of Italy but very common in France, obviously in Normandy but even at Cluny, the most famous abbey in the West during the Middle Ages. As a matter of fact, the head of the diocese of Aversa at this time was a Cluniac monk from Normandy named Guimund. It would not be an accident if the ambulatory of the cathedral in Aversa, consisting of seven cross-vaulted covered bays supported by strong pillars, bore a strong resemblance to the Anglo-Norman buildings in Canterbury, Norwich, and Gloucester. Nor would it be a coincidence if the ambulatories in the cathedral of Acerenza and the church of Santissima Trinità in Venosa, which are twins of the one

Cloister of the monastery of Santa Sofia in Benevento.

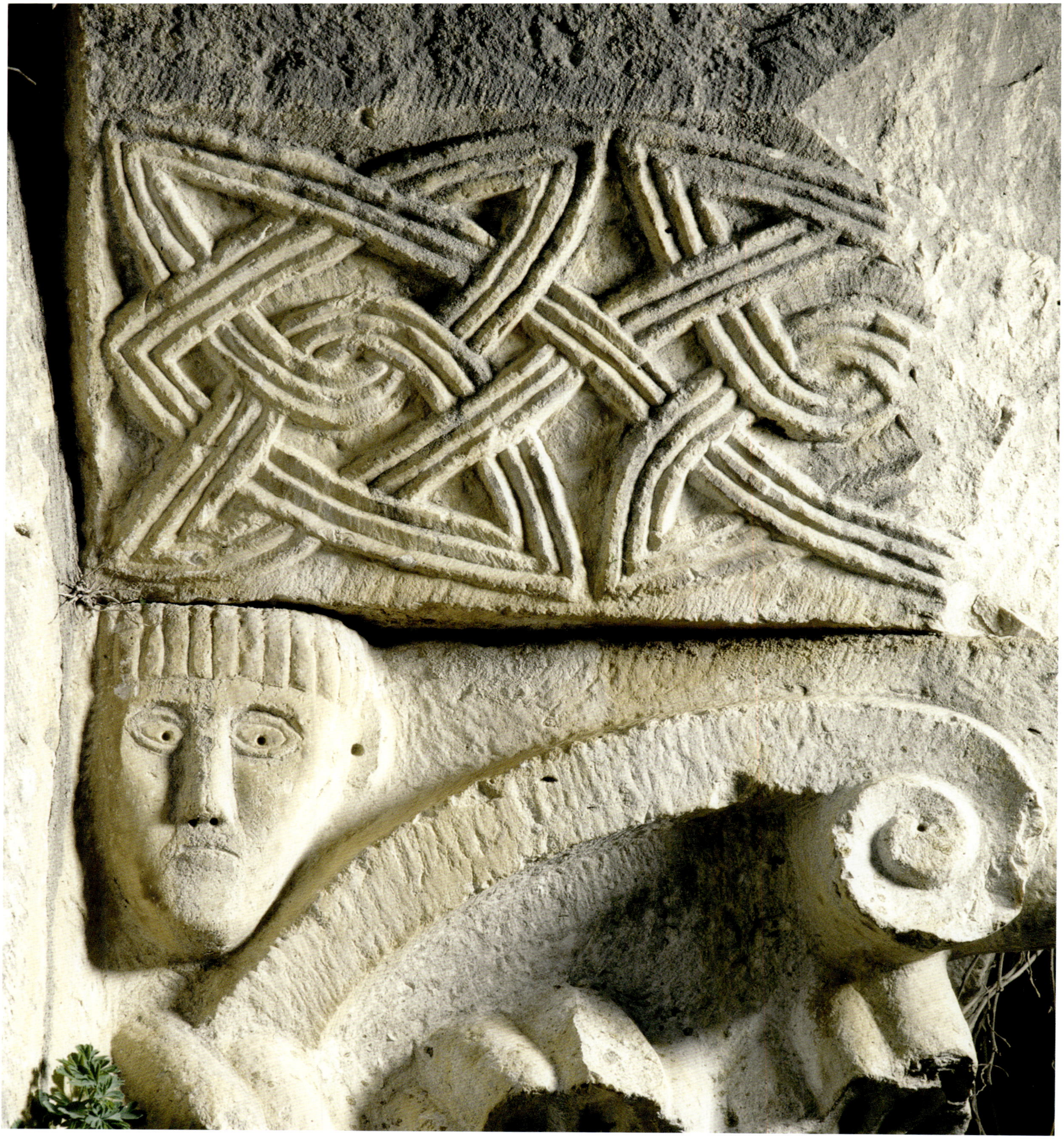

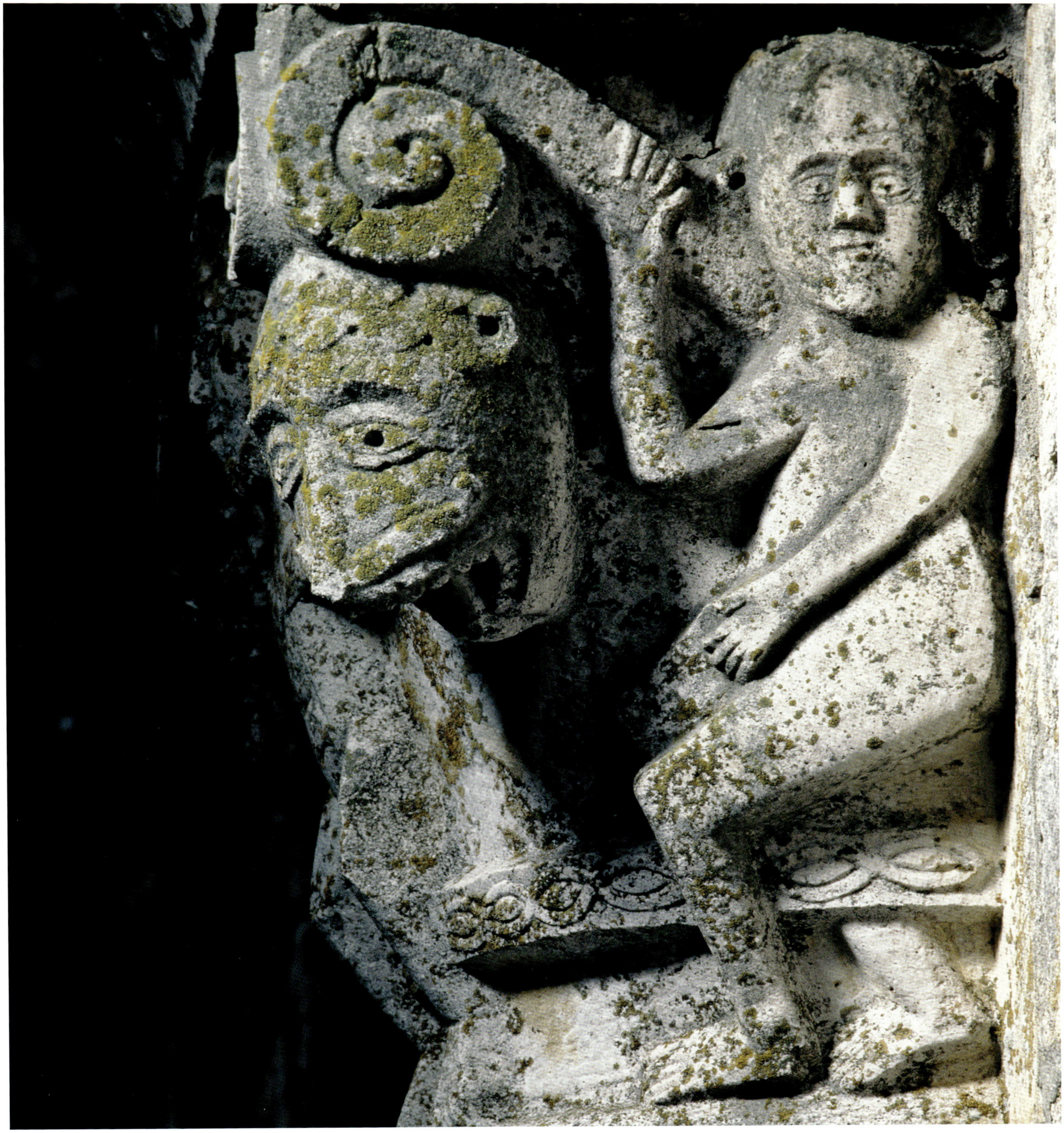

in Aversa, were found in buildings constructed at more or less that same time and in areas where episcopal and clerical affairs were administered by Benedictines of Norman extraction.

A sculpture workshop of high quality must have worked on the construction of Aversa cathedral, as shown by the relief with a knight and a dragon that art historians have called the most beautiful sculpture of its time in southern Italy (F. Abbate), and even a "medieval Picasso" (F. Bologna). Although its subject is not clearly identifiable—it may be St. George and the dragon, or perhaps Siegfried and the dragon Fafner—the design clearly refers to the struggle between good and evil. It possesses the fabled grandeur of a Norse saga, with its echoes of a natural world that is mysterious and unyielding in which the spectre of evil, tamed by the knight, appears in all its intense beauty. The reliefs carved by this extraordinary atelier are often compared to the reliefs on the portico of the cathedral of Cerinola, built between 1087 and 1094 by a bishop named Bernard. The portico contains sculptures belonging to the phase of the work that was overseen by Bernard, more or less the same period in which the cathedral of Aversa was built. In these sculptures, placed on the jambs of one of the portals, motifs derived from Sassanid art can be seen in the stylized curls of the horse's mane, and motifs derived from Arabic art can be seen in the definition of the bodies and heads, while the expressive manner of the saw-toothed figures with large whiskers recalls the dragon in Aversa.

In 1071 the basilica of the monastery of Montecassino was consecrated in a magnificent ceremony attended by high prelates, princes, and counts that marked its

this page and opposite:
Bas relief (with detail) of a knight and a dragon. Eleventh century. Cathedral of Aversa. The stone slab, which was perhaps the jamb of the cathedral's portal, depicts an enormous monster run through by a knight.

preceding pages:
Capitals with anthropomorphic and geometric motifs. Twelfth century. Abbey church of Santissima Trinità in the town of Venosa in Basilicata. Stimulated by diverse influences, the Normans chose the ones they liked the most, not hesitating to introduce Nordic elements with results that were unusual, archaic in feeling, and at the same time innovative.

following pages:
Two panels with scenes of men fighting dragons. Details from the architrave of the side portal of the church of San Benedetto in Brindisi. Late eleventh century. Images such as these could easily be used to symbolize the struggle between good and evil and therefore became a recurring artistic motif.

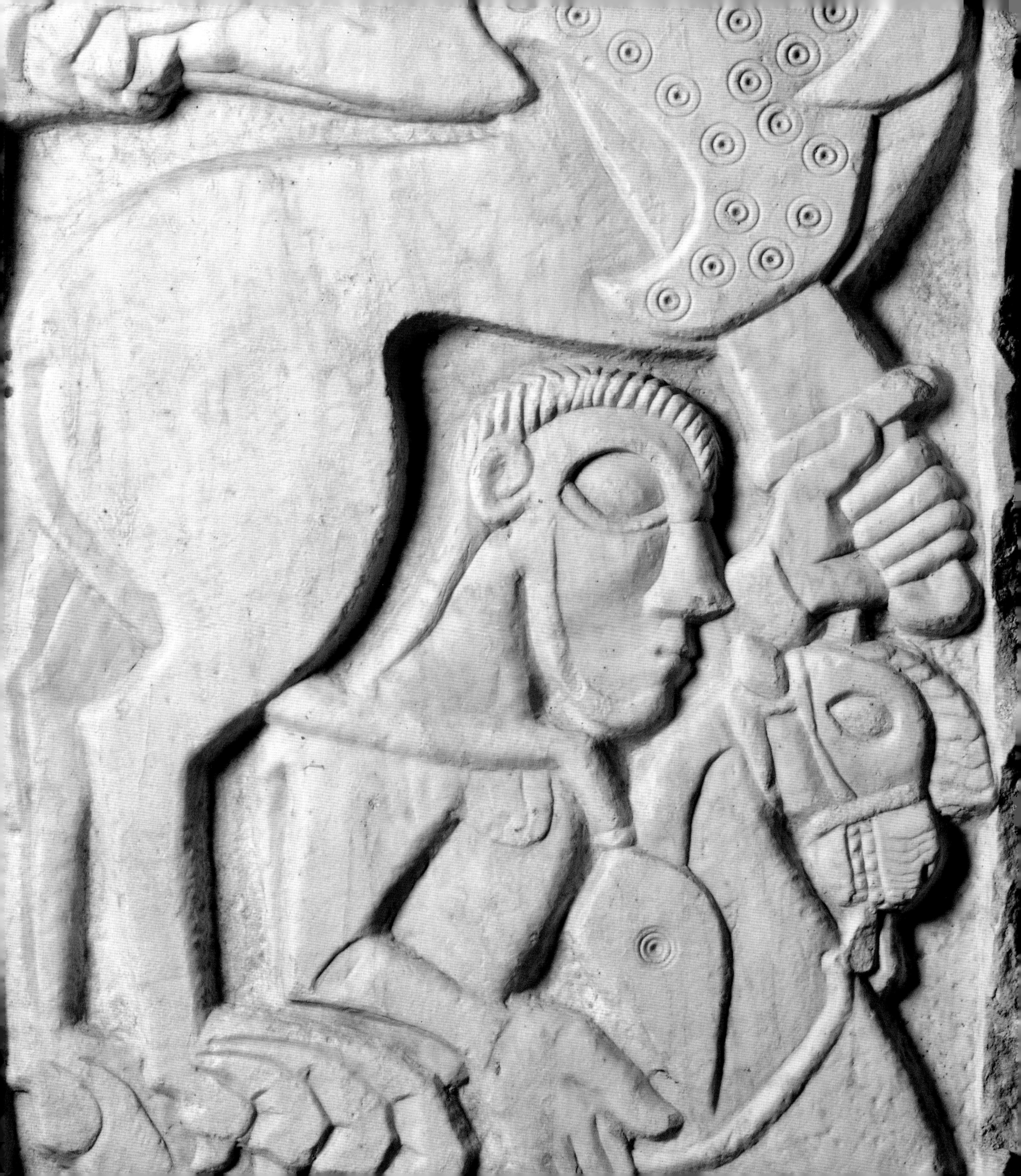

210 . ADELE CILENTO

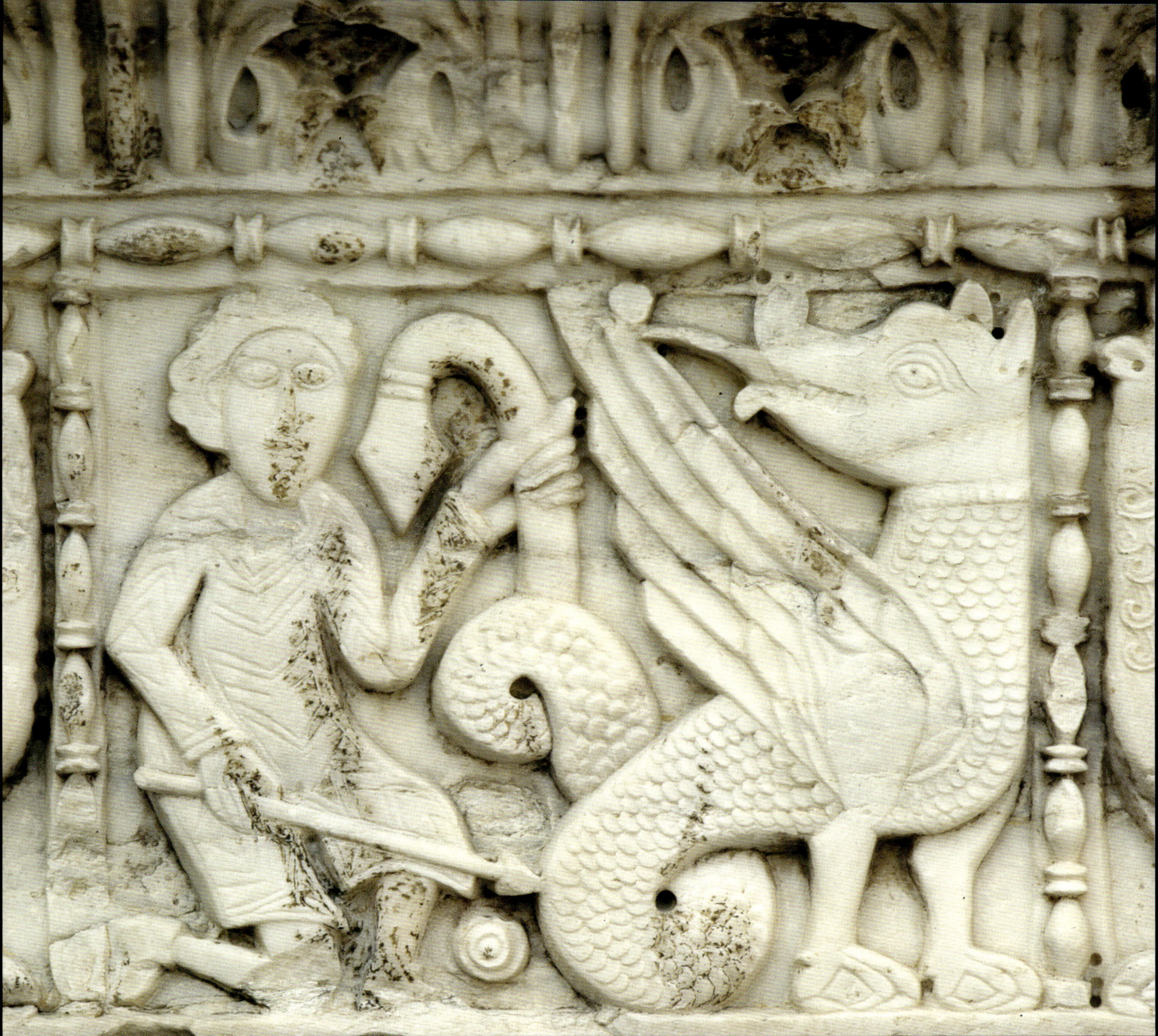

212 . ADELE CILENTO

NORMAN SICILY . **213**

above:
Winged dragon, detail of a mosaic on the architrave of the cathedral of San Cesareo in the town of Terracina in Lazio.

left:
Marble slab depicting a dragon, once part of the pulpit of the cathedral of San Giovanni del Toro in the town of Ravello in Campania. Dating to 1272, it is now in a local museum.

Sanctissimi Ecclesiæ Doctoris Gregorii Papæ
ad Leandrum Episcopum Hispalensem Epistola
in expositionem libri Iob.

EVE
RENTIS
SIMO
ET S̄C̄ISSIMO
FR̄I LEANDRO
CO EP̄O·
GREGORI
SERVVS
SERVORV̄ DĪ;

Knight on the back of an imaginary animal. Detail of the portal of the church of San Marcello Maggiore in Capua. Twelfth century.

Reliefs depicting strangely-shaped animals on the lunette of the left portal of the church of San Giorgio in the town of Petrella Tifernina in the region of Molise. Thirteenth century.

opposite page:
Illumination in a twelfth-century manuscript of a letter from Pope Gregory I to St. Leander, bishop of Seville, now in the municipal library of Dijon.

complete reconstruction by Desiderius, the abbot of the monastery and leader of a reform movement whose most active members belonged to the Benedictine order. It was this same Desiderius who had been of great help in reaching an accord between the papacy and the Normans. The cultural preferences of this abbot leaned markedly in the direction of Byzantium, but not completely. He also looked to England, as can be seen by the presence in Montecassino of an English goldsmith, documented in 1063, and by the various manuscripts from the British Isles in the monastery library, including a set of the Gospels made in Winchester. According to Leo Marsicanus, who wrote a history of Montecassino and later became bishop of Ostia, Desiderius hired expert artisans from Amalfi and Lombardy for the basilica's

Detail of an anthropomorphic decoration on a marble capital made into a basin for holy water. Abbey church of Santissima Trinità in the town of Venosa in Basilicata. Thirteenth century.

opposite page:
Grotesque masks and zoomorphic motifs carved on marble columns in the abbey of Sant'Adriano in the town of San Demetrio Corone in Calabria. Twelfth century.

great workshop, and others came from Constantinople in order to put mosaics on the walls and pavements. The basilica was severely damaged by an earthquake in 1349, many times rebuilt, and finally—as is well-known—completely destroyed by bombing in 1944. Hardly anything is left of the extraordinarily splendid structure and furnishings, except for a famous bronze door and some Byzantine capitals. Nevertheless, the memory of its magnificence survives in the codices produced in the *scriptorium* of the abbey during its long rule by Desiderius, a period that ended when he became Pope Victor III. Furthermore, the overall plan of the basilica, along with its structural and decorative solutions, became an architectural and stylistic model for many churches in southern Italy.

A very early example of that is provided by the cathedral in Salerno, which was built through the joint efforts of the archbishop, Alfano, and Robert Guiscard, who had made the city his residence. Alfano, who was bishop of Salerno from 1058 to 1085, had been a monk in Benevento and Montecassino, becoming a friend of both Desiderius and Hildebrand of Soana, the future Pope Gregory VII. Together with

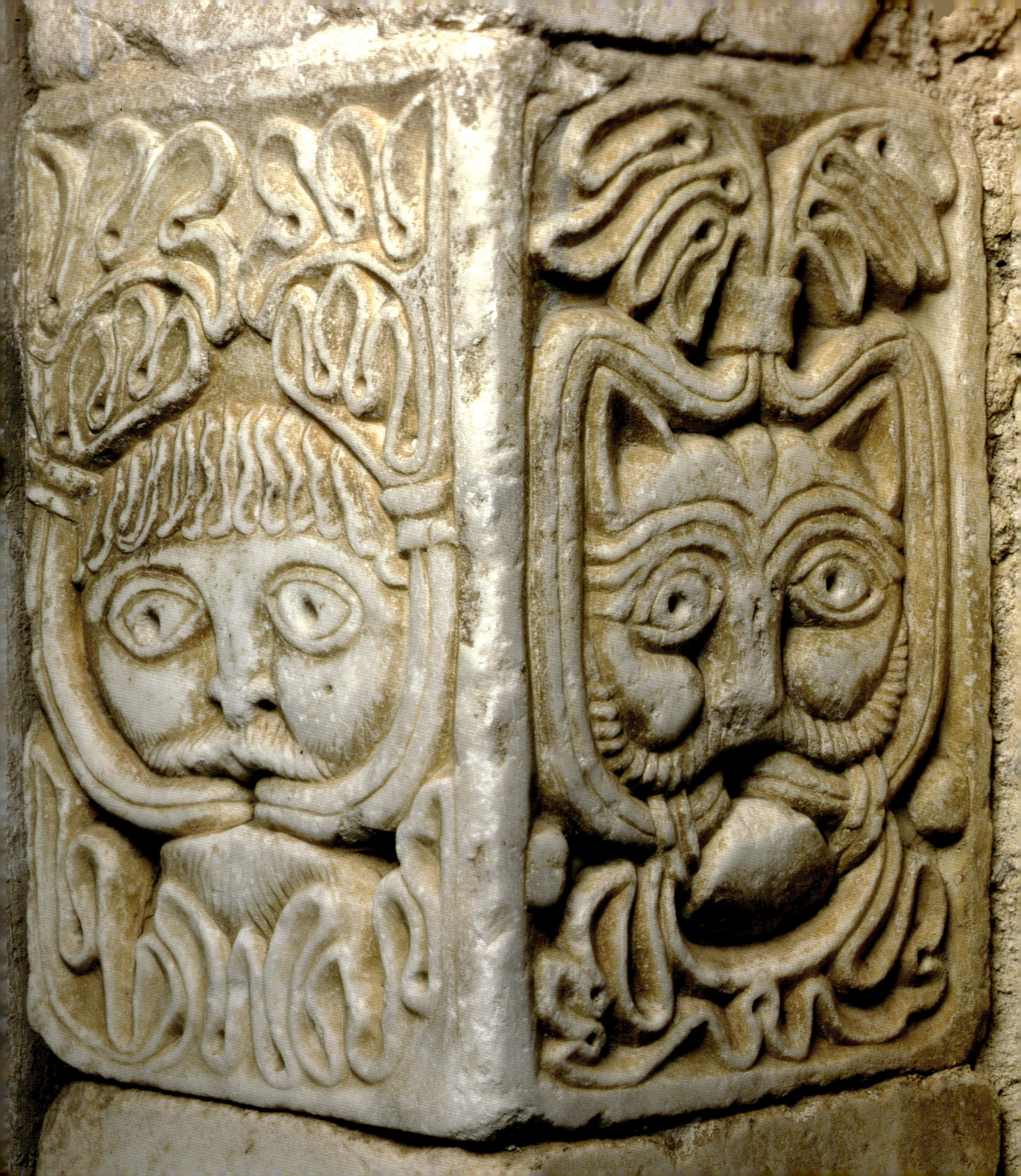

Capital with zoomorphic decoration made into a basin for holy water. Found in the abbey church of Santissima Trinità in the town of Venosa in Basilicata, but likely originated elsewhere.

Hildebrand, who was in exile in Salerno under the protection of Robert Guiscard, Alfano would consecrate the rebuilt cathedral sometime after 1078, i.e. shortly after the Norman conquest of the city. Alfano's cathedral expanded on the early Christian plan used at the abbey in Montecassino, and in a similar way he re-used columns and classical capitals taken from elsewhere, along with other ancient objects that were adapted for a variety of purposes. Islamic inflections are noticeable even in the lions placed next to the jambs that guard the entrance portal of the church. Also of Islamic influence are the star-shaped ornaments that decorate the interlaced arches of the bell tower, constructed afterwards in the mid twelfth century. If the choice of architectural and decorative elements was due to the sensibilities of Alfano, the actual site of the cathedral was chosen by Robert, due to the needs of town planning and also perhaps for symbolic reasons. In fact, the construction of the Norman cathedral disturbed the

opposite page:
Bishop Hildebrand of Soana meets Prince Richard I of Capua. An illustration from the Regesto di Sant'Angelo in Formis. *Twelfth century. Archives of the Abbey of Montecassino.*

Baptismal basin made from a single stone. Late twelfth century. Church of San Giorgio in the town of Petrella Tifernina in the region of Molise.

NORMAN SICILY . 219

R:
chardo;
prceps
p̃mus.

hylde
brand:
ap:

Commucatione dõm p̃mi Richardi prcpis

area's original urban plan and made it the true hub of the city. It was not by accident that Robert chose Salerno as his first capital, preferring it to Bari, a city that was too Byzantine because it had been the seat of the *catepanato*.

Following the political fragmentation caused by the Normans with their creation of numerous individual counties, Apulia experienced a definite revival of its civic consciousness, something that would give great impetus to the construction of cathedrals as a way of causing the new social forces in the city to consolidate around the figure of the bishop. At the same time, Apulia would suffer all the repercussions of the conflicts between its cities and the Normans, especially after the reunification and centralization of the kingdom in Sicily. The moment of greatest zeal in the construction of cathedrals

Two column-bearing lions placed on each side of the central portal of the cathedral in the town of Sessa Aurunca in Campania. Twelfth century.

in Apulia came during the fifty years between the conquests by Robert Guiscard and the coronation of Roger II, when the removal of the center of political power in the duchy, first to Salerno and then to Palermo, deprived Bari of its role as capital and encouraged the emergence of other cities. Among these was Canosa, the favorite city of Bohemond, who built his mausoleum there, right next to the cathedral. Bohemond had become fascinated with the Orient and its Islamic and Byzantine influences during the First Crusade and the years that followed, and he wished to create a monument that would serve as a reminder of that world. The mausoleum, with a quadrangular plan and enriched on the outside by marble facings decorated with blind arcades, originally had a pyramid-like roof that was typical of Oriental funerary architecture (not the small cupola seen today), especially that of Syria, a place that Bohemond knew quite well.

If for the regions of Campania and Lazio the model for religious buildings was the abbey church of Montecassino, for Apulia it was the basilica of St. Nicholas in Bari. Following the legendary theft of his relics from the city of Myra, in modern-day Turkey, the bones of this miracle-working saint arrived in Bari in 1087. In order to house them, a suitable sanctuary was built—and even the story of its construction is full of legendary and controversial details—, one large enough to accomodate a great flood of pilgrims. It was located near the abandoned complex that contained the abbey of the *catepanato*, a fortress that was the seat of the Byzantine administration. There is still much debate among scholars about the architectural solutions used in the renovation of the basilica and about the events of its construction, which occurred in open competition with the nearby cathedral. A theory that considers the current appearance of the church to be the result of a series of incoherent additions has recently been replaced by one that sees the demolition of the Byzantine complex as having been less extensive, with the new basilica taking advantage of the older structures, incorporating and adapting them to new uses. Like the cathedral, the basilica has a women's gallery, which cannot be used, with large three-mullioned windows. An alternation of solid

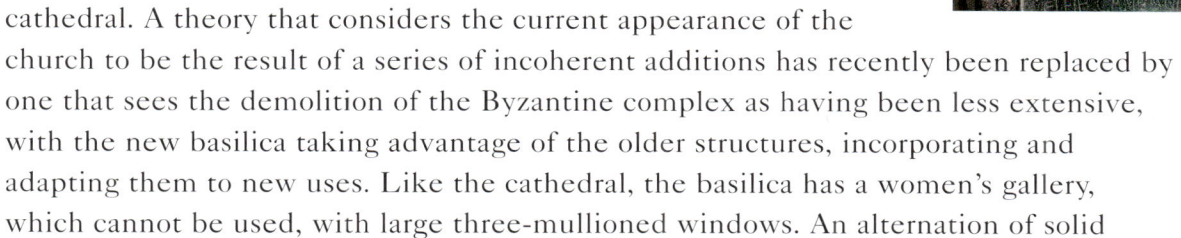

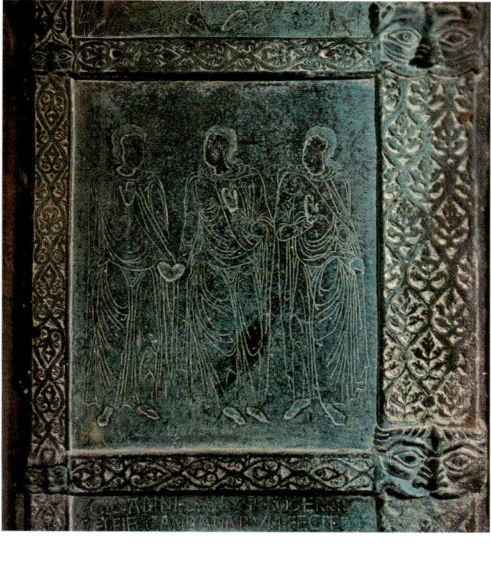

Two panels from the bronze door of the tomb of Bohemond I. Above, a panel in relief depicting Bohemond II, Tancred, and William I; the work of Ruggero da Melfi, c. 1120. On the left, a panel with a lion's head surrounded by inscriptions and ornaments in Arabic letters; unknown artist, eleventh century.

Detail from the portal of the cathedral of Trani. Founded in 1097, the cathedral was built primarily between 1159 and 1186 by Bishop Bertrand II.

opposite page:
Bishop's throne in the cathedral of San Sabino in the town of Canosa, in Apulia.

structures with the elegant flow of the arcades provides a feeling of space. The sculptural ornament that decorates the windows, the iconostases, and the portals makes the structure more graceful, interrupting the linear simplicity of the shapes in a refined way. Not even the cathedral in Bitonto (a city to the west of Bari), which is modelled on the church of St. Nicholas, even if on a reduced scale, achieves the special aesthetic dimension of the basilica in Bari.

St. Nicholas was also especially venerated in Trani, where a cathedral was dedicated to him. It had three naves that each ended in an apse, similar to the abbey of Montecassino. A particular characteristic of this cathedral was the use of a system of paired columns to support the arches of the nave, a motif that was already well-known in early Christian architecture but which became widespread during the Crusades. The royal stateliness of San Nicola di Bari would be softened in Trani, resulting in more graceful rhythms. The blind arcade on the facade projects just the smallest amount so as not to disturb the play of light on the facade itself. Even the bronze door, executed by Barisano da Trani, becomes part of this atmosphere of serene luminosity.

NORMAN SICILY · 223

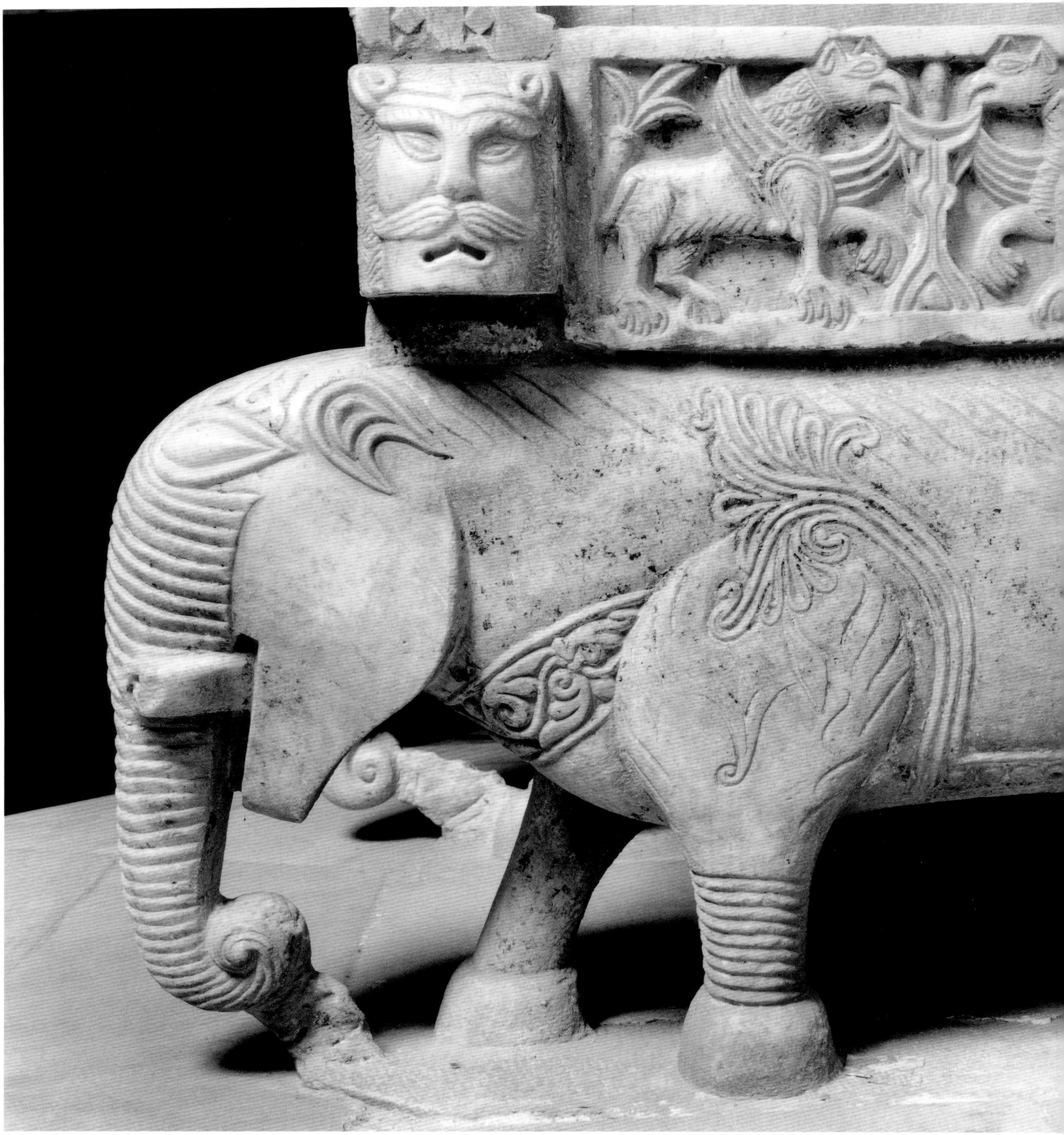

Detail of the bishop's throne in the cathedral of San Sabino in the town of Canosa, in Apulia. Commissioned by Ursone, who was bishop of Bari and Canosa from 1078 to 1089, it is the work of the sculptor Romualdus. The throne is extraordinarily expressive, combining refined geometric forms with elements dear to the symbolism of the Romanesque such as gryphons and decorations in the shape of an animal's head, in this case a lion. Possessing great impact because of its size, it is made even more monumental by the elephants on which it rests, appropriating a motif typical of Islamic bronzes and ivories.

Two panels from the bronze door of the cathedral of Trani showing St. George and St. Eustace. The door is by Barisano da Trani, who also created the doors for the cathedrals of Ravello and Monreale. He used both Byzantine and Romanesque models with great skill.

opposite page:
Detail of the bronze door of the cathedral of Ravello, with refined floral and animal ornamentation, by Barisano da Trani (1179).

In 1093 the cathedral in Troia was rebuilt on the classic plan of a Latin basilica. The exterior is very original, with a facade of two stories, the lower of which is animated by the play of blind arcades that end in an ornament of circles and lozenges. This design had earlier been used in Santa Maria di Siponto, a square-plan building in a Middle Eastern style of which only the second floor remains, although it must originally have had an appearance similar to the cathedral in Troia. Even though the plan of the basilica of San Nicola di Bari had the greatest influence, there were several types of churches in Apulia during the Romanesque period and even the successful design featuring multiple cupolas on a single axis would continue to be used in combination with other elements. Churches with three cupolas, of which the center cupola was highest, included San Francesco a Trani, the somewhat later cathedral of Molfetta, and perhaps San Leonardo a Siponto, which had a hospital for pilgrims annexed to it, something that was typical of those ecclesiastical complexes that were run by orders of knights. These philanthropic institutions were usually placed along the routes to the Holy Land. Important examples in Apulia were the church of San Giovanni al Sepolcro in Brindisi and Santo Sepolcro in Barletta.

With regard to religious politics, Robert Guiscard quickly put into effect that which was expected of him as a result of his investiture by the pope. Within just three years, he arranged for the arrival in Calabria of Benedictine monks from the abbey of Saint Evroult-sur-Ouche in France, led by Robert de Grandmesnil, for

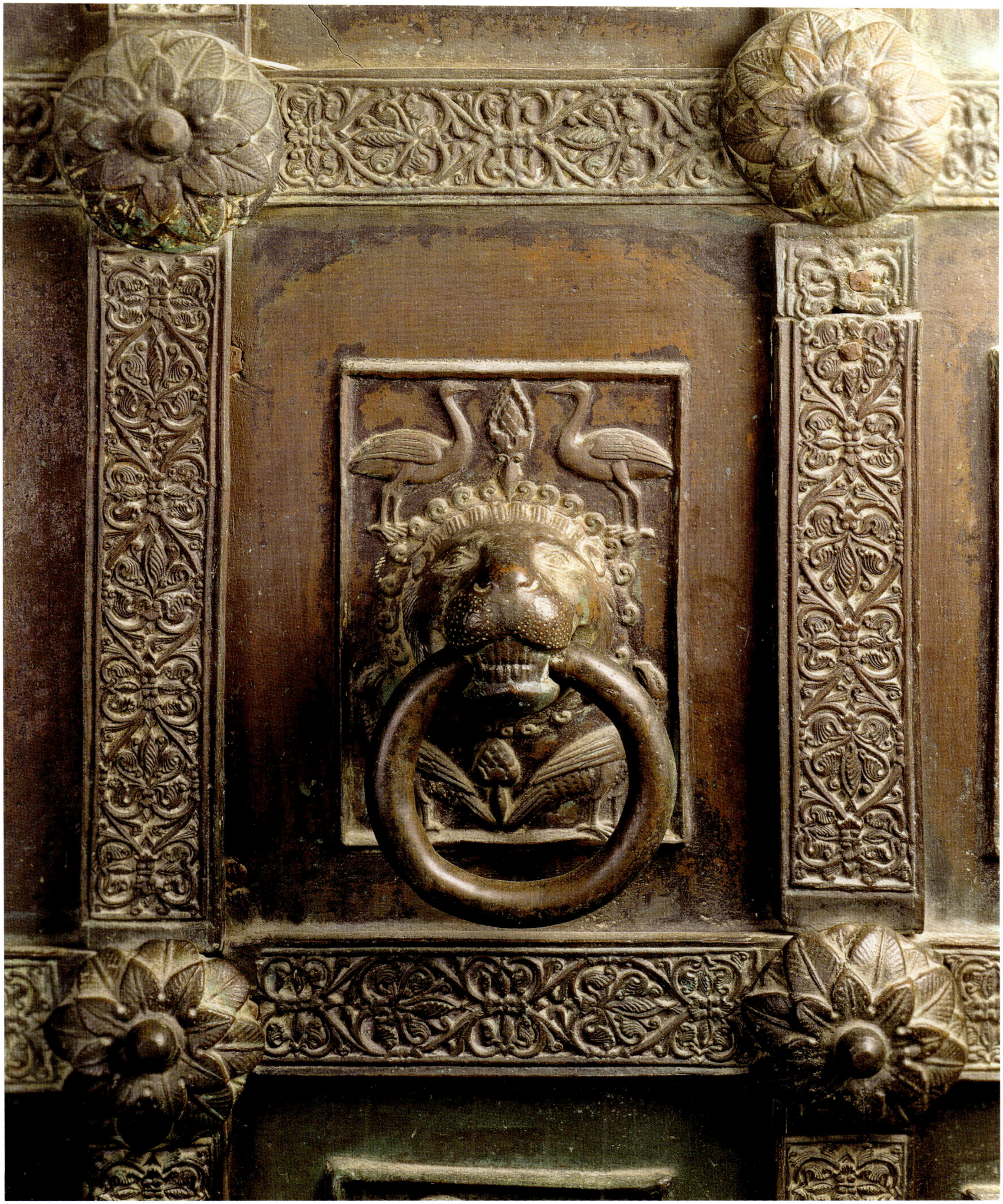

On the extreme southern slopes of Mt. Gargano in Apulia, in an area that is barren and very steep, is the abbey church of San Leonardo a Siponto. Built near the end of the eleventh century, it was the seat of the Teutonic Knights, who restored it in a Levantine style.

opposite page:
Central nave of the Basilica of the Holy Sepulchre in Barletta, in northern Apulia. The church dates to the eleventh century and was several times expanded over the course of the thirteenth.

following pages:
The castle in Caccamo, about halfway between Palermo and Cefalù, is first mentioned in the founding charter of the monastery of San Bartolomeo in Lipari, with Messer Goffredo Sageyo as lord of Caccamo. The site was considerably altered during the Swabian period.

the purpose of establishing new religious institutions that would follow the Latin rite. The zeal of these Latin clergymen and the strong Byzantine cultural influence that was still felt in Calabria combined to produce a very original architecture in which Byzantine and Italo-Greek architectural elements, such as interior wall hangings and exterior courses of alternate-colored bricks, were mixed with others from northern Europe, almost as a symbol of the coexistence of two churches and two rites, the Greek and the Latin. The use of construction materials, which for the most part were very plain and bare, was typically Byzantine in color and ornament, while the shape of the projecting apse and the stateliness of the buildings—to the extent they can be deduced from the plans—show a Benedictine influence from north of the Alps. Unfortunately, almost all of these architectural examples have been greatly modified in their original structure or even reduced to ruins, sometimes as a result of the earthquakes which often devasted the region. This was the fate of the great abbey of Santissima Trinità di Mileto, founded between 1063 and 1070 by Robert Guiscard immediately after he completed his conquest of Calabria. The abbey was placed under the direct control of the pope, as was customary with the largest Christian abbeys. The magnificent abbey church was consecrated in 1080 and chosen by Roger as the mausoleum of the younger branch of the de Hautevilles. Roger was buried there in 1101, next to his second wife Eremburga and to Simon, his first son by Adelaide, his third wife. The monastery, as the beneficiary of such high patronage, quite quickly became a large and powerful feudal domain. In fact, the de Hautevilles favored this type of ecclesiastical dominion because it helped them reinforce their ties to the papacy and was also a way for them to undermine the power of the secular feudal lords. The abbey, which began to decline during the

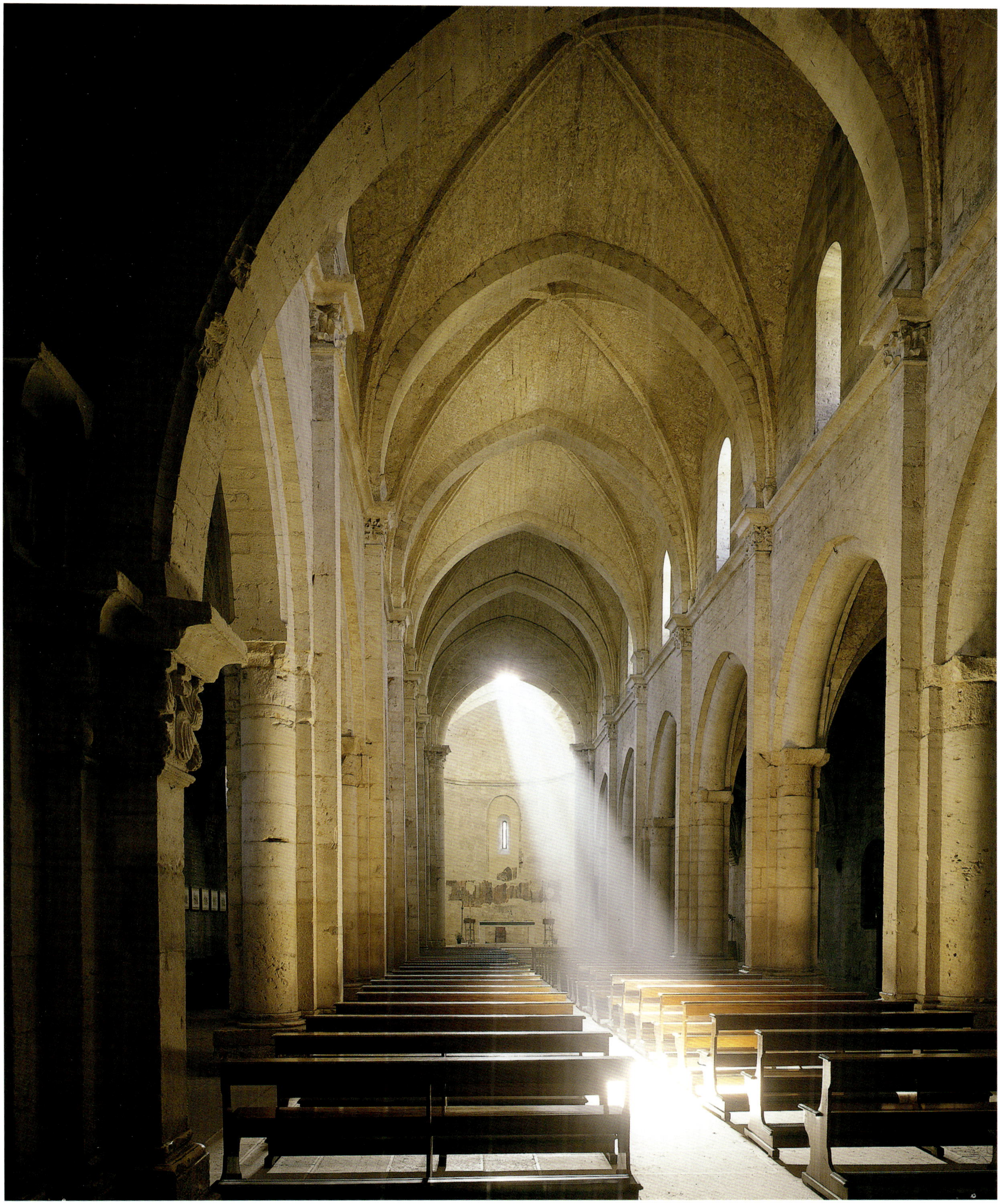

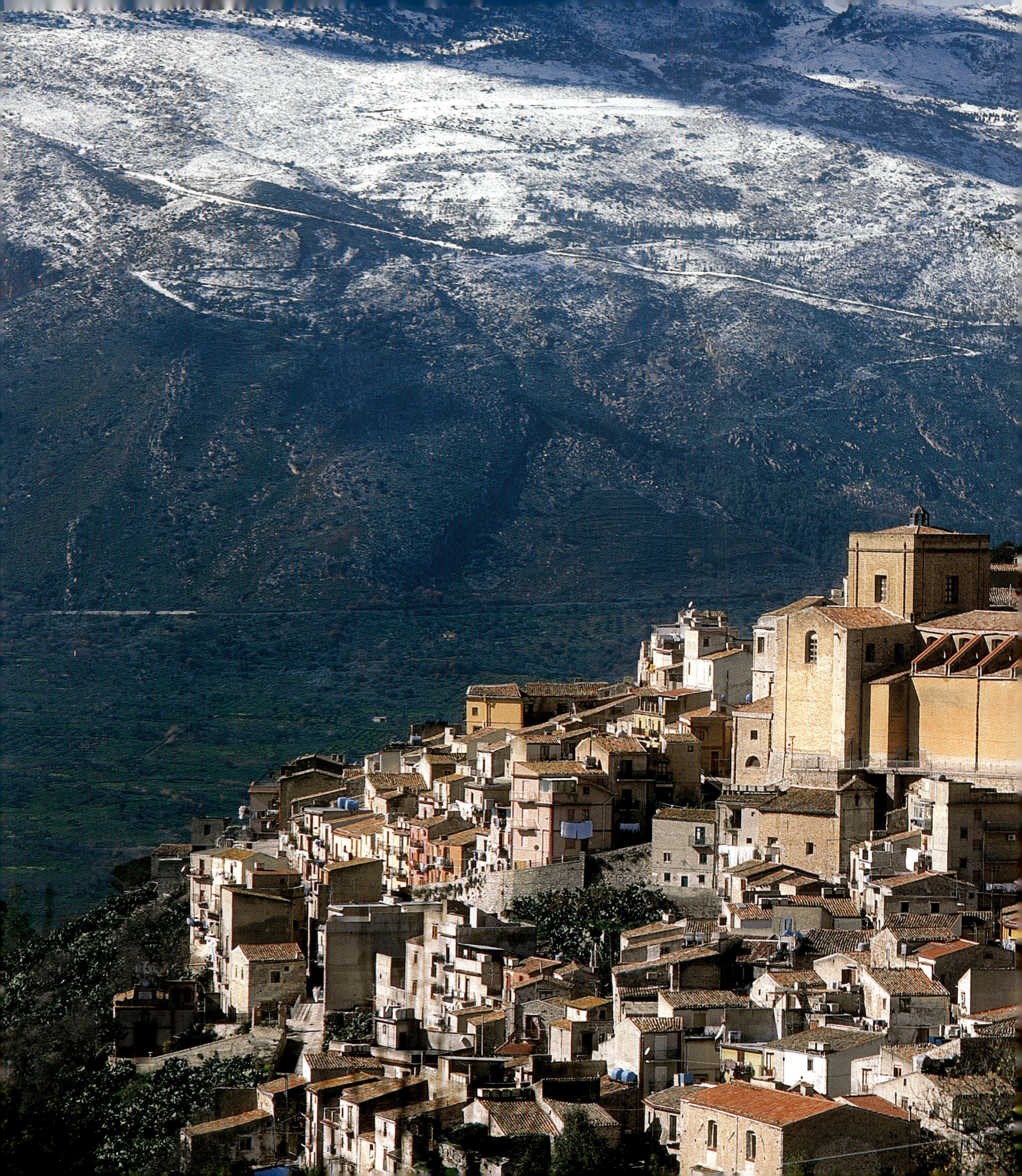

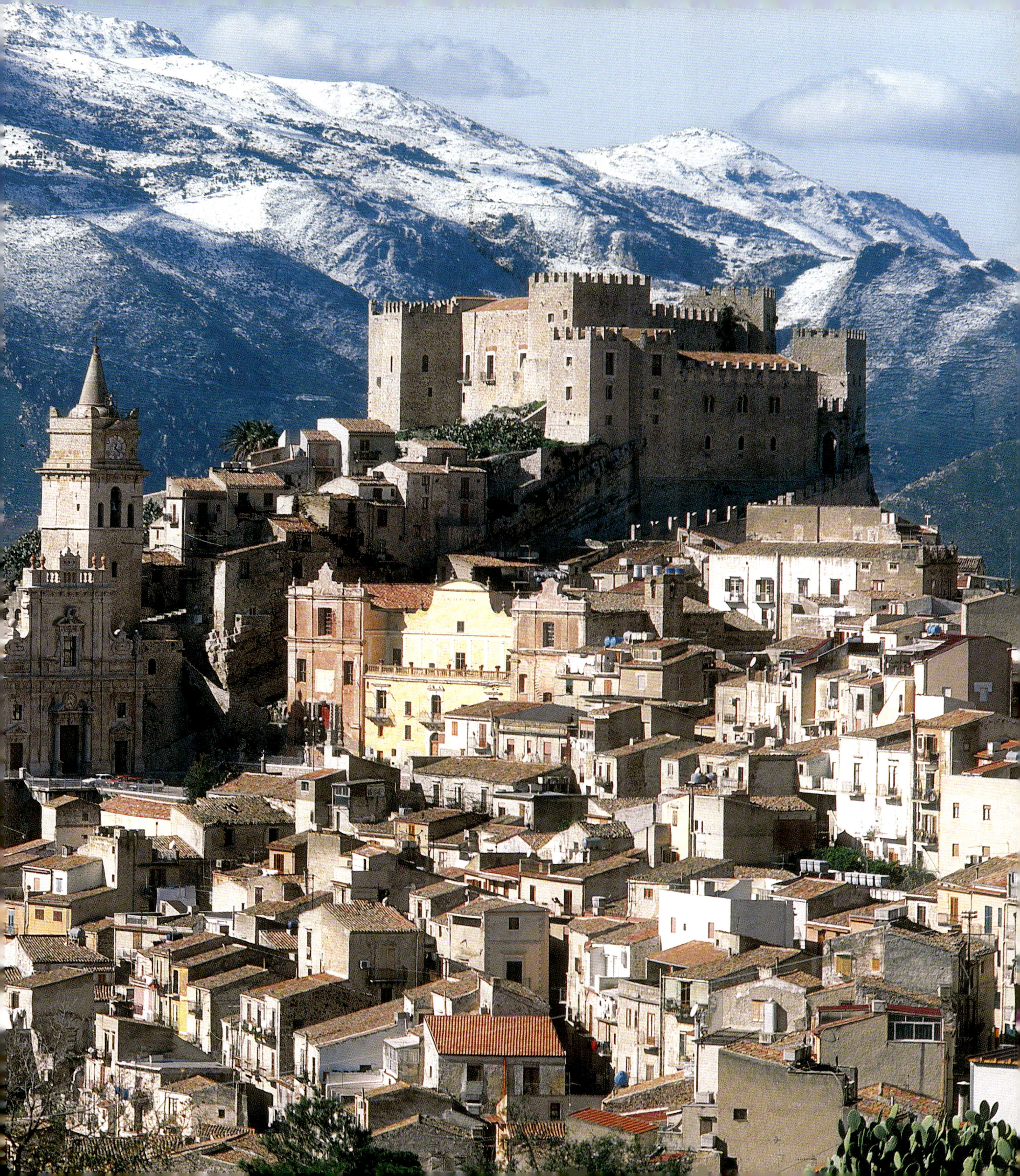

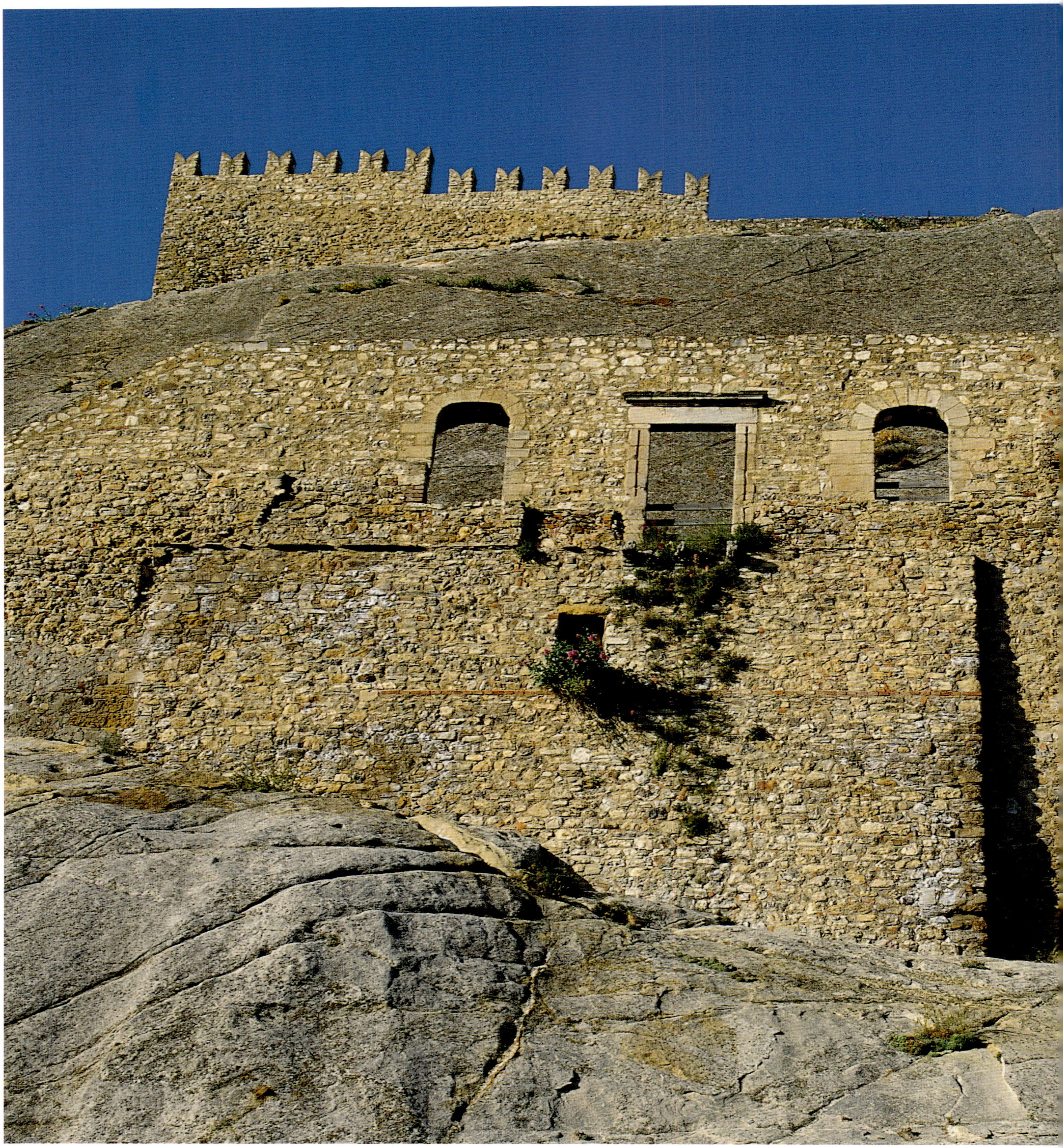

Passageways in the fortress of Sperlinga carved out of the living rock.

The castle of Sperlinga, a town in the province of Enna. The town is mentioned in a charter granted by Roger I and in a grant of privileges by the diocese of Troina in 1081. It was the residence of the widow of William de Hauteville and of his sons Hugo, Richard, and Robert, and also of a chaplain named Eriberto. The geographer Idrisi described the castle as opulent and surrounded by fertile and abundant land.

The cathedral of Gerace, the largest in Calabria. Although it was consecrated in 1045, one can see from the crypt that its construction began in the late Byzantine period and continued up until the early Norman era, as indicated by the characteristic arrangement of the apses in a typically French style that was brought to Italy by the Normans.

time of Frederick II, was destroyed a first time in the earthquake of 1659 and then totally devastated in 1783.

As the cathedral in Reggio Calabria was also destroyed, in the tremendous earthquake of 1908, the only cathedral founded by the Normans to survive in Calabria is the one in Gerace, an important city under Byzantine rule which, thanks to its strategic position on the road that connected Apulia and Sicily, achieved its greatest magnificence with the arrival of the Normans. This imposing structure, on which work began sometime between the end of the eleventh and the start of the twelfth century, is more than two hundred thirty feet in length and provides another interesting variation on the blending of architectural traditions that was typical of the ecclesiastical construction favored by the Normans. The plan is that of a basilica with three naves. It does not follow the traditional layout but rather that of northern Europe. The colonnade, consisting of columns brought from the Orient and recycled, is interrupted in the middle by a massive pillar that recalls examples from northern Europe, in the same way that the structure of the crypt draws on German prototypes. This blending of styles is also seen in the fact that in this church, despite a plan that was inspired mostly by Latin and north-European models, the liturgy continued to be performed according to the Greek rite up until the fifteenth century.

From the start of their occupation, the Normans aimed to establish military settlements throughout the territory, building castles that would function as defensive structures as well as elegant residences, and also as a means of controlling the local population. A symbol of defense and sometimes of repression, the Norman castle was almost always located outside the town center, close to or astride the walls. But the castle was also a defense against those same Normans by local rulers who were in periodic conflict with one another and in conflict with the greater authorities against which they often and willingly rebelled, heedless of the oaths of feudal loyalty which they had sworn.

In this environment of fragmented power, the building of fortifications became widespread and frantic, all of them arranged in similar ways given their common purpose and similar topographic conditions. Among their main characteristics, besides the location, is that they were based on a square tower with their merlons perpendicular to the curtain wall of the bastions and not in an overhang. Such was the case with the castle in Aversa built by Count Rainulf Drengot, and also with the castles in Melfi, Gioia del Colle, and Ariano, which was one of the most important

The castle of Agira, in the province of Enna, was mentioned in 1094 as a fief of Count William and later of his son Robert. It was most likely built over a preexisting Arab fort.

centers of power in all of southern Italy and the place where Roger II convened the first parliament of his reign. Many of these castles, which were considerably transformed during the Swabian era, were built more for the purpose of ensuring the obedience of the people than for defending them, perhaps because the people hated the castles, especially in the cities where municipal pride was strong. An example of this is the Norman castle in Bari, constructed after the reconciliation between Bohemond and his half-brother Roger Borsa, on the occasion of which the two princes exchanged control over the cities of Cosenza and Bari. Each having promised the people of his city not to build a castle, they broke their promises and Bohemond soon built a new fortress in Bari. Its exact location is not known, but most likely it was outside the town center. Some time later, right after the conquest of Bari in 1131, which ended almost twenty years of relative autonomy for the city, Roger II hired Arab workmen for the construction of a new castle, again outside the city, in the Swabian style that has come down to us today. The Norman castle in Bari would be destroyed many times, until in 1155 William I considered an assault on it by rebels from Bari to be an offense against himself as sovereign and the city was razed to the ground.

The castle of Bari. This imposing fortress was built by Frederick II of Swabia between 1233 and 1240 over the preexisting Byzantine and Norman fortifications of the eleventh and twelfth centuries.

opposite page:
The city of Enna sits on top of a mountain with a commanding view of the entire island, a place of symbolic as well as strategic importance known as the "umbilicus" of Sicily. On the summit, the tower built by Frederick II of Aragon stands out at a height of almost eighty feet. The building, which is octagonal and has rooms covered by umbrella vaults, is typical of its period, although likely also the result of a thirteenth-century restoration of a much older fortress.

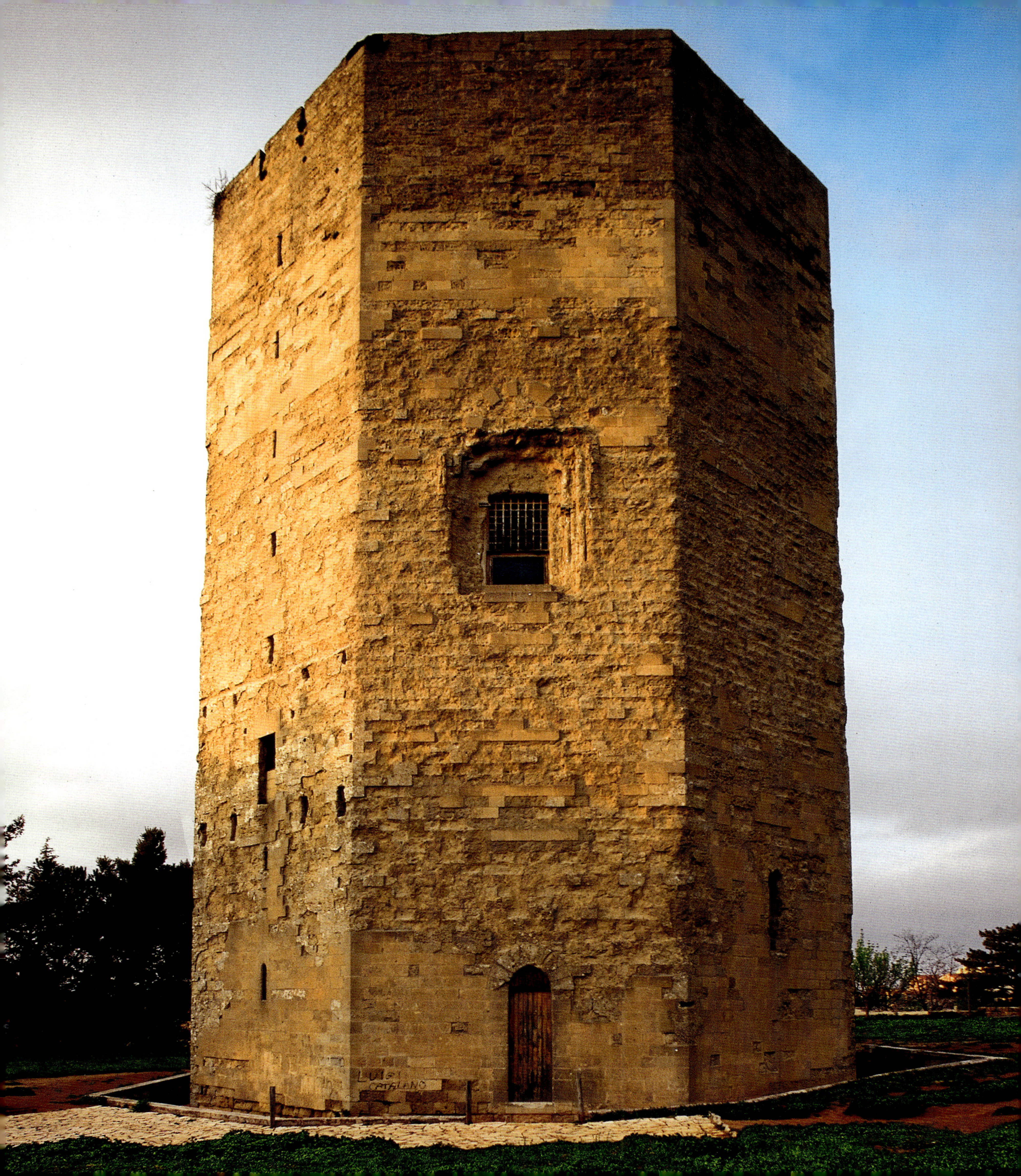

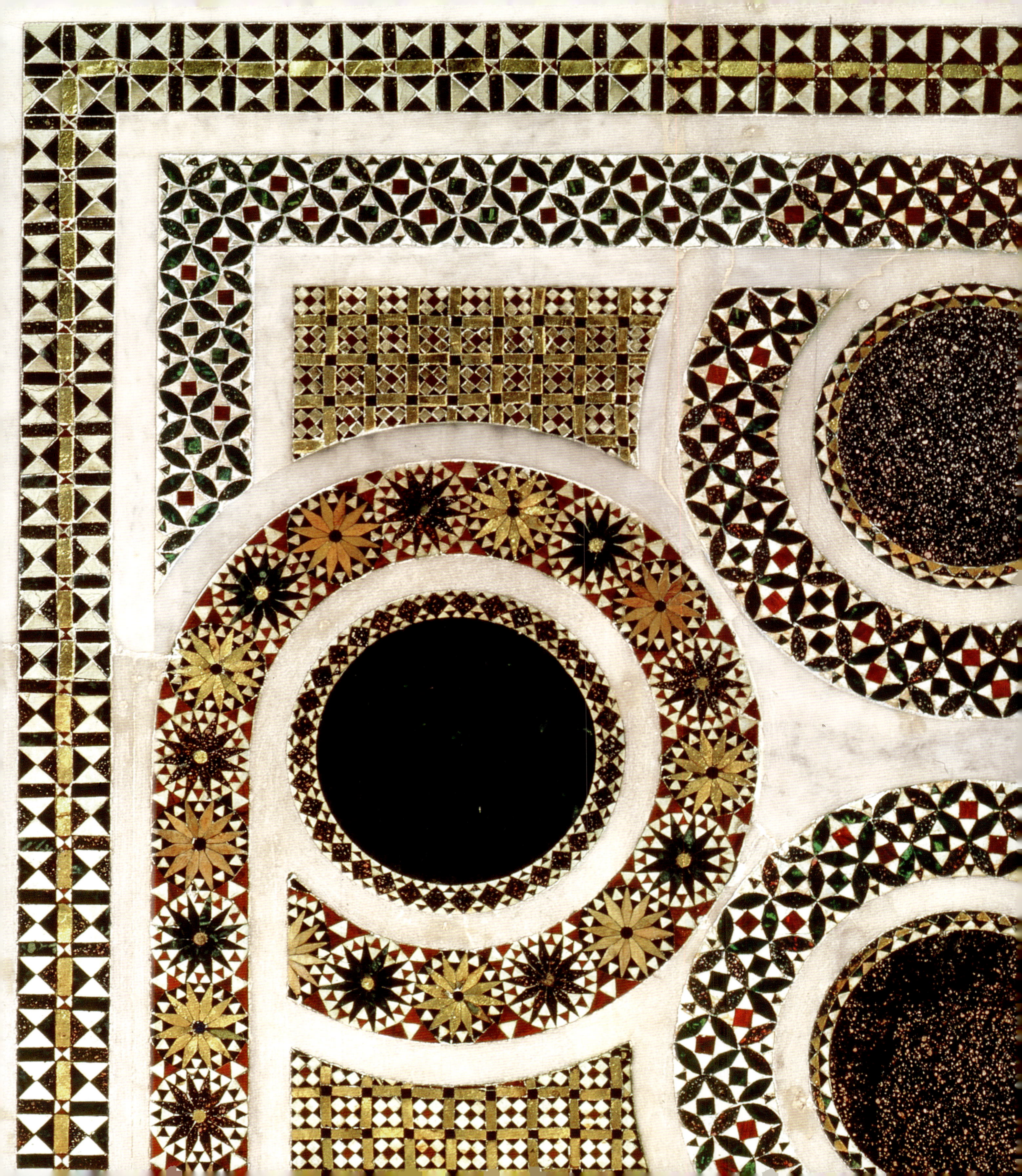

THE KINGDOM OF
A THOUSAND
COLORS

THE REUNIFICATION OF THE KINGDOM OF SICILY

Even though Adelaide was able to continue the policies of her husband Roger I in governing Sicily, there were many problems in the duchy of Apulia and the principality of Capua after the death of Robert Guiscard. A conflict between his children Bohemond and Roger Borsa gave unruly nobles an opportunity to join together in dangerous factions that were loyal to one or the other of them. The quarrels between the brothers would never be settled, despite the fact that Roger Borsa was at some point able to make the reluctant nobles submit to him. As a result no single figure was able to impose his feudal authority on that part of the Italian peninsula, and it suffered moments of great anarchy. There is little information about the last years of Roger Borsa's rule, except regarding his donations to churches and monasteries, among them the sumptuous abbey of Cava de' Tirreni, near Salerno, where even today—in memory of the gifts received—the monks recite a prayer for his soul every evening. On his death in 1111, Roger Borsa was buried in Salerno in the cathedral that his father had built and which today contains his sarcophagus. Some weeks later came the death of Bohemond, his half-brother and rival and a hero of the First Crusade. Bohemond was buried in Canosa, in a mausoleum that abuts the outside wall of the cathedral and is probably the oldest surviving example of a Norman tomb in southern Italy. Bohemond had married Constance, the daughter of King Philip I of France, in 1106, and she became ruler of Taranto as regent for their young son Bohemond II. The successor of Roger Borsa was his son William, who showed himself to be completely incapable of resisting the rebellious barons and was forced to cede Calabria and his other holdings to his cousin Roger II of Sicily. William died without heirs and Bohemond II renounced any claim to his grandfather Robert Guiscard's possessions in Apulia, preferring to rule the lands in the East conquered by his father Bohemond during the First Crusade. This left Roger II as sole ruler of all the territory conquered by the de Hautevilles.

Roger's first step was to seek the support of the church. Arriving in Salerno with a fleet of seven ships, he forced its citizens to acknowledge him as their ruler and was annointed by the bishop with the title "Duke of Apulia." The ceremony performed by the bishop was highly symbolic. It served to legitimize Roger's authority and to guarantee his superiority over the other Norman princes. His second act was to swear allegiance to Pope Honorius II, who in Benevento invested him with the duchies of

The tomb of Bohemond I in Canosa, a prime example of the artistic-cultural syncretism of the Norman period. It recalls Byzantine Greece, the Islamic world, and ancient Rome, with a specifically southern Italian element in its link of cathedral and dynastic tomb, consistent with the Norman ruler's desire to receive a burial worthy of a bishop.

preceding pages:
A detail of the polychrome mosaic pavement in the church of Santa Maria dell'Ammiraglio, also known as La Martorana, in Palermo, built by George of Antioch, the admiral of Roger II, in 1143.

Capital in the crypt of the cathedral of Sant'Agata dei Goti with a depiction of a Norman knight. Twelfth century.

Apulia, Calabria, and Sicily, as Pope Niccolò II had done previously for Robert Guiscard. In order to impose his sole authority over the entire territory, and to assure the support of the feudal nobility, Roger made separate treaties with the barons of Apulia and Calabria, requiring them to swear allegiance to him and to his two sons.

The ambitious duke also had more lofty goals. After the death of Honorius II, he benefited by making a decisive change in his plans, with the purpose of altering the institutional structure of the Norman possessions. Taking advantage of the election of an anti-pope by the Roman nobility and a small group of bishops, Roger did not miss the chance to offer his support in exchange for confirmation of his rights over the duchy of Apulia and the other lands. But above all, as payment for this support and loyalty, Roger obtained from Pope Anacletus II the crown of the Kingdom of Sicily, Calabria, and Apulia, as well as royal power over all the lands that had been ruled by the earlier de Hautevilles, along with Naples, Benevento, and the principality of Capua. Roger's political actions reveal the reasoning behind them, which was to seek on the universal level of an authority such as the papacy a legitimate right to the territories he had conquered, as well as a legal guarantee of the legitimacy of his rule over the other Norman lords, just as Robert Guiscard had done.

The only thing missing was a solemn ceremony, a highly symbolic act that could communicate, with the potency of an emblematic event, all the worth and merit of that royal title. So in Palermo, in the cathedral that had formerly been a mosque, with his feudal vassals from Apulia and Calabria in attendance, on Christmas Eve in 1130

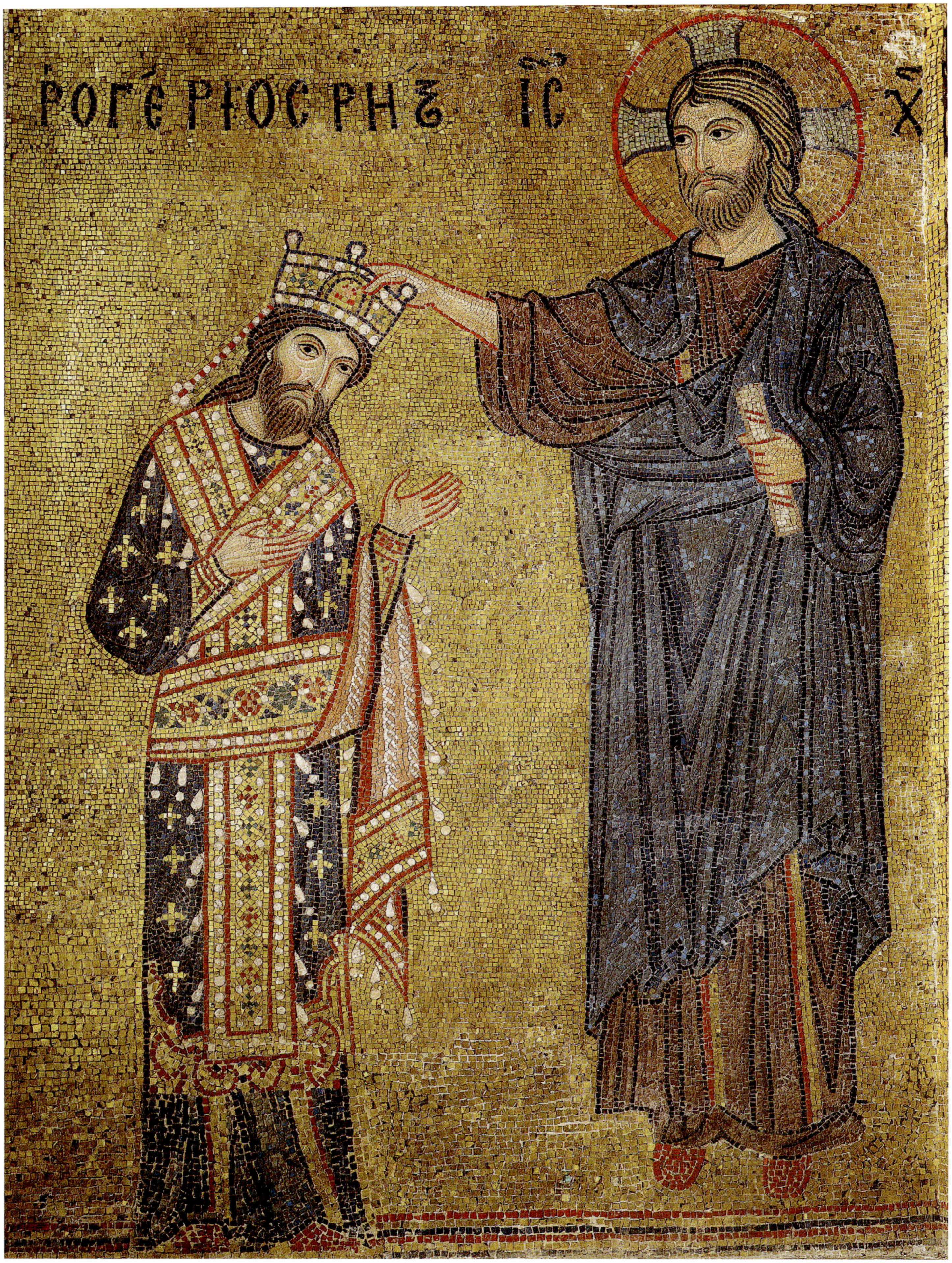
ΡΟΓΕΡΙΟϹ ΡΗΞ
ΙϹ
Χ

Prince Robert of Capua and Ivone, his treasurer, in an illustration from the Regesto di Sant'Angelo in Formis. Twelfth century. Archives of the Abbey of Montecassino.

opposite page:
The coronation of Roger II (1095-1154), in a detail from the Byzantine mosaics on the interior of the dome of the church of Santa Maria dell'Ammiraglio, also known as La Martorana, in Palermo. During a period in which the Byzantine empire still considered itself to be the direct descendant of ancient Rome and the inheritor of its imperial authority, the Norman rulers of Sicily sought a mantle of legitimacy that would allow them to exercise in the West the power and influence which was seen to be weakening in the Byzantine East. For this reason they wished to present themselves in a manner which emphasized that their dynasty was sacred and immune from attack.

Roger II was annointed with the sacred oil by the cardinal of Santa Sabina, who had been sent especially by Anacletus II, and received the royal crown. The legendary pomp and magnificence of that moment are immortalized in a mosaic in the Church of the Martorana that shows Roger in the act of receiving the Greek crown with pearl pendants not from the pope or his representative but directly from Christ. And this depiction, even if it was created some twenty years after the event, presents a complete account of the young king's political vision. It was the expression of a sovereignty that drew on two traditions, in which the symbolic forms came from the Orient and the legal concepts from the West.

Despite his coronation, Roger II had to endure ten years of extremely hard fighting before he could consider that his authority was unquestioned. He fought against Pope Innocent II, with whom he reached an agreement only in 1139; against the rebellious barons—especially Geoffrey of Conversano, Robert of Capua, and Rainulf of Alife—who were deeply resentful of the de Hauteville family and opposed any attempt at a centralization of power; and against the German emperor Lothair III, who did not look with favor on the creation of a strong monarchy in Italy.

In view of these difficulties, and of his need to strengthen his role as sovereign through legislative activity, Roger had the idea of issuing a comprehensive law code that would legitimize his royal authority over all the territories of the kingdom. So in 1140 he enacted the series of laws known as the Assizes of Ariano, after the town of that name near Benevento. It is a compilation that confirmed the prerogatives of royal power, first of all the right of the monarch to give directives for the organization of the state and to guarantee peace and justice. Roger's desire to centralize power at the expense of the Norman barons, who wished to maintain their independence, is evident throughout, as is his awareness that he governed a multiethnic state with distinct legal traditions. Based to a large extent on the law codes of Justinian, the Assizes reflected French, Norman, Byzantine, and Muslim influence. In forty-four sections it touched on questions of public, private, ecclesiastical, and penal law, and for that reason is correctly considered as the best example of territorial legislation based on Roman law.

In foreign policy, Roger II showed himself to be a ruler equally interested in extending his power and his ideology. In 1147 he told Louis VII, the king of France, that he would contribute a fleet to the Second Crusade. This was a clever move, since Roger already controlled the islands of Malta, Pantelleria, and Djerba, as well as the city of Tripoli in Libya, and it would provide the opportunity for an open attack on the Byzantine empire. And as a matter of fact Roger revealed his intentions with a naval attack in the Ionian Sea off the west coast of Greece that conquered the island of Corfu. He then went to the Aegean Sea and the island of Euboea. On the mainland he sacked Athens and its surrounding areas as far as Thebes, from which he carried off the Jewish women who worked in the region's famous manufacturing centers. But the results were only temporary because, as a result of the Second Crusade, which was a complete failure, the Byzantines allied themselves with Venice and in 1149 Roger was expelled from Corfu. Even though Roger's campaign in Greece was brief, it lent resonance and prestige to the kingdom of Sicily in terms of the balance of power in the Mediterranean. It also underlined the difficulties faced by the Byzantine empire, including its possible disintegration, aggravating its internal tensions and jeopardizing its dominance of the seas.

Islamic art had already made its presence felt throughout Italy, from Venice to Sicily, by the middle of the eleventh century. Two examples among many are the bishop's thrones illustrated here. On this page is the eleventh-century "throne of St. Peter" in the church of San Pietro di Castello in Venice, the back of which is constructed using a stele of Islamic origin from the Seljuk period decorated with tendrils, floral and star-shaped motifs, and an engraved inscription. On the opposite page is the twelfth-century bishop's throne in the cathedral of the town of Calvi Vecchia, in Campania. It is decorated with highly stylized animals and ornamental motifs that recall models found on Iranian-Islamic textiles and bronzes.

But it was with his policies at home in Sicily that Roger II showed his gifts as a statesman to their fullest extent. He organized the basic structure of the kingdom and made it an important European power. Contrary to the situation in a modern state in which the prince retains all power and rules through his officials, the Norman monarchy did not eliminate the various jurisdictions in the kingdom. Roger created a system of local bureaucracies whose purpose was not to eliminate the power of his feudal vassals or of the various cities, but simply to control them and to make it plain that his royal power was paramount. He tried to design the machinery of power in such a way as to maintain an equilibrium between the king and his vassals, thanks to a central bureaucracy that was under his direct authority. Roger found both Greeks and Arabs among the government officials in Sicily and Calabria at the time of the conquest, and it is difficult to ascertain the exact duties of each, as their titles and positions were often improvised. Along with titles of Arab origin there were others, such as *protonotarius*, derived from the administration of the Byzantine empire, as well as some of Norman origin, such as *camerarius*, although they did not necessarily carry the same meanings as previously. The ancient Byzantine titles also continued to be used in Apulia, but again with new meanings. In Campania, however, the administrative structures of the Longobard principalities were preserved. While the administration of most areas on the mainland remained in the hands of the nobility, at the royal court in Sicily the supply of expert bureaucrats of Greek, Arab, and even Latin origin was the decisive factor. And while Roger I and Adelaide made use of local officials in governing Troina and Messina, Roger II created a royal curia, or court, in Palermo with positions for various officials, chief of which was the *amiratus*, a kind of prime minister. After 1140 there was a palace chancellery which worked tirelessly to draw up documents in all three of the kingdom's languages. There is a depiction of this intense activity in the illustrated chronicle of Pietro da Eboli that shows pairs of Greek, Arab, and Latin notaries hard at work.

THE IMAGE OF THE SOVEREIGN

If one thinks about the figure of Roger II, the first image that comes to mind is without doubt the one in the mosaic in the church of Santa Maria dell'Ammiraglio in Palermo. This church, which sometime later took the name of the nearby monastery of La Martorana, was founded by the king's prime minister, George of Antioch. Sometime between 1146 and 1151, in what was to be his family church, George placed a depiction of himself and the sovereign in whose service he became wealthy. This is not an official portrait of Roger, but an image that reflects the way in which the church's patron saw his king. Nevertheless, it is likely that Roger knew about and possibly saw the portrait while it was being made and that the ideology expressed in the mosaic had his approval. In the mosaic, which is located in the narthex of the church, Roger wears the ceremonial costume of a Byzantine emperor, itself derived from the costume of a Roman consul. Its main accessory was the *loros*, a sash that fastened round both shoulders, the hips, and the left forearm. It was worn over a rich tunic embroidered with pearls and gold, with a dark blue undergarment. Depicted with a beard and hair down to his shoulders, Roger appears similar to the figure of Christ, which is placed noticeably higher up, and shown in the act of crowning him. Roger thus resembles Christ, from whom he receives the crown, according to a Byzantine ideology that gave the sovereign a status halfway between God and men. It is, obviously, a very idealized depiction that reflects the imperial

George of Antioch, the great admiral of Roger II, prostrate in front of the Madonna in the act known as proskynesis, *in a detail from one of the two dedicatory panels in the church of Santa Maria dell'Ammiraglio in Palermo.*

iconography of Byzantium. There was a similar portrait in a mosaic in the cathedral of Gerace, in Calabria, but it has unfortunately not survived.

This image of Roger II can, however, be compared to another which is preserved in the basilica of St. Nicholas in Bari. On an enamel plate placed in the ciborium, the king is portrayed wearing those same imperial garments and holding a globe in his left hand, while St. Nicholas, dressed as a bishop, is shown in the act of crowning the king. In this case, however, the crown is of the western type and the emperor, in addition to

Diadem traditionally attributed to the coronation of Roger II performed by the anti-Pope Anacletus II in the basilica of San Nicola in Bari in 1131.

the globe, carries the processional banner with the cross of Constantine, another symbol that was dear to the Greeks. As the enamel plate is worked in two different techniques, one typically French (*champlevé*) for the emperor and the other typically Byzantine (*cloisonné*) for St. Nicholas, it is thought that the plate was made by a workshop in Apulia, where eastern and western elements were often combined. This image also dates to the 1130s, when Roger's royal title was still in dispute. It therefore, above all else, had to communicate to the people of Apulia the legitimacy and sacredness of the new monarchy.

Seals and coins also provide standardized images of the ruler. He is always depicted with the symbols of authority recognized in Byzantium: a crown with pendants, a globe in the right hand, and a banner in the left. The letters appearing on the seals affixed to documents were, most importantly, in Greek. On the gold *tarì* coins minted in Sicily, however, there are phrases in Arabic that praise the sovereign with formulas that combine Muslim and Christian titles, such as *King Roger, the sublime, ruler by the*

248 . ADELE CILENTO

grace of God (Allah), which is seen on coins produced after 1130. But if there are many examples of an idealized image of Roger, that cannot be said of his actual appearance. The chroniclers tell us little about that, except that he had an impressive physique and a voice that was a bit hoarse. More was said about his inner nature. His contemporaries produced a very precise portrait of his character, and in describing it, besides attributing to him all the virtues that a ruler could possibly have, they emphasized some of the particular traits of his personality, about which his actions also provide eloquent testimony.

According to the chroniclers of the time, Roger was prudent and cautious, given to weighing risks, and the secret to his success was an ability to wait quietly for just the right moment and then to act quickly. All those who have tried to describe Roger have emphasized these qualities. But to this steadiness of purpose were added some shortcomings on the battlefield. Roger was not a great warrior, and he took actual command of his army on few occasions, preferring to leave that to his generals. Or it may be that the historical sources have simply preferred to emphasize not so much his physical strength as his shrewdness and cunning. Another quality often noted was his clemency, which he combined with a stern manner. The chronicler Alexander of Telese wrote that "both in public and in private he controlled every act of familiarity, sociability, and courtesy between people, such that everyone was always in fear of him." At least during his youth, Roger was also hot-tempered and passionate, and at times this led him to acts of excessive cruelty. In 1138, driven by an overwhelming hatred for Rainulf of Avellino, who had betrayed him, Roger committed an act of great

Roger I, the Great Count, along with his brother Robert Guiscard, nurtured the dream of unifying southern Italy. His bold temperament and authoritative manner were inherited by his son Roger II who, thirty years after the death of his father, turned Palermo into the brilliant capital of a united and prosperous kingdom.

opposite page:
Enamel plaque depicting San Nicola placing a crown on Roger II. Twelfth century. Museo della basilica di San Nicola, Bari.

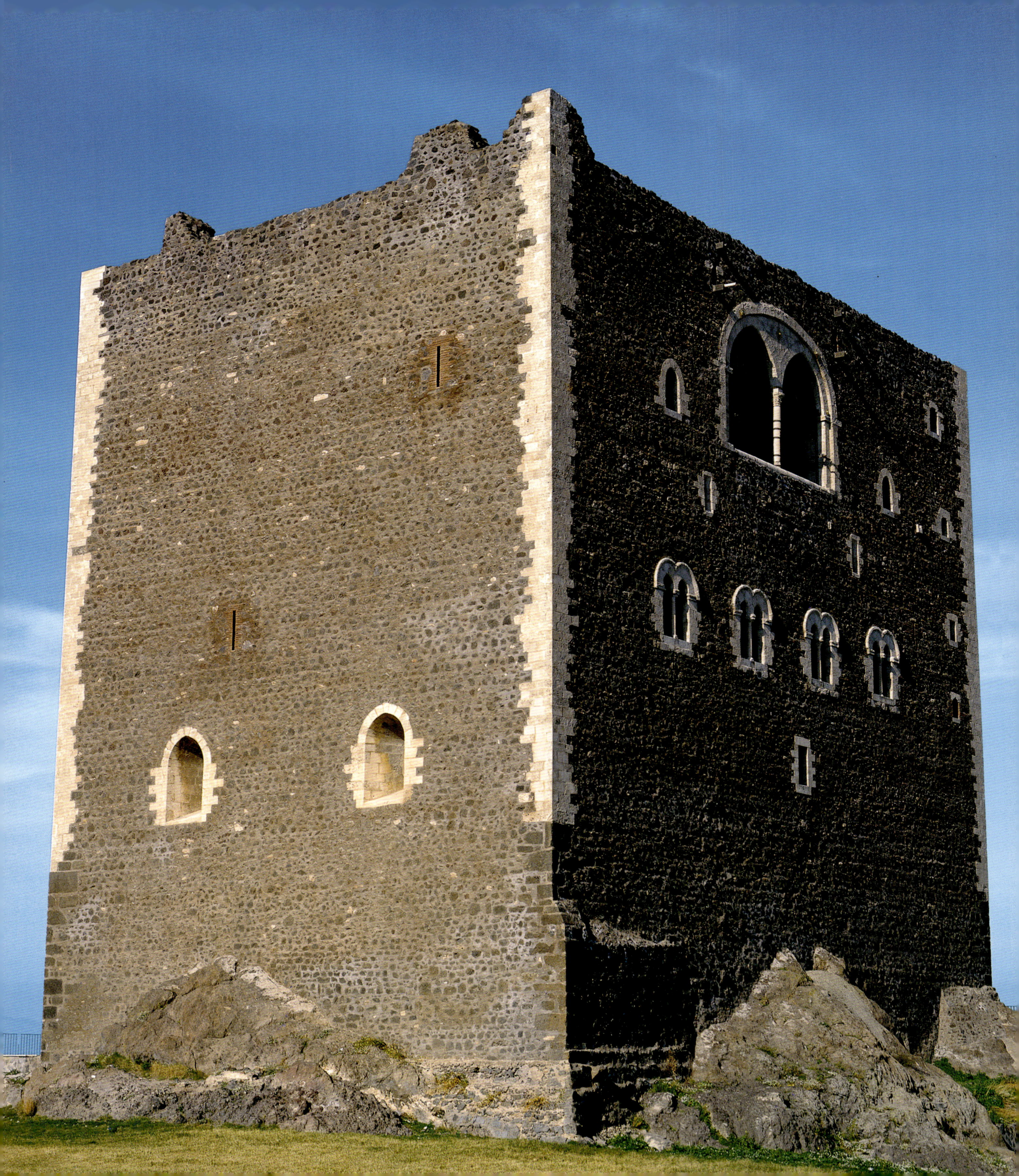

impiety and desecrated his corpse. Over time, Roger learned to balance daring with caution, at least according to an account of him from the 1140s onward, when, at the height of his glory, he learned the subtle art of diplomacy. This was what brought German counts and bishops to Sicily, along with the patriarch of Jerusalem and the king and queen of Spain, all of whom were welcomed by Roger's brilliant oratory. Moreover, a certain liking for oratory and rhetoric, and for art and science, had always accompanied his political activities, and this caused him to invite noted intellectuals and artists to Sicily.

A COSMOPOLITAN AND ELEGANT COURT

For this reason Roger's court was attended by government officials, clergy, and men of culture from all over the Mediterranean as well as northern Europe, France, and England. It developed an atmosphere that was highly cosmopolitan, of which Sicily and the king himself, and his exploits, were often the center of attention. It was in fact Roger's lively curiosity above all that stimulated the creativity of the people with whom he surrounded himself. It was Roger, for example, who, after years of his own study, commissioned a map of the world with illustrations and commentaries by the Arab geographer al-Idrisi. Production of the work began in January 1154, after fifteen years of preparation. If we can believe al-Idrisi, Roger was not just a client, but was deeply interested in geography and the natural sciences. Despite any possible exaggeration by al-Idrisi regarding his patron, it is plausible that Roger developed these interests as a result of contact with the Arab world, something that was in fashion in Europe during the twelfth century. Besides, al-Idrisi was not the only Muslim at Roger's court, as we have the work of at least six Arab poets in Sicily who sang the praises of Roger, his palaces, and his gardens.

The presence at the court of eunuchs, who also played a significant role in the Byzantine empire, was due to Arab influence. But a harem, in the strict sense of the term, probably did not exist, contrary to prior belief, or at least there is no evidence that the apartments for the women and for the eunuchs who served the king and queen were kept strictly separate from other parts of the palace.

As regards Byzantine culture, there were famous theologians at court, such as the monk Filagato da Cerami, who preached in Calabria and in the cathedral of Palermo, and Nilo Doxopatres, who had been a deacon of Hagia Sofia in Constantinople and a notary for the patriarch before coming to Palermo. Roger gave Nilo the task of compiling a list of patriarchal sees along with their history and that of each local diocese. His work, which has not survived, may have been conceived as a kind of

opposite page:
The castle of Paternò, a town west of Catania, was built by Roger I in 1073, as chronicled by Geoffrey Malaterra. It is the only Norman castle in Italy that has remained unchanged, and one can admire the perfect Anglo-Norman style of the tower. It is in the typical shape of a donjon, *the massive inner tower set within the walls of a medieval castle.*

this page:
Detail of a mosaic decoration in the Room of King Roger in the Palazzo dei Normanni (also known as the Palazzo Reale) in Palermo.

this page and opposite: Two ivory chess pieces, a knight and a king. They show a clear Norman influence, and are similar to the medieval chess pieces believed made in Norway that were discovered in the famous archaeological find on the Isle of Lewis, in the Outer Hebrides of Scotland, in the early nineteenth century. Sicilian, eleventh century. Museo Nazionale del Bargello, Florence.

atlas of ecclesiastical geography, in a sense a pendant to the work of al-Idrisi, although it probably also served to demonstrate to the pope that his primacy was not universally acknowledged.

Little is known about the ceremonies at court. In order to produce the sumptuous garments worn there, there was a palace workshop that employed Arab, Greek, and Jewish artisans who worked on luxury goods such as jewelry, textiles, ivories, and enamels. It was a kind of workshop, or *ergasterion*, like the one in the palace in Constantinople, and its first workers were probably artisans brought to Sicily from Greece by George of Antioch after his expedition of 1147. The fabrics produced there which have survived are few in number but quite important, for example a round-shaped fragment with gold lions on a blue ground. But the most unusual piece by far, a triumph of the entire tradition of luxury goods production in Byzantium, is the famous robe of Roger II, a large mantle completely embroidered in gold on a ground of bright red. It would later be worn by the Swabian emperors during their coronation ceremonies and is today preserved in the Kunsthistorisches Museum in Vienna along with other symbols of Roger's reign. A combination of Byzantine textile techniques and Arab embroidery, the robe shows two lions standing over two camels with a palm tree in the center. The lion would become the heraldic animal of the de Hauteville dynasty and the chroniclers often compared Roger to a lion. The robe is embellished with pearls, and its symbolic value is emphasized by a series of small lace patterns that echo the universal symbols that have been used on imperial robes since ancient

NORMAN SICILY . 253

ADELE CILENTO

times. On a long strip that runs along the upper border of the robe an inscription in Kufic script is embroidered in gold:

> "This was made in the royal workshop (*tiraz*) for the good fortune and highest honor and perfection and strength and best and skill and prosperity and sublimity and glory and beauty and attainment of security and hope and the goodness of the days and nights without end and without interruption, for the power and the safekeeping and the defence and the protection and the good fortune and the salvation and the victory, and ability. In the capital of Sicily in the year 528."

The year 528 is understood as meaning after the Hegira, or the flight of Muhammad from Mecca. It corresponds to 1133 A.D.

Norman ceremonial sword.

opposite page:
The glove of Frederick II.

256 . ADELE CILENTO

Mantle of Roger II, King of Sicily. The Kufic letters along the border explain that this precious handmade article of red silk was woven in the royal workshop where "perfection and excellence reside." The decorative motifs of facing lions, the tree of life, palmettes, stars, and camels are of Middle Eastern origin and were brought to Sicily by the Arab artisans who produced the robe. The inscriptions indicate that the robe was made in Palermo in the year of the Hegira 528, which corresponds to 1133 A.D. Kunsthistorisches Museum, Vienna.

STYLES: NORDIC SHAPES, ARABIC LINES, BYZANTINE LIGHT

With the establishment of the kingdom, the de Hautevilles attained a rank and magnificence previously unimaginable, with great ideological and propagandistic impact. This is the notion of kingship that the Normans conveyed to the various ethnic groups under their rule, which they consecrated in monumental buildings and which they promoted by means of carefully chosen images and symbols. It is no accident that the notions of kingship championed by Roger II and William II have been favorite subjects for study by historians and scholars of art.

Just a few months after his coronation in Palermo, Roger II began work on the church that would be identified with him the most, the cathedral in Cefalù. The building itself was completed within a year, while the pictorial decoration and furnishings took much longer. Research has definitively established that Sicily's great mosaics, not only those in Cefalù but also those in the Cappella Palatina, the Church of the Martorana, and the cathedral at Monreale, were created by Greek workmen summoned to Sicily direct from Byzantium who brought with them the most refined and up-to-date artistic trends. In the case of Cefalù the intermingling of styles was particularly fluid. Mosaics that were classically Byzantine were used to decorate a cathedral created on Benedictine and Cluniac models, while the shapes of the transept and the apse, and the structure of the towers that flank the portico on the facade, are especially Norman in character. The same blending of styles is apparent in the languages used for the inscriptions that accompany the great figure of Christ Pantocrator. Depicted in the double role of stern judge and divine giver of blessings, Christ is surrounded by a golden radiance and an intense sparkling of colors that together inspire both a fear of punishment and the promise of eternal salvation. The trusses are decorated with a series of motifs running one right after another that include scenes of music and dance as well as animals and imaginary beings. Secular in character, they recall an Arab tradition that, according to descriptions in the Koran, favors this type of representation as a symbol of the delights of Paradise. Even if the pictures on the ceiling of Cefalù are likely the work of Muslim artists from Fatimid Egypt, it is not necessarily true that these motifs are directly derived from Arab culture, because the theme of the pleasures in the life of the prince had become part of the common figurative culture of much of the Mediterranean world and was widespread even in Byzantium.

The Cappella Palatina, which is part of the Palazzo Reale and dedicated to St. Peter, shares certain important characteristics with the interior of the cathedral of Cefalù. Each has three naves articulated by a series of pointed arches supported by recycled columns brought from elsewhere and ending in a slightly raised sanctuary. A splendid mosaic adorns the pavement with geometric patterns and animals in a kind of symbolic representation of the virtues that a true Christian must cultivate. The walls

opposite page:
The cathedral of Cefalù. Cefalù was the city most loved by Roger II, which he chose for his residence, the osterio magno. *The day after his coronation, Roger ordered his Arab architects to begin its construction. In this way he fulfilled a vow he had made while threatened with shipwreck during a storm on a voyage from Salerno to Sicily, after which he landed safely near Cefalù.*

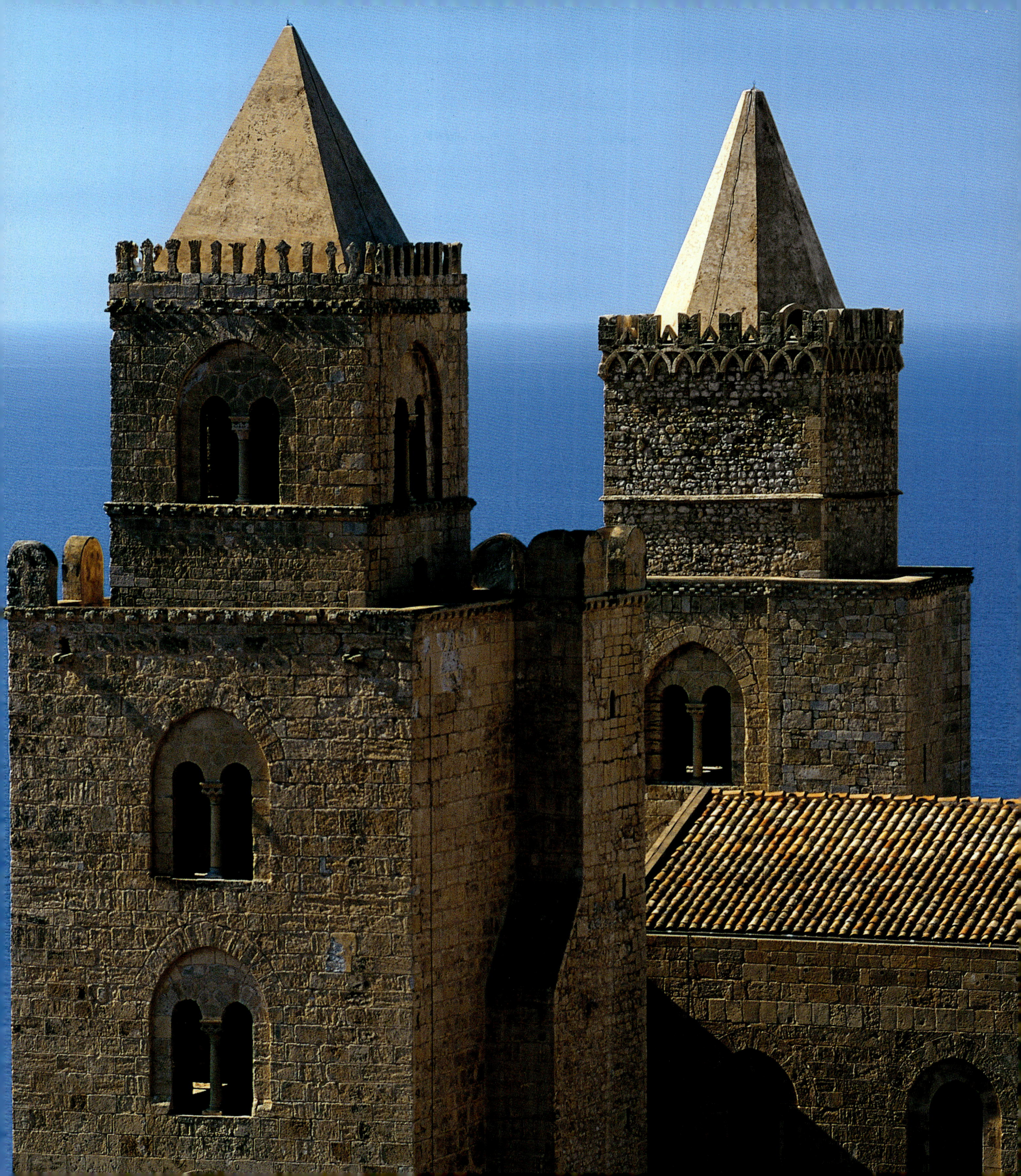

260 . ADELE CILENTO

The magnificent Christ Pantocrator in the apse of the cathedral of Cefalù. Completed around 1148.

The interior of the cathedral of Cefalù, divided into three naves by a total of sixteen columns with carved capitals that support pointed arches.

NORMAN SICILY . 261

above:
Interior view of the cathedral of Monreale, facing the facade. Construction of the cathedral began around 1180 on the order of William II, the grandson of Roger II, and was finished during the reign of Tancred. A masterpiece in which elements of Islamic and Byzantine culture blended with Romanesque architecture, it is one of the most splendid and magnificent churches built during the Middle Ages. The interior, which has three naves, is completely covered with some sixty thousand square feet of gold and colored mosaics executed by both local and Greco-Byzantine craftsmen. Late twelfth, early thirteenth centuries.

opposite page:
Apse of the central nave with Christ Pantocrator above the Virgin and Child enthroned with angels and apostles.

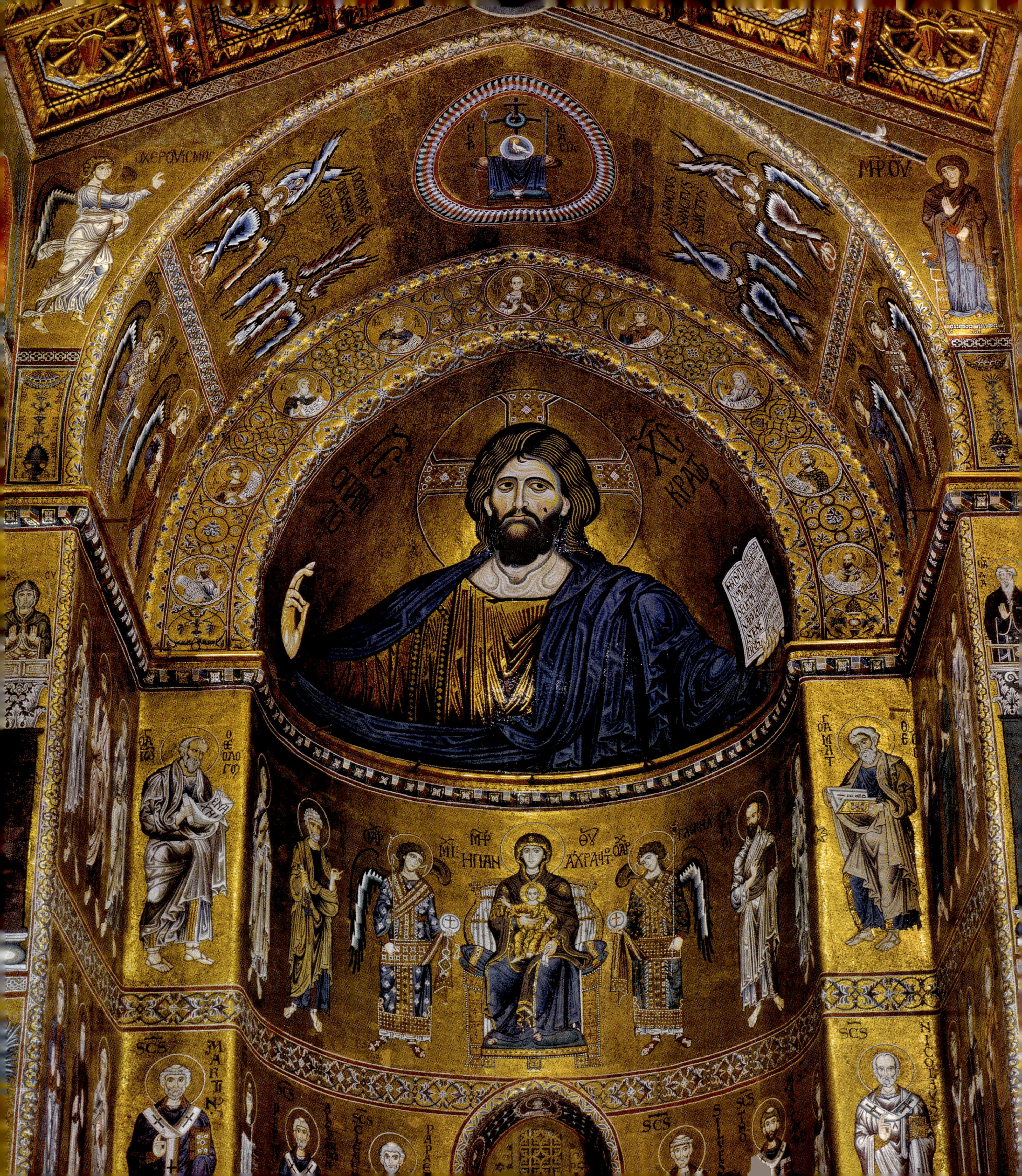

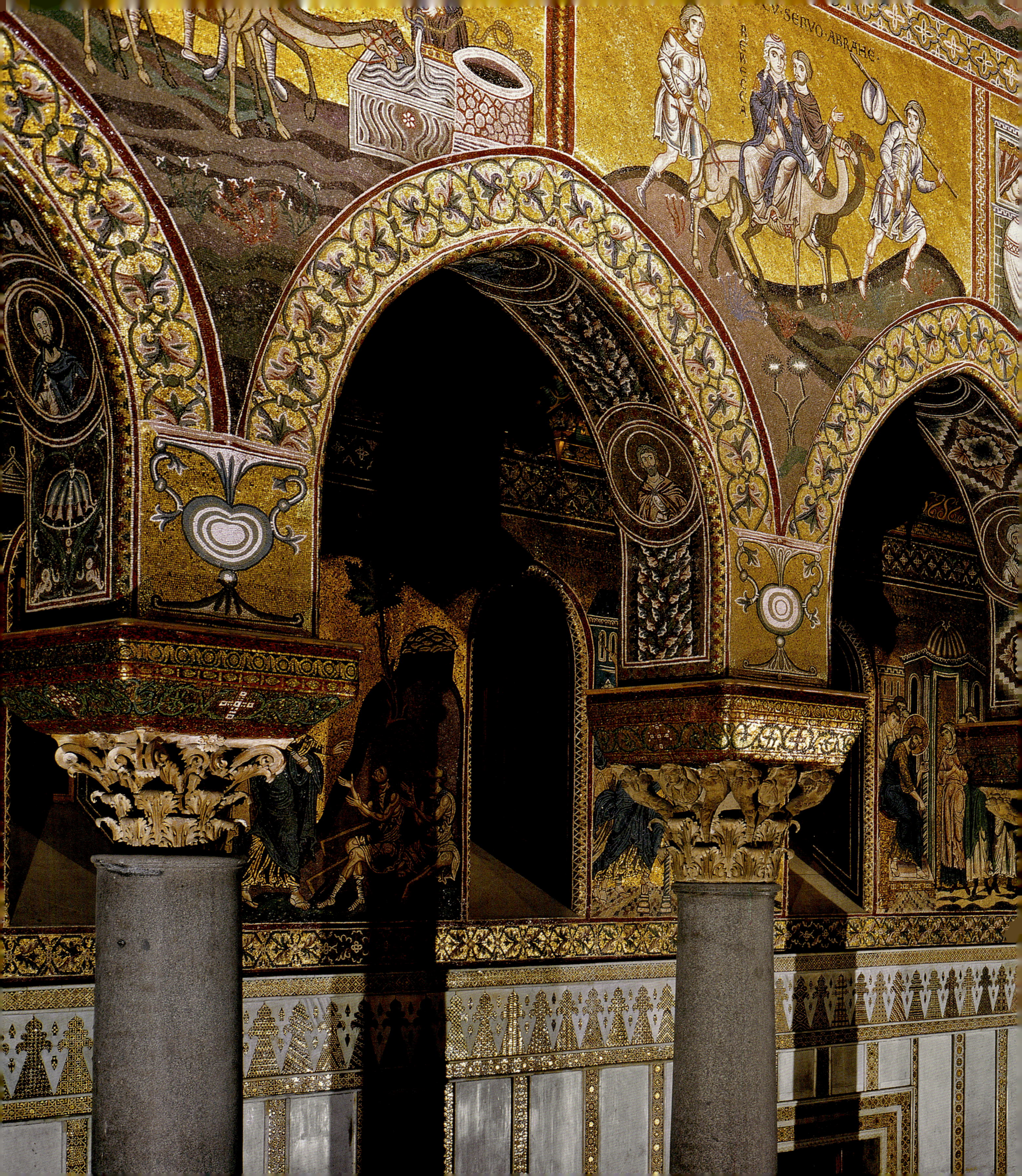
REBECCA
SERVO · ABRAHE ·

Cathedral of Monreale, left-hand wall of the central nave facing the apse, with stories from the Old Testament. In one, Rebecca, having left her father's house, rides on the back of a camel to the house of Abraham in order to become the wife of his son Isaac. In another, Isaac, now old and blind, promises a blessing to his son Esau if he will go hunting and prepare a meal for him.

Cathedral of Monreale, right-hand wall of the central nave facing the apse, with episodes from the story of Noah. The first illustrations depict the flood and the ark, followed by Noah making a sacrifice, and then by the drunkenness of Noah.

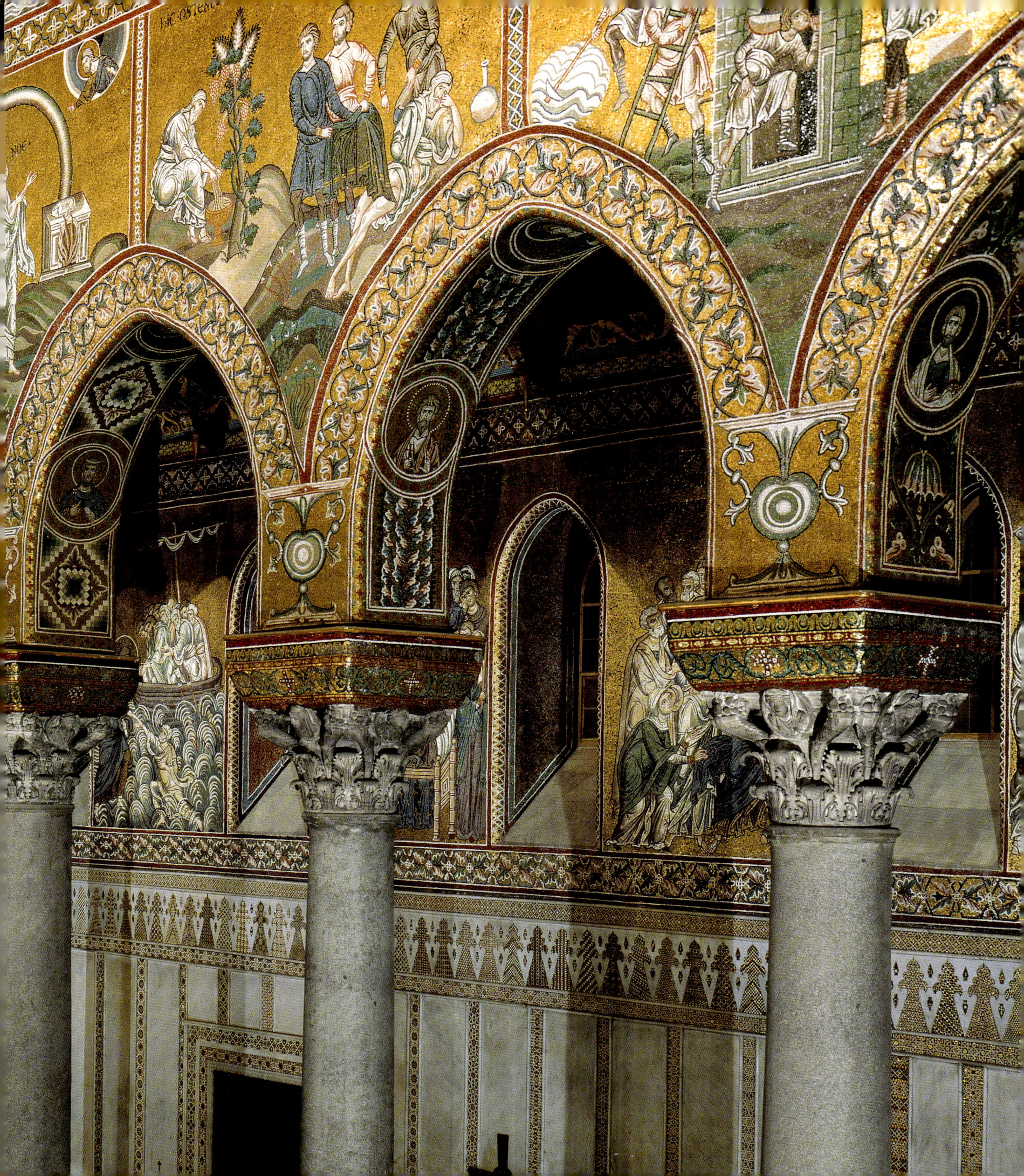

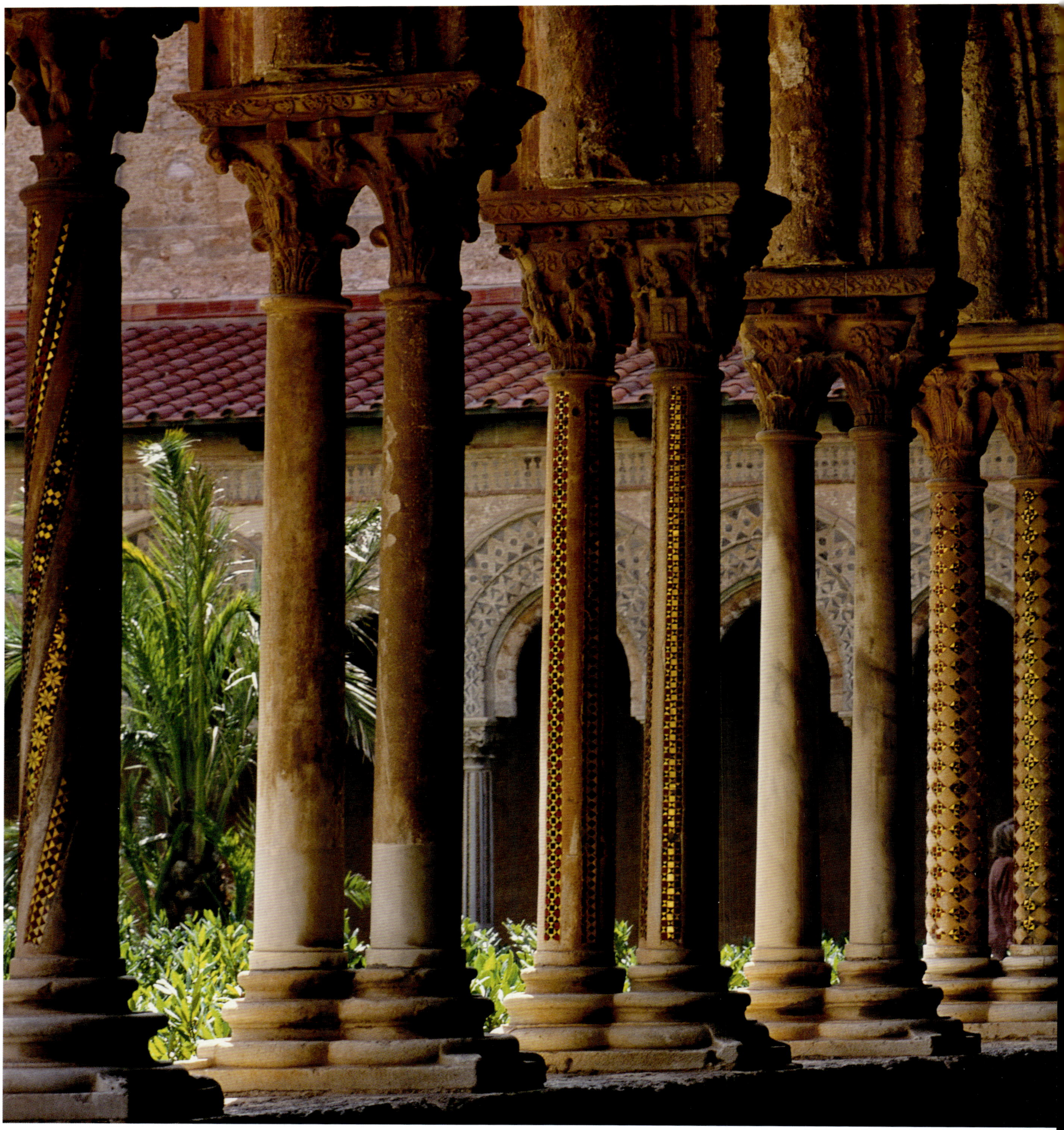

above and left:
Twin columns in the cloister of Monreale, embellished with elaborate capitals and encrusted with polychrome mosaics. Last quarter of the twelfth century.

One of the muqarnas *on the ceiling of the Cappella Palatina in Palermo.*

opposite page:
Located in the Palazzo dei Normanni (also known as the Palazzo Reale), the Cappella Palatina displays a magnificence worthy of the emperors of Byzantium. Built between 1132 and 1140 by Roger II to serve as the court chapel, it is completely covered by mosaics. Those near the altar were begun first, followed by the mosaics of the cupola and the drum, which were completed in 1143, the work of Greco-Byzantine mosaicists. The mosaics in the central nave with stories from the New Testament are from 1154 to 1168. Alongside the extraordinary mosaic decoration is the stupendous wooden ceiling that is remarkable for its great beauty, with its painted figures and Kufic inscriptions, executed by Fatimid workmen in the twelfth century.

of the church are decorated with one of the most extraordinary mosaic cycles in Sicily, according to an iconographic program that seems to have been worked out by Roger II and his most intimate advisors. Work began with the mosaics over the altar, and by 1143 those of the dome and the drum were finished, except for the busts of the prophets, which were added later. Executed according to the most classic Byzantine figural typologies and construction techniques, these mosaics are without doubt the most deeply Greek-influenced in the entire decorative scheme of the Cappella Palatina. Their proportions and positioning were carefully studied so that the sovereigns, who sat on the royal platform, were able to see them. As in Cefalù, the ceiling of the Cappella Palatina is painted in the Muslim style, although it is more precious and elaborate. The decoration is a type known as *muqarnas* that features stalactites and carved honeycombs. This technique, which is both decorative and structural, and originated much earlier in Persia and other parts of Asia, is also found in many other royal buildings in Palermo. Amidst the thousand colors in which it appears suspended, the ceiling resembles a precious and luminous jewel box that evokes a supernatural atmosphere, recreating the dazzling richness of the Garden of Eden. An extremely refined Easter candelabrum echoes the preciousness of the whole of the interior. It is covered by a sinuous vine-shoot of acanthus leaves, among which

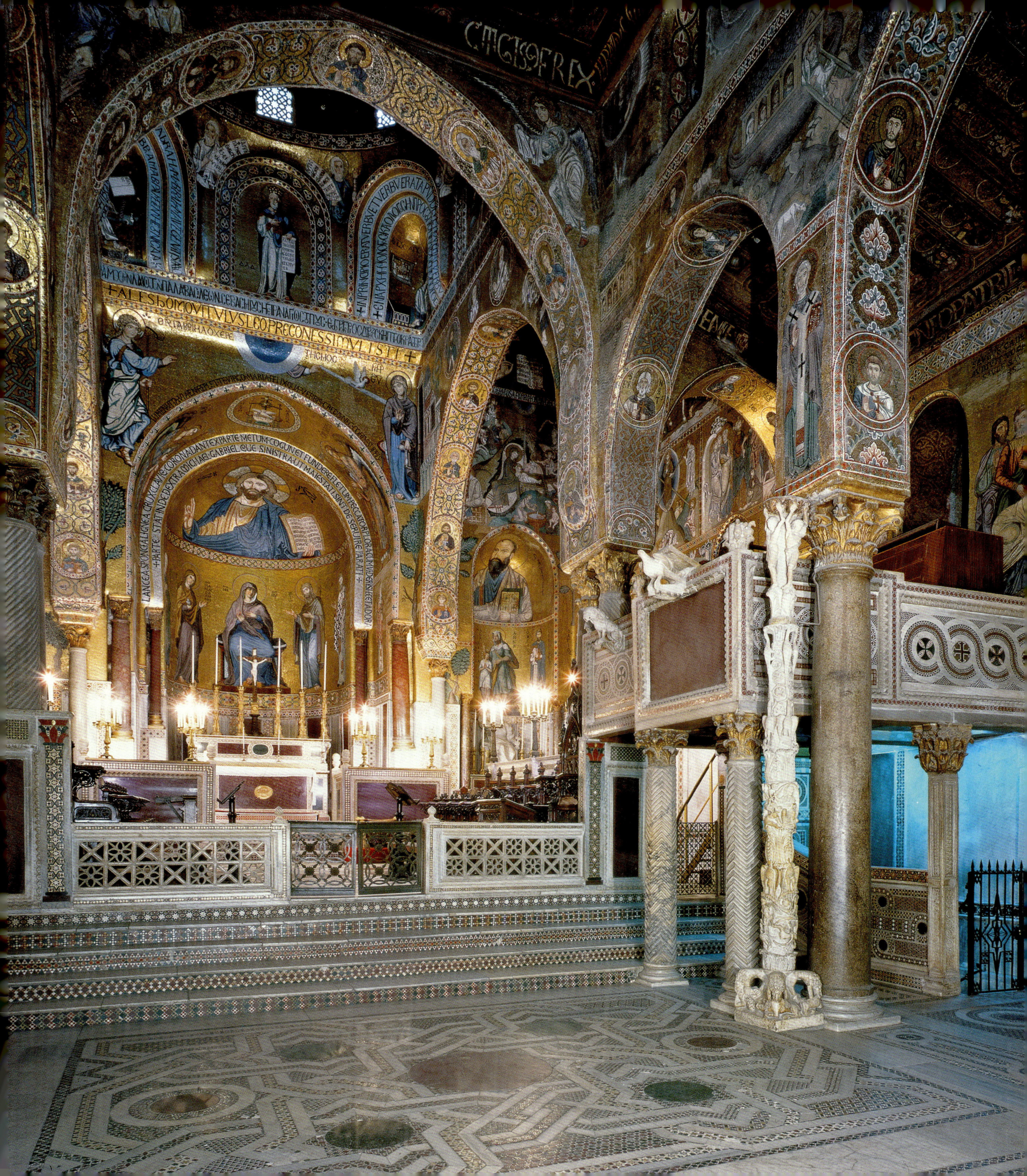

small figures are nestled, in a style similar to the classicizing taste current in Campania at the time.

The mosaic decoration in the Cappella Palatina has a sequel in the pictorial cycle in the church of Santa Maria dell'Ammiraglio, which was founded by George of Antioch in thanks to the Madonna for protecting him while at sea. The church, which has a square Greek cross plan, is divided into four arms covered with barrel vaults and a central dome supported by four columns. Both the architectural plan and the extensive mosaics make careful and precise references to Byzantine culture. The mosaics in La Martorana, as the church is also known, including the very famous ones of the coronation of Roger II and of George prostrate in front of the Madonna—the typical Byzantine act of *proskynesis*—, are of the highest quality and greatest elegance.

The great flowering of Arab-Sicilian culture is seen above all in a sumptuous series of royal residences, palaces, and pleasure pavilions with gardens. Besides the Palazzo Reale, there are the castle of Favara, the palace of Altofonte, the palace of La Zisa, and La Cuba, all of them examples of this great moment in Norman secular architecture, evidence of its originality and of its Fatimid inspiration. Rising on the site of the Cassaro (Arabic for "castle"), the name by which the palace of the Muslim emirs was known, the Palazzo Reale has often been described in both Arabic and Latin texts that give an impression of its former sumptuousness. Conceived as a fortress, but with all the comfort and luxury suitable to a king and his court, the palace dominated the entire city, as we are told by Ugo Falcando, a twelfth-century historian of the Sicilian monarchy. It consists of a complex of buildings which over time have undergone many substantial modifications. On the basement level of the so-called "Pisan tower" is the room that contained the treasury, and above it is the room in the tower in which Roger probably often resided. In an adjacent building on the south side known as the Torre Gioaria were the king's private rooms. All were richly decorated with mosaics, as can be seen in the Stanza di Re Ruggero, or Room of King Roger, which was probably completed under William I. The king's apartments were connected to the upper floor of the Cappella Palatina, so that he and his family could have direct access to the royal gallery that was located on its northern side in order to follow the religious ceremonies without being seen by the other believers.

Also connected to the Palazzo Reale in a practical way was the church of San Giovanni degli Eremiti, constructed between 1142 and 1148 in order to provide a cemetery for members of the court, although not for the king, as the great monumental project of Cefalù had been reserved for the tomb of Roger II and that of Monreale for William II. Built on the order of Roger II and at his expense, the church is constructed of blocks of squared volcanic rock, so that the walls are smooth and the overall structure is linear and flawless, with a purity of form that

An angel. Detail of a mosaic in the arch that leads to the apse of the Cappella Palatina, Palermo.

opposite page:
Christ Pantocrator surrounded by angels and archangels. Mosaic in the dome above the main altar in the Cappella Palatina, Palermo.

following pages:
General view of the architecture and mosaics that, in the words of Guy de Maupassant, make the Cappella Palatina "…the most beautiful that exists in the world, the most astonishing religious treasure ever dreamed by man or made by the hand of an artist."

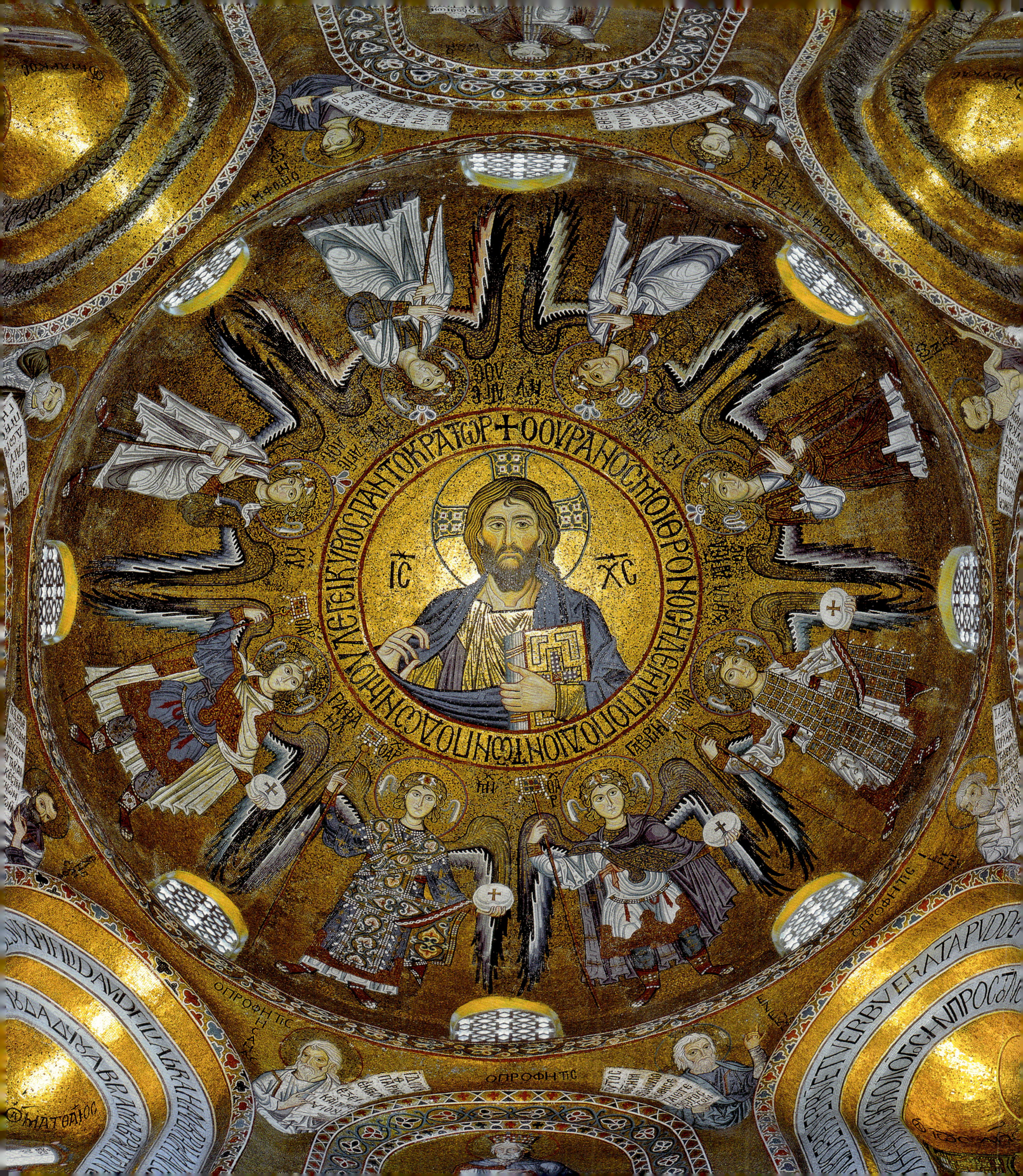
IC
XC

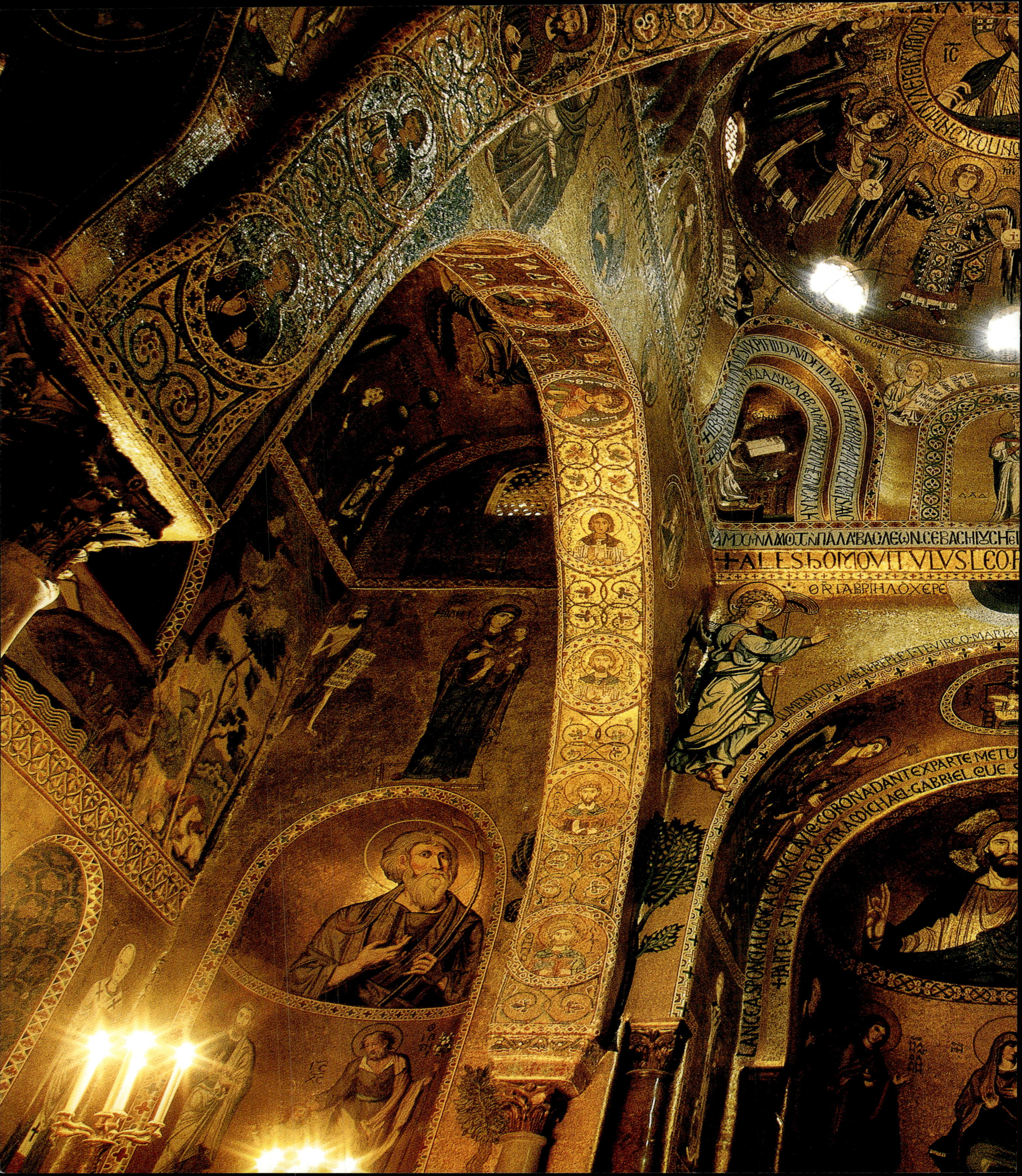

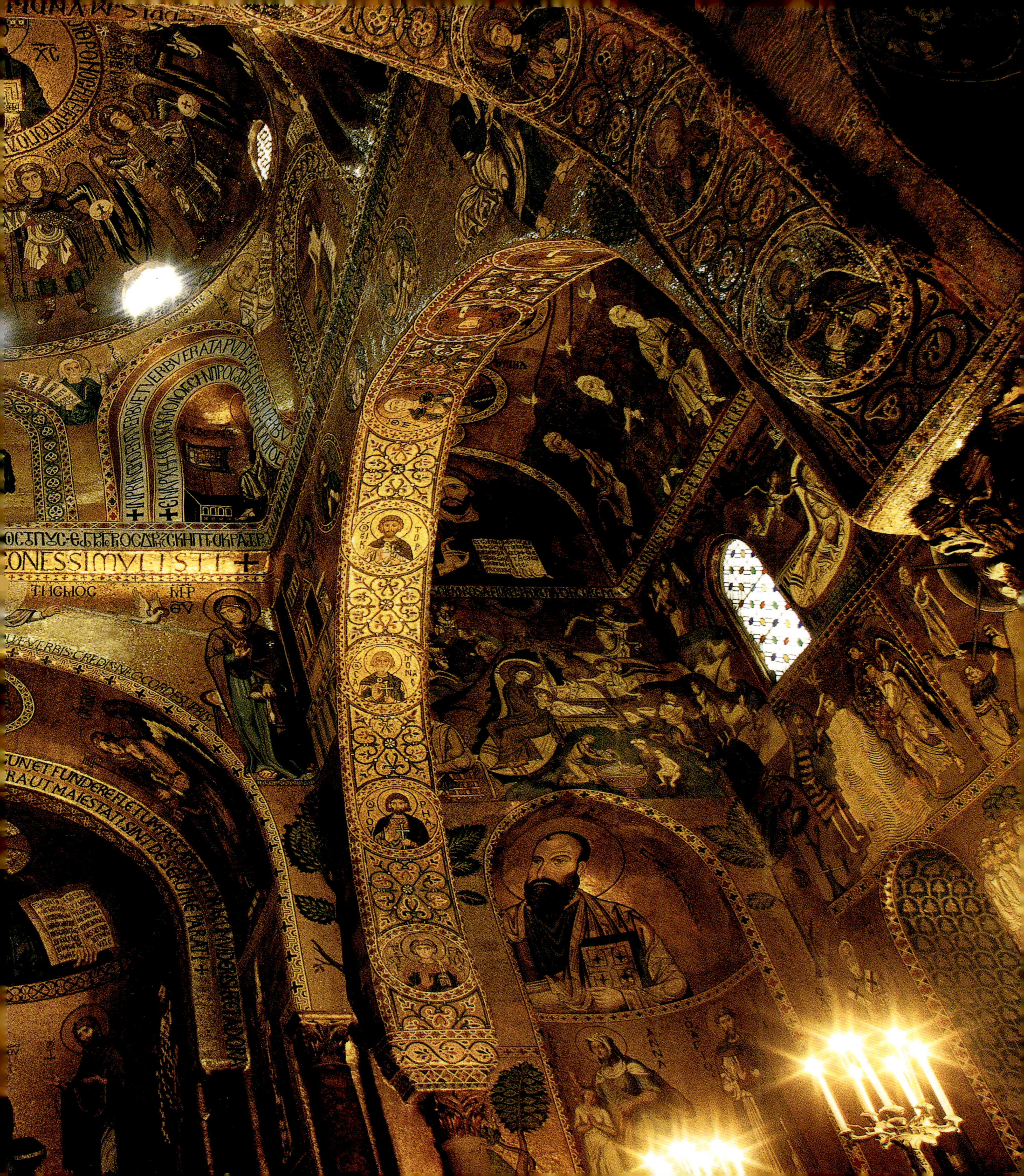

276 . ADELE CILENTO

Mosaic showing St. Peter and St. Paul in one of the side naves of the Cappella Palatina. Completed in the fourteenth century, it was among the last of the mosaics to be executed.

The royal throne, placed in front of the main apse. Above is a mosaic showing a seated Christ with the apostles Peter and Paul on either side. The ruler and his family usually observed liturgical services from the tribuna regia, *or royal tribune, a sort of balcony or elevated platform that connected directly to their private apartments. In this way they were shielded from the eyes of others and could also enjoy a view of the mosaics.*

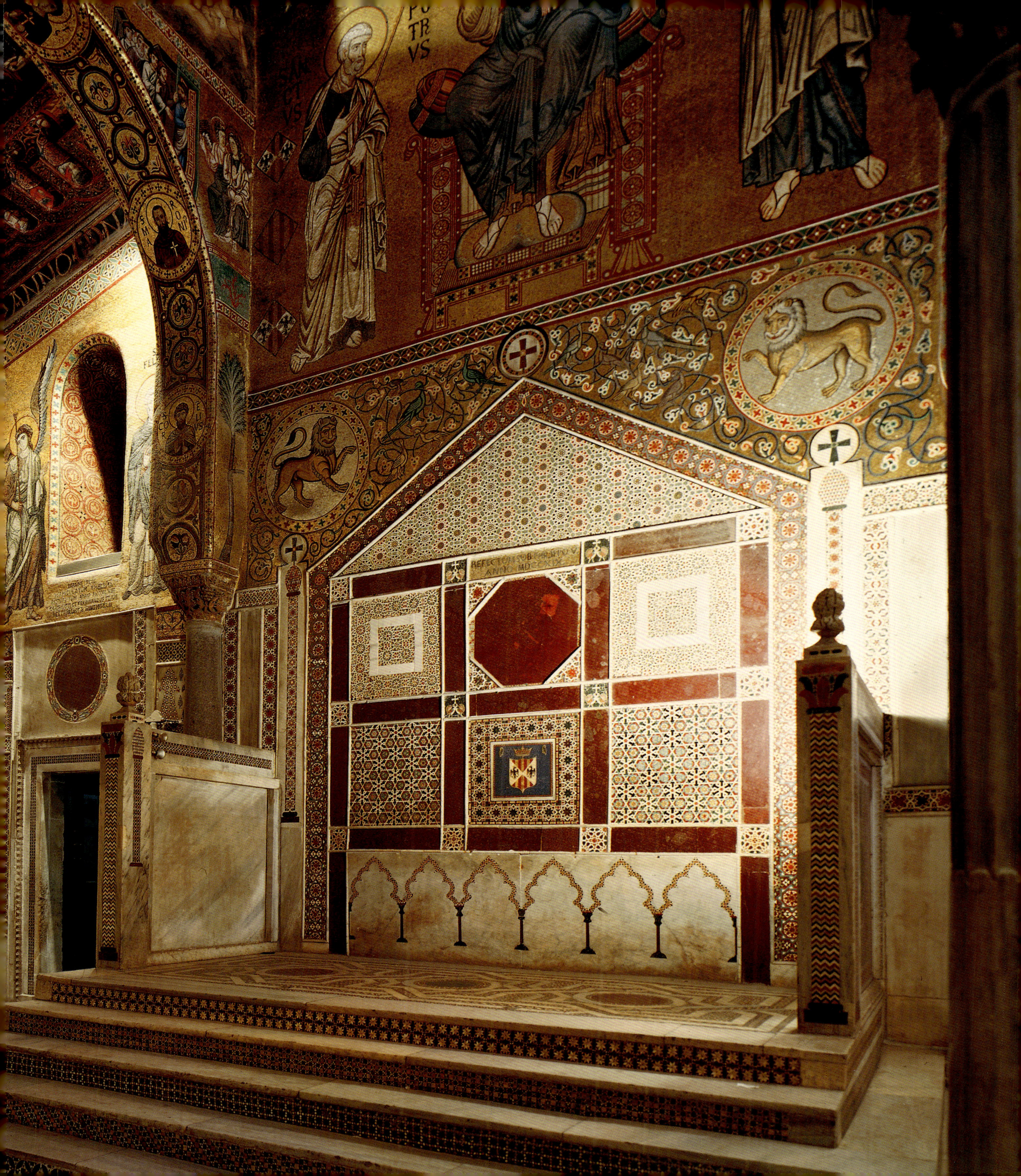

this page and opposite: *Two mosaics in the church of Santa Maria dell'Ammiraglio in Palermo. One shows George of Antioch, the patron of the church, at the feet of Mary, to whom the church is dedicated. The other shows the archangel Gabriel dressed in the kind of sumptuous clothes worn by the emperors of Byzantium.*

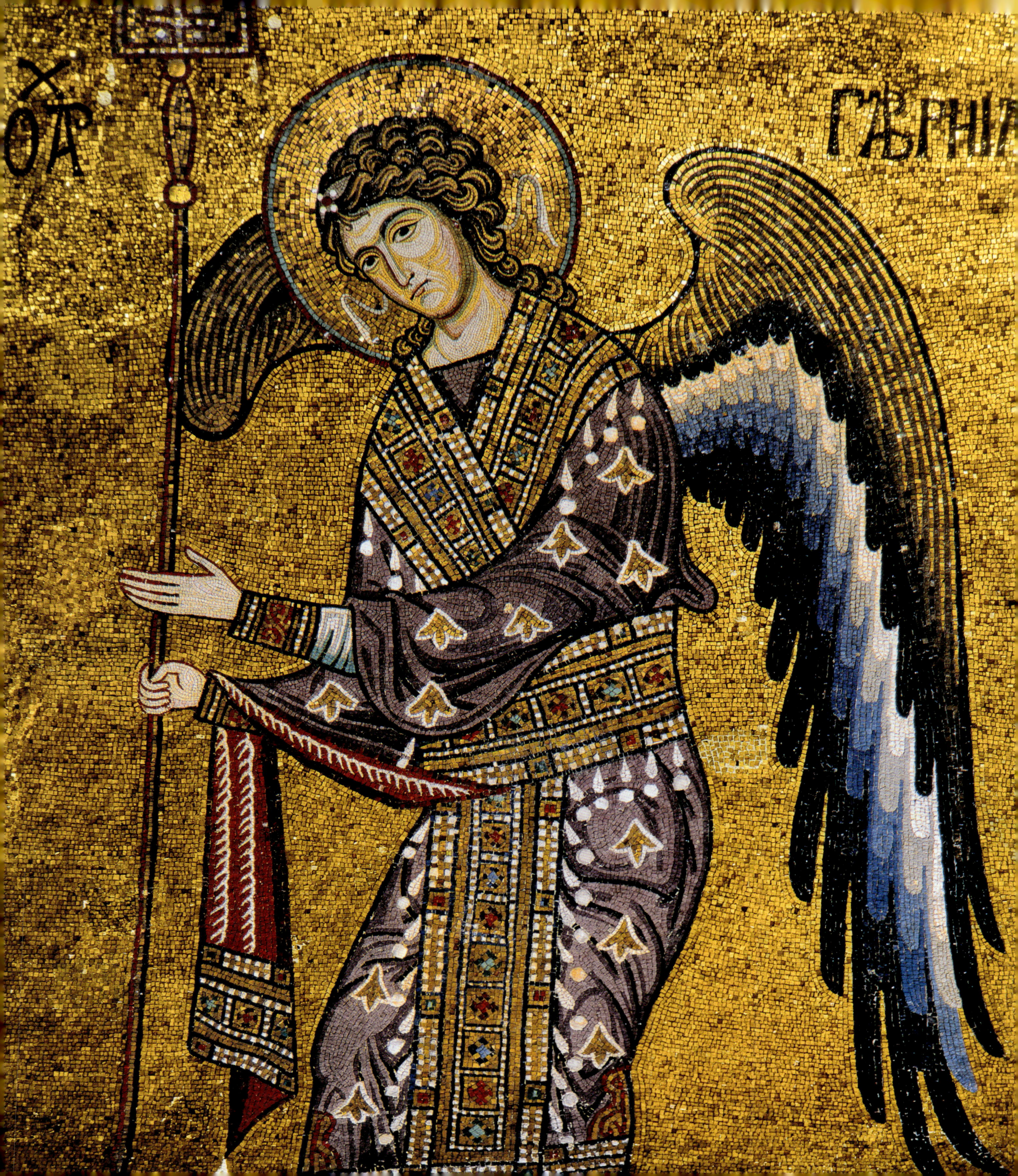

280 . ADELE CILENTO

opposite page:
The Room of King Roger, in a part of the Palazzo Reale known as the Torre Gioaria that was used as a private residence by the king and his family in which they loved to spend their free time, surrounded by musicians, poets, and men of science. In such a setting, Greek mosaicists from Byzantium working with Arab and Persian motifs were able to produce a unique decorative space that was a kind of earthly paradise in which deer, lions, and leopards mingled in scenes of the hunt set among palms and leafy trees laden with colorful fruit.

above:
Mosaic with leopards facing each other and various kinds of plant life. Room of King Roger in the Palazzo Reale, Palermo.

ADELE CILENTO

Another view of the mosaic decoration in the Room of King Roger. Begun by Roger, the decorative work was likely completed during the reign of William II. It is interesting to note that for some images the iconography draws on Christian subjects such as deer and peacocks, and for others on Persian subjects such as palm trees, lions facing each other, and peacocks again, although this time as part of floral arabesques.

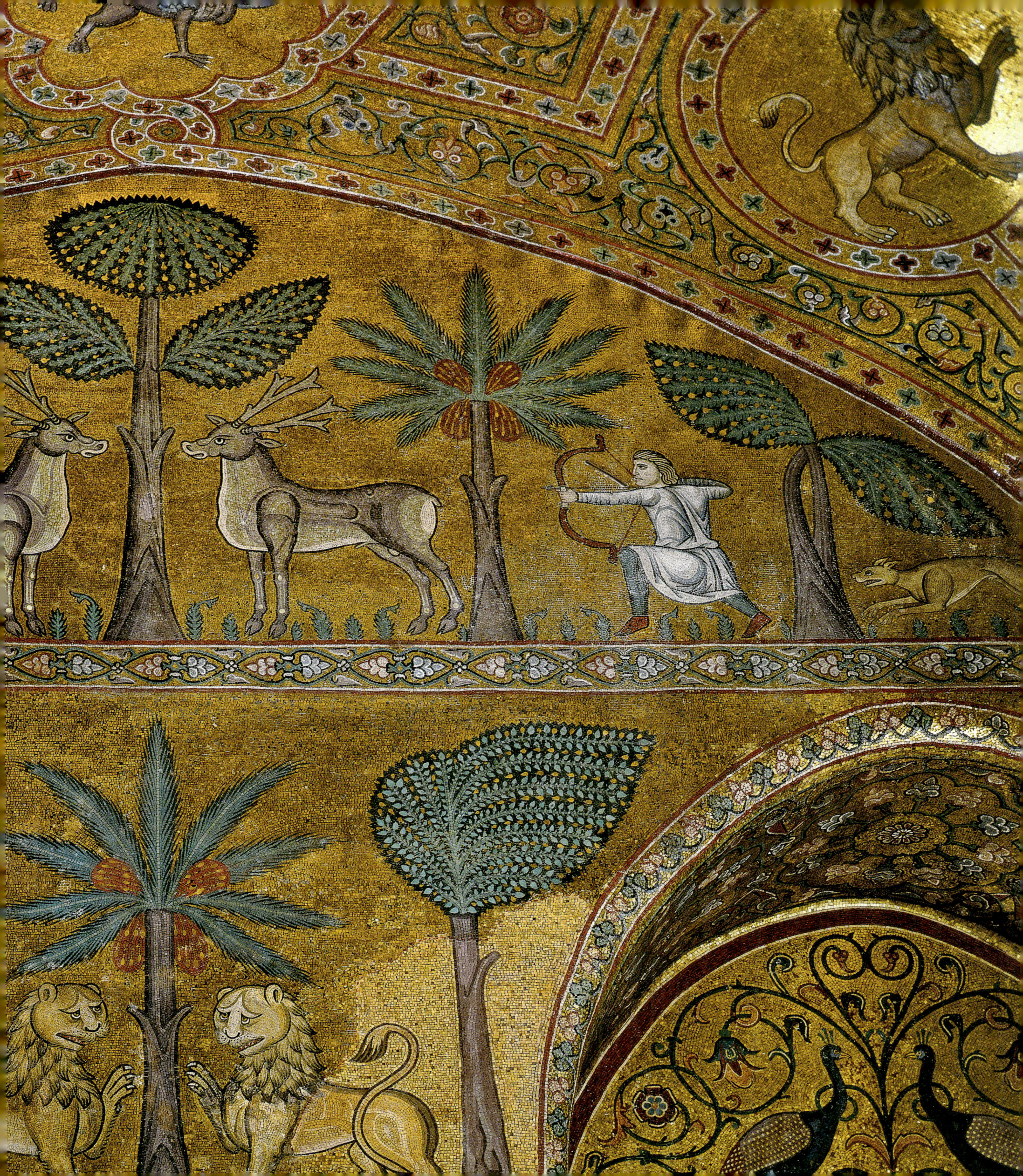

The church of San Cataldo, built in 1160 on the order of Maio of Bari, the chancellor of William I.

opposite page:
La Cubola, or the small Cuba, surrounded by the lush vegetation of the park built by William II, a remnant of the Islamic world of Sicily that has survived up until today.

refers to the geometric symbolism of Fatimid culture. The decidedly Islamic character of the exterior is in contrast to the interior in which Byzantine elements and motifs predominate. Among these are the domes laid out on an axis, identical to those in the church of San Cataldo, which may have been built by the chancellor to William I.

Famous places of delight, built by the successors of Roger II, La Zisa and La Cuba were constructed between 1164 and 1180. Made from smooth blocks of limestone, La Zisa has the typically solid and geometric appearance favored by the Fatimids, embellished only by a series of arches within which the windows open. The main room consists of a hall used for festivities and audiences that would astonish anyone who entered it, finding himself in front of a great fountain (from which the building takes its name) that poured water over the floor by means of a small channel. A more monumental variation on La Zisa is La Cuba (or Cubba), of which today only the outer walls remain. One of the pavilions (known as a Cubula, or small Cuba) from the extraordinary park that adorned the building still survives. In contrast to these two residences that were completed during the Norman period, La Favara, which was built by Roger II, made use of a suburban residence constructed just after the year 1000 by the Muslim emir Giafar. The building rises evocatively in the middle of an artificial lake called "Maredolce" ("sweet sea"). In its shape and the layout of its rooms, which open onto an internal courtyard, it recalls the desert castles of the Umayyads.

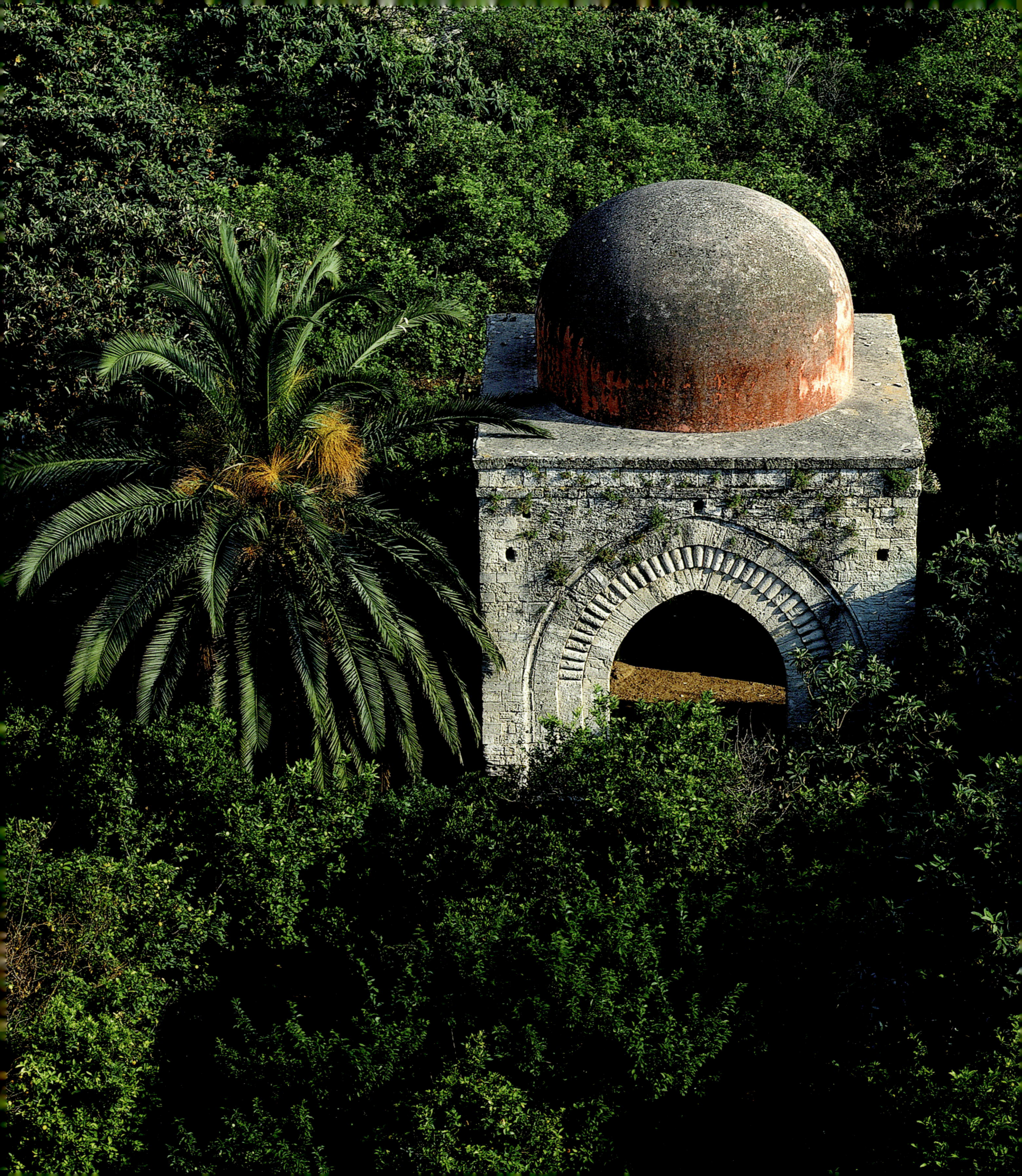

ναυμαχία

ρ̣ιοϲ ταυροϲ δε χερρόννηϲοϲ ὁ ἐνεϲθλ̣..
πιννηι τοῖϲ πελαγεύϲι τὸν ἀ̣..
τοῦ ἱεράκοϲ με δαλίτοροϲ δρι̣..
αυλοί· οἱ βάρβαροι· ϲεβρα̣.εϲτε ἀρι..
λένται· ἱμοϲροί· ἐηριμοντοϲ δρ...
λουτοϲ αυρος· θυμα ϲαμφρα̣..

HEIRS AND DESCENDANTS

THE LAST NORMAN RULERS

When Roger II died in February 1154 at the age of fifty-eight, rule passed to his last-born son William, the only one of his sons to survive. Despite his great political success, Roger had to pay, in the words of one chronicler, "the price of destiny" in his emotional life. His first wife, Elvira, the daughter of King Alfonso IV of Castile-Leon, died in 1135 after having given him five sons, of whom four were to die between 1138 and 1149. Roger then married Sibyl, the sister of Duke Eudes II of Burgundy, in 1149, but she died barely a year after the wedding. With his last wife, Beatrix of Rethel, Roger had one child, a daughter named Constance, who was born just a few months after his death and would be the last Norman heir to pass on the kingdom of the de Hautevilles.

William I was made co-ruler by his father in 1151, but international politics and the frequent disorder caused by struggles among various factions of the nobility would make this one of the most complex and difficult periods of the Norman monarchy. Among the causes were strained relations with the papacy. From the moment in 1155 that Frederick Barbarossa ascended to the throne of the Holy Roman Empire, the pope began to look with interest on an alliance with him in the hope of reducing the power of the Normans, especially their control over the churches of Sicily. But the accession of Barbarossa also opened up the possibilities of anti-Norman alliances between powers in the West and Byzantium. In fact, the Byzantine emperor Manuel I Komnenos, who had not been pleased by Roger II's attack on the Greek coasts, entered into negotiations with Barbarossa for the purpose of creating a grand coalition aimed at undermining the rule of the de Hautevilles. Faced with the prospect of a combined German-Byzantine attack, William resorted to diplomacy. But internal problems caused by the unresolved complaints of the nobility and the cities caused the

preceding pages:
Naval battle between opposing Norman factions in an illustration from the Greek manuscript Oppian. *Eleventh century. Biblioteca Marciana, Venice.*

above, left:
Detail of the sculptural decoration on the facade of the basilica of San Nicola in Bari, construction of which began under Abbot Elia between 1087 and 1089.

opposite page:
Exterior view of the basilica of San Nicola in Bari.

below:
The central nave of the basilica of San Nicola in Bari.

situation to come to a head, added to which was a long illness that William suffered at the end of 1155. This was a moment of great crisis for the Norman monarchy, but it was resolved through the energetic action of the king as soon as he recovered.

The tradition that ascribes a series of negative characteristics to William—on the basis of the period's only chronicle—, such that he deserved the nickname "the Bad," should not be accepted completely. After a period of some months during which the government was under the control of his chancellor, Maio of Bari, and the nobles on the mainland had withdrawn their obedience to him, William assembled an army and a fleet and went back on the offensive with a combined land and sea operation against the strongholds of the rebellion. First was Brindisi, where he burned the castle, and then Bari, which he razed to the ground with unprecedented violence, sparing only the basilica of San Nicola. It was then on to the Campania, where William blinded Robert, the prince of Capua, who was accused of high treason, and sent the other rebels into exile. In the end, he forced even the pope, Adrian IV, to grant him investiture and all the privileges regarding the new episcopal sees that had been denied to his predecessors. In addition, by means of treaties with Genoa and Byzantium, William restored Sicily's prestige in the Mediterranean. In the last years of his reign, William dedicated himself above all to luxury and ostentation, abandoning himself to a dissolute life at court and preoccupying himself with the construction of La Zisa. So perhaps there is little exaggeration in this description of the funeral of the forty-year-old sovereign, which took place in Palermo on May 7, 1166:

> "…above all there were the Muslim women who dressed in sackcloth with dishevelled hair and night and day went up and down the streets of the city in processions. They were preceded by great numbers of maidservants who sang mournful dirges accompanied by tambourines, and the entire city resounded with their laments."

After a few years in which William's wife, Margaret of Navarre, ruled as regent, his son William II assumed the throne. In contrast to his father, William II was known as "William the Good." He was known especially for his beauty and elegance, which were praised by all the chronicles of the time: "So handsome that it would not only be impossible to find someone more handsome, but even his equal," in the words of Ugo Falcando, who described the young king as he passed through the streets of

Two gryphons on the portal of the cathedral in Ruvo.

opposite page:
The central nave of the cathedral in Ruvo. It is one of the most outstanding Romanesque monuments in Apulia. Twelfth century.

Palermo on his horse on the day of his coronation. But as was always the case in the descriptions of medieval sovereigns, the external beauty was said to be an image of their justice and generosity and of all the gifts that a ruler was supposed to possess. William II, like his father, seemed to be very attracted to Muslims and their way of life, following Muslim customs in eating, dressing, and taking concubines, but without hiding his deep attachment to the Catholic church. Indicative of this attitude of broadmindedness and tolerance—which was not free of a certain skepticism—is an anecdote related by the Arab traveler and geographer Ibn Jubayr. It seems that during an earthquake the king called upon desperate Christians and Muslims "to each pray to the God he adored and in which he believed; whoever had faith in his God—he made clear—would enjoy peace in his heart."

During his rule, William II always had two influential people at his side: Matteo d'Aiello and the English bishop Walter Ophamil. They were responsible for the idea of a strategic marriage between his aunt, Constance de Hauteville, the daughter of Roger II, and Henry, the son of Frederick I Barbarossa. In short, apart from the laudatory tones of the chroniclers, the policies of William II did succeed in giving the kingdom a period of peace, the beneficial effects of which appear even greater when compared to the tumultuous years that preceded it as well as those that followed.

Events that were then taking shape on the international scene, with complicated plots involving a balance of power between states, local rulers, and the church, would cause a gradual dissolution of the power of the de Hauteville line, but not a

King Tancred in Palermo. A page from the manuscript of Peter of Eboli. Twelfth century. Burgerbibliothek, Bern.

dissolution of the kingdom which they had created. William II died without heirs in November 1189, but his vassals had previously sworn at an assembly in Troia to recognize Constance as his successor in case he left no children. Opposed to this, the nobles of the court, supported by certain members of the royal family, elected Tancred, the illegitimate son of Roger III (the eldest son of Roger II), as successor. Tancred was born in Lecce, on the Italian mainland, around 1138, but had been brought up at court in Palermo, and was later sent back to the mainland as the king's lieutenant. But his election was an unlawful act, because the monarchy in Sicily, since its beginning, had been dynastic and not elective. Meanwhile, the German emperor was preparing an expedition to southern Italy. While Frederick I Barbarossa was on his way to the Holy Land to take part in the Third Crusade, his son Henry VI, who had married Constance in Milan in January 1186, came to Rome in order to receive the

Illustrated miniature from the Book of the privileges of the city of Palermo. *Biblioteca Comunale, Palermo.*

imperial crown from the pope. This coronation by the pope did not help Henry overcome the distrust of any large number of the Norman feudatory lords, or help him intimidate Tancred, who held firm and was determined to defend his crown. Nevertheless, a series of fortuitous diplomatic events, including the premature death of Tancred, allowed Henry VI to assemble an imperial army, supported by a fleet from Pisa and Genoa, and to advance towards Sicily.

On December 25, 1194 in Palermo, Henry finally succeeded in having himself crowned king of Sicily and Apulia, obtaining the *Sicaniae Regni Corona*, the crown which for sixty years had been held by the de Hautevilles. The next day, his wife Constance, who was on her way to join him in Sicily and had stopped in the small town of Jesi, on the Italian mainland near Ancona, gave birth to a son. This son, Frederick II, made possible the unification of the kingdom of Sicily with an empire that stretched from Germany to the north of Italy. Meanwhile, Henry rid himself of all the relatives of the de Hautevilles. The worst fate suffered was that of Tancred's son, William III, who was blinded and castrated and taken to a castle in Germany. Having eliminated all dynastic rivals, Henry VI was preparing himself for an alliance with the pope and promising to launch a new crusade when he died suddenly in 1197.

The following year, Constance, who was now queen of Sicily, crowned her young son Frederick II as co-ruler. Little more than three years old, Frederick was head of both an empire and a kingdom. But much time would pass before he could receive his inheritance, years in which a paramount role would once again be played by a pope, Innocent III, a man of outstanding personality. But meanwhile the Norman dynasty of the de Hautevilles had found an heir, and Sicily had a new king.

THE LAST RADIANCE OF AN EXTRAORDINARY ARTISTIC ADVENTURE

In 1174 William II founded the Benedictine monastery of Santa Maria la Nuova in Monreale ("royal mountain") just outside Palermo. Like the cathedral of Cefalù, it was meant to represent the physical symbol of his ideological propaganda, and to be the last step in the process of the Latinization of the kingdom carried out by the Normans. To this ambitious project, which envisioned the construction of a monumental building of great size and extraordinary beauty, William added a series of donations and privileges that would make the abbey of Monreale one of the largest of all ecclesiastical dominions. Endowed with vast territories that extended even to Apulia, along with castles, ships, boats for catching tuna, mills, and factories for processing sugar cane, the abbey was completely exempt from taxes and was given legal jurisdiction over the area as well. Monreale was thus on the way to becoming a power of the first rank that combined church and royal palace. Just as Roger II had hoped to be buried in Cefalù (although his remains were instead placed in a large porphyry tomb in the cathedral of Palermo), so did William dream of having a royal mausoleum, and Monreale in fact contains the sarcophagi of both William I and William II.

A series of original solutions, even if partly derived from other Norman buildings, were adopted for the individual parts of this large architectural complex. First of all is the facade, set between two towers similar to those of Cefalù but showing in its plan a

opposite page:
Throne of St. Elia, a bishop's throne in the basilica of San Nicola in Bari.

Detail of the rose window of the cathedral in Ruvo.

NORMAN SICILY

The Cloister of Paradise in Amalfi, built between 1266 and 1268 by Archbishop Filippo Augustariccio, is in the form of a peristyle with twin columns that support sharply pointed interlaced arches.

development similar to the original abbey of Montecassino. Not seen before in Sicily was its use of a quadriportico, which has not survived, something that was also typical of Montecassino and other Benedictine buildings. The three-apse structure is exceptional, based on elements that jut out with great formal elegance, and embellished with a series of interlaced arches that seem to run one after another. This motif is certainly of Arab derivation, but also well known in the English Romanesque. According to some art historians, it was brought from northern Europe to southern Italy by the Normans, along with other decorative motifs. The pointed arches are accentuated by cornices and distinguished by ornaments made of polychrome stone inlays. This use of color in the stone inlays was well known in Campania, in the churches and palaces of Salerno, and above all on the Amalfi coast, in both Amalfi and Ravello, areas of strong Byzantine influence. It was not by chance that this polychromy is found in the architecture of Byzantine monasteries in Calabria and Sicily. At the two entrances the bronze doors play off each other. The main door on the facade is by Bonanno da Pisa and the other door, by Barisano da Trani, opens onto the left-hand nave. Both are works of great merit due to their technique and luminous effect, a natural complement to the radiance of the interior. In the Middle Ages, great attention was paid to the doors of religious buildings. Bronze was the preferred material, for its prestige, as it was often used in classical antiquity, and for its intrinsic value. It was also a metaphor for durability, a quality well-suited to the entrance to a sacred place. In particular, the door by Barisano is practically a replica of the door made by him for the cathedral in Trani, as can be seen in the odd detail of the panels that are the same on both sides, so that the view is the same whether open or shut.

The bell tower of the cathedral in Amalfi, in an Arab-Byzantine style, dating to sometime before 1180.

Inside the church, the iconographic grid of the mosaics was inspired by the tradition of Montecassino, although with an obvious connection to the subjects depicted in the Cappella Palatina. The events of the Old Testament unfold in the central nave, with the stories of Christ in the side aisles. A large Christ Pantocrator dominates the interior of the dome, while the side apses contain depictions of scenes from the lives of the apostles Peter and Paul. William II is shown twice: being crowned by Christ—same as his grandfather Roger II in the church of Santa Maria dell'Ammiraglio—and offering a model of the basilica to the Virgin Mary. Despite the fact that the mosaicists who were called to carry out this magnificent project came from Byzantium, the layout of the mosaics, which in fact completely cover the architectural surfaces, breaks from the Byzantine idea that there should be an absolute integration of architecture and ornament. Something almost absolutely new

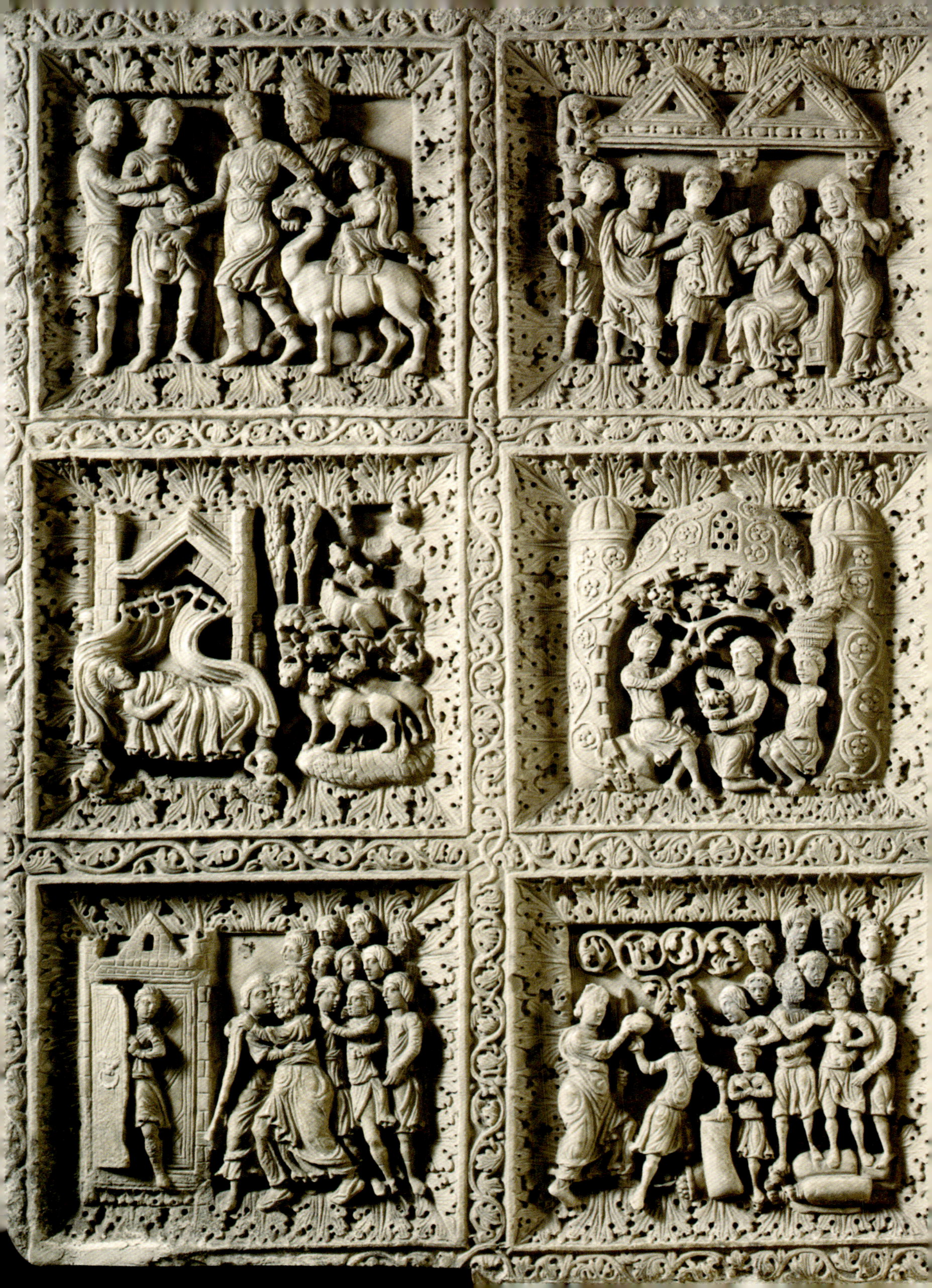

NORMAN SICILY · 299

The pulpit of Alfonso da Termoli in the cathedral of San Giovanni del Toro in the town of Ravello, in Campania. Twelfth to thirteenth century. It is in a Byzantine style embellished with geometric inlays of Islamic inspiration and applied ceramic material of Syrian or Egyptian origin from the late Fatimid period.

opposite page:
Spiral column with polychrome mosaic inlays in an Arab-Byzantine style by Niccolò di Bartolomeo, who was born in Foggia, in Apulia, and active in Campania between the twelfth and thirteenth centuries. Museo del Duomo, Ravello.

is seen in the almost eighty thousand square feet of mosaics in Monreale: the mosaics spread out and multiply, creating the majestic impression of a totality, the effect of a dream or of a prolonged moment of rapture.

The feeling that one is in the middle of a garden in paradise is also experienced in the cloister, with its highly decorated capitals supported by columns often embellished with thousands of gold and multicolored tesserae. Even the cloister has some unusual architectural features, such as the small, jewel-like courtyard around a fountain that recalls the intimacy of the Muslim gardens and royal palaces of Palermo in which one could seek solace. The capitals are of incredible variety, with their many elegant sculptures executed by workmen from every part of Sicily and elsewhere, so that the capitals in the cloister of Monreale speak different languages. Some have a classical tone, others are more Byzantine, and still others seem to have assimilated aspects of Provencal Romanesque. Among all the types it is possible to identify, in the capitals that depict stories from the Bible, the hand of an artisan from Campania, perhaps the same one who executed the stories of St. Peter on the central arcade of the portico of the cathedral in the town of Sessa Aurunca. This same artisan was responsible for two marble slabs with the stories of Samson and Joseph in the church of Santa Restituta in Naples. These two masterpieces of Neapolitan Romanesque sculpture are for various reasons closely connected to the capitals in Monreale, with the same double cornice

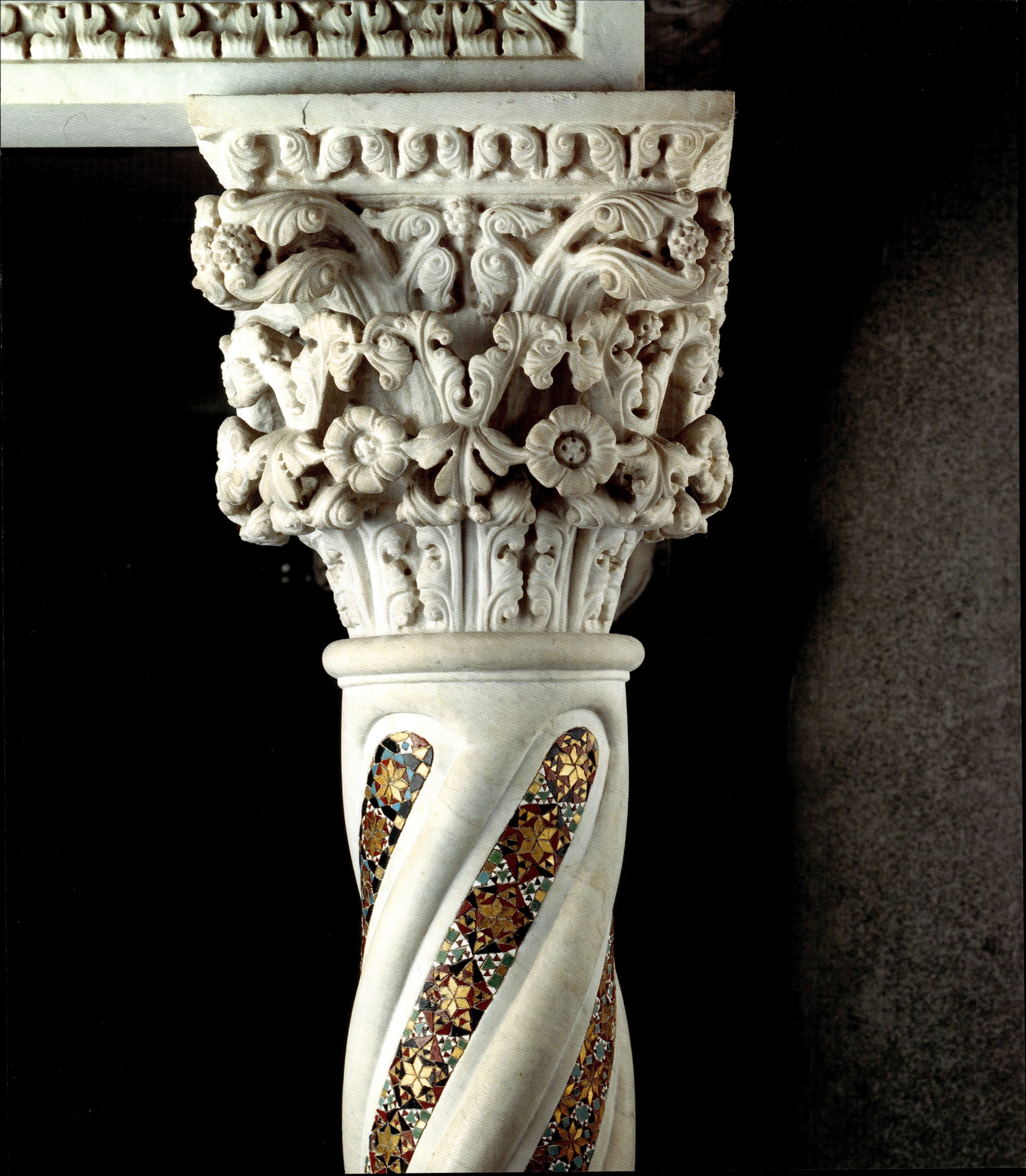

ROMOALD SECVND

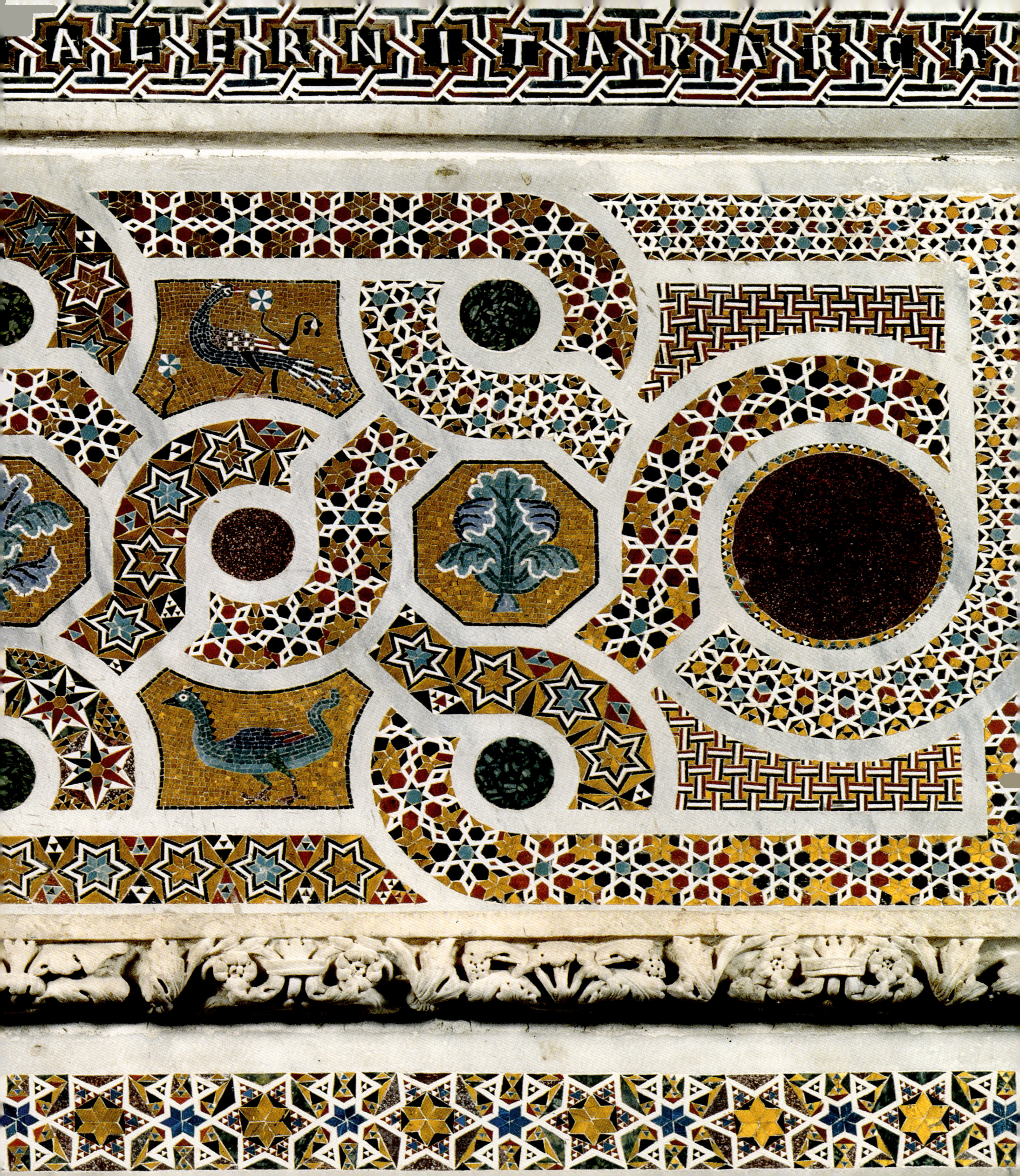
ALERNITANARCH

The two pulpits of the cathedral of Salerno. On this page, the one donated by Archbishop Romualdo II Guarna in 1181. On the opposite page, the one donated some decades later by Archbishop Nicola d'Aiello.

preceding pages: Mosaic panel with floral and geometric ornament, enriched with figures of gryphons and peacocks, part of the pulpit illustrated on this page.

with friezes of vine-shoots and acanthus leaves. There is an oriental appearance to these precious ornaments, perhaps Hellenistic more than Byzantine, while the figures have a fluidity of gesture that is classical in nature.

Also linking Monreale to the region of Campania are two pulpits from the cathedral in Salerno that were commissioned by two members of the court in Palermo: Matteo d'Aiello, who was himself from Salerno and an important part of the Norman government under William I and William II; and the archbishop Romualdo Guarna, a very broadminded intellectual and student of medicine who was bishop of Salerno from 1153 to 1181. The pulpit of Archbishop Guarna, square in shape, is located on the left side of the church, while the pulpit of d'Aiello is on the right and rests on twelve columns that culminate in the same number of Corinthian capitals. They are both of great originality and perfection, as can be seen in the circular mosaic decoration, the interlaced geometric motifs, and the polygonal rosettes (in Guarna's pulpit) inspired by the Byzantine ornament in the abbey of Montecassino. There is also a strong echo of Provencal sculpture, especially in the figures on the capitals of

NORMAN SICILY . 305

d'Aiello's pulpit, while a more Islamic quality is found in the motifs of the marbles, which are very luminous and embellished with enamel and glass tesserae. These two pulpits are something new and are the first examples of a type of pulpit with mosaic decoration that began to spread in Campania and the lower part of Lazio between the twelfth and thirteenth century. Among the significant examples is the pulpit of San Giovanni in Toro at Ravello, which develops an extremely lavish mosaic ornament, enriched by the insertion of ceramic basins of Islamic manufacture. Once again, in the blending of styles, tendencies, and taste, we see a reflection of the many artistic expressions and cultures found in the kingdom of Sicily.

Mosaic slab depicting birds and flowers, originally part of the pulpit in the cathedral of Ravello, created by Niccolò di Bartolomeo in 1272. It uses ceramic tessera imported from Syria. Museo del Duomo, Ravello.

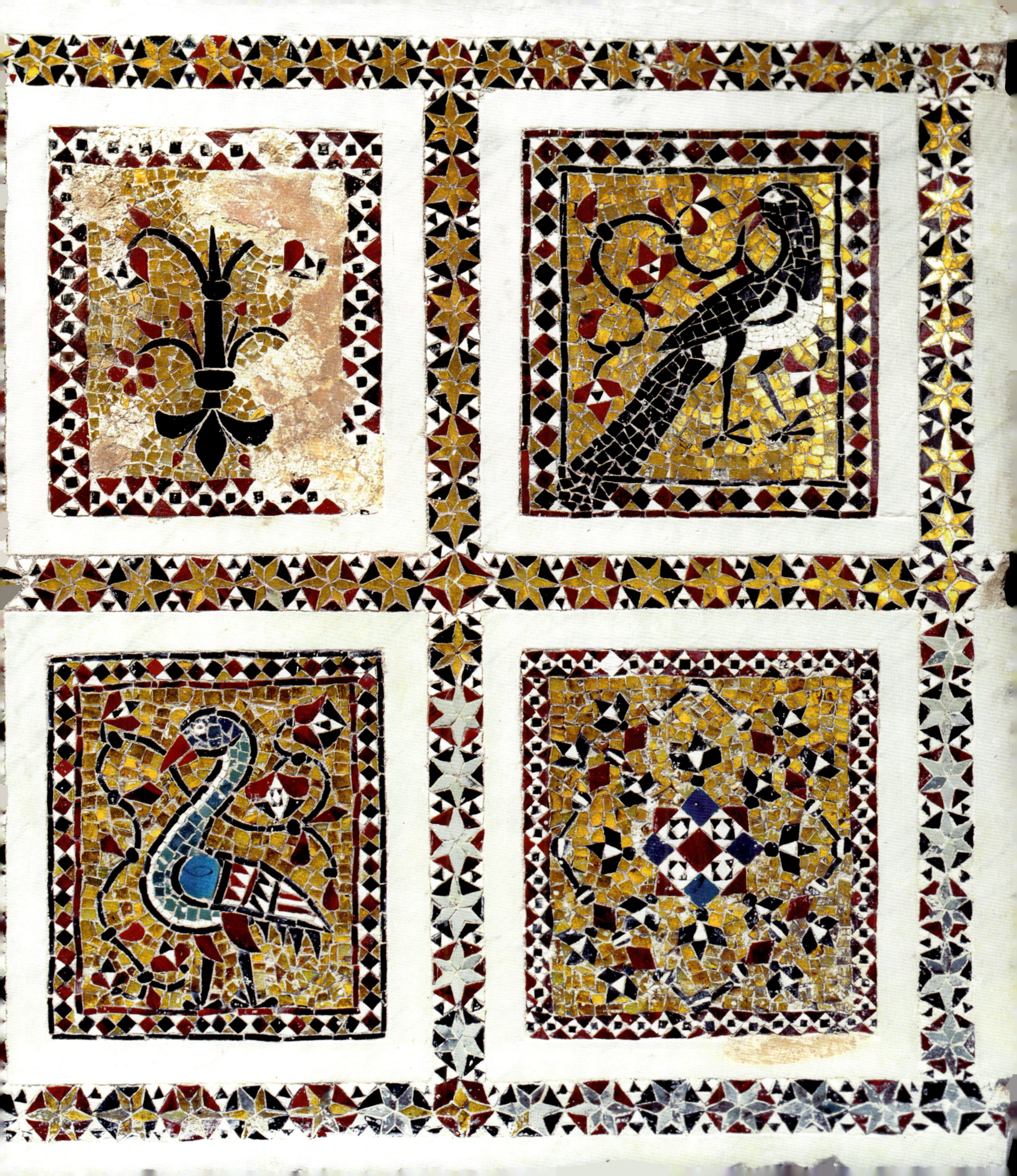

BIBLIOGRAPHY

MUSLIM SICILY

Ahmad, Aziz. *A History of Islamic Sicily*. Edinburgh: Edinburgh University Press, 1975.

Amari, Michele. *Storia dei musulmani in Sicilia*. New edition annotated by C. A. Nallino, 3 volumes. Catania: R. Prampolini, 1933-1939.

Benigno, Francesco. *Storia della Sicilia*. volume 1: *Dalle origini al Seicento*. Rome: Laterza, 1999.

Bresc, Henri. *Arabi per lingua, Ebrei per religione*. Messina: Mesogea, 2001.

Corrao, Francesca Maria. *Poeti arabi di Sicilia*. Milan: Mondadori, 1987.

Del nuovo sulla Sicilia musulmana. Rome: Fondazione L. Caetani-FLC, 1995.

Gabrieli, Francesco, and Umberto Scerrato. *Gli Arabi in Italia*. Milan: Garzanti-Scheiwiller, 1979.

Pellitteri, Antonino. *I Fatimiti e la Sicilia (sec. X)*. Palermo: al-Farabi, 1997.

Rizzitano, Umberto. *Storia e cultura nella Sicilia Saracena*. Palermo: Flaccovio, 1975.

NORMAN SICILY

Abbate, Francesco. *Storia dell'arte nell'Italia meridionale. Dai Longobardi agli Svevi*. Rome: Donzelli, 1997.

Houben, Hubert. *Roger II of Sicily: a ruler between East and West*. Trans. Graham A. Loud and Diane Milburn. New York: Cambridge University Press, 2002.

Kensington, M. *Storia dei Normanni*. Ariccia: Rusconi Libri, 2005.

Licinio, R., and F. Violante, ed. *I caratteri originari della conquista normanna. Diversità e identità nel Mezzogiorno (1030–1130)*. Bari: Dedalo, 2006.

Martin, Jean-Marie. *Italies normandes, XI–XII siècles*. Paris: Hachette, 1994.

Matthew, Donald. *The Norman Kingdom of Sicily*. New York: Cambridge University Press, 1992.

Roberto il Guiscardo e il suo tempo. Bari: Dedalo, 1991.

Ruggero il Gran Conte e l'inizio dello Stato normanno. Bari: Dedalo, 1991.

Tramontana, Salvatore. *Il mezzogiorno medievale: normanni, svevi, angioini, aragonesi nei secoli XI-XV*. Rome: Carocci, 2000.

———, *La monarchia normanna e sveva*. Turin: UTET Libreria, 1994.

PICTURE CREDITS

Archivio Fotografico UniCredit Group: p. 17, p. 43, p. 47, p. 82, p. 85 top, p. 85 bottom, p. 98, p. 99, p. 102, p. 104, p. 105, pp.106–107, p. 108 top, p. 108 bottom, p. 109, p. 111, p. 112 top left, p. 112 top right, p. 112 bottom left, p. 113, p. 117, p. 124, p. 125, p. 126, p. 127, p. 128, p. 129 top, p. 129 bottom, pp. 130–131, p. 186, p. 223, p. 244, p. 245, p. 247, p. 270, p. 285, p. 297, p. 300.

Archivio IGDA (Picture Library): p. 25 top, p. 25 bottom, p. 28, p. 29, p. 30, p. 34, p. 35 top, p. 35 bottom, p. 41, p. 42, p. 44, p. 63, p. 84, p. 86, pp. 88–89, p. 96, p. 114 top, p. 122, pp. 134–135, p. 137, p. 155, p. 169, p. 172, p. 201, p. 213, p. 214, p. 228, p. 229, p. 234, p. 236, p. 237, p. 249, pp. 276–277, p. 292, p. 293, p. 296, p. 301.

Archivio Magnus: p. 18, p. 46, p. 51, p. 53, p. 76, p. 110, pp. 118–119, p. 157 left, p. 157 right, p.171, p. 202, p. 203, p. 226 left, p. 226 right, pp. 230–231, p. 251, p. 269.

Archivio Oronoz (Madrid): p. 11, p. 27, p. 37, p. 74, p. 75, p. 77, p. 78, p. 97.

Alfio Garozzo: pp. 4–5, pp. 6–7, p. 8, pp. 12–13, p. 54, p. 55, pp. 56–57, p. 58–59, p. 62, p. 68, p.69, pp. 70–71, p. 72, p. 90, p. 91, p. 103, p. 116, pp. 120–121, p. 123, p. 176, pp. 178–179, p. 184, p. 190, p. 191, pp. 192–193, p. 196, p. 197, p. 199, p. 222, pp. 232–233, p. 233, p. 235, p. 259, pp. 268–269, p. 284, p. 288 top, p. 288 bottom, p. 289, p. 290, p. 291, p. 294.

Hirmer Verlag: pp. 224–225, p. 295.

Melo Minnella: p. 10, p. 20–21, p. 60, pp. 64–65, p. 114 bottom, p. 115, p. 250, p. 260, p. 272, pp. 274–275, p. 276, p. 281.

Kunsthistorisches Museum (Vienna): p. 194, p. 195, p. 254, p. 255, pp. 256–257.

Luciano Pedicini: p. 1, p. 45, p. 138, p. 139, p. 141, p. 144, p. 166, p. 167, p. 168, p. 170, p. 173, p. 174, p. 175, p. 183, p. 200, p. 204 top, p. 204 bottom, p. 205, p. 206, p. 207, p. 208, p. 209, p. 210, p. 211, pp. 212–213, p. 215 top, p. 215 bottom, p. 216, p. 217, p. 218 top, p. 218 bottom, p. 220 left, p. 220 right, p. 221 top, p. 221 bottom, p. 227, p. 240, p. 241, p. 248, pp. 298–299, pp. 302–303, p. 304, p. 305, pp. 306–307.

Rabati & Domingie Photography: p. 159, p. 177.

The Picture-Desk (London): p. 22, p. 23 left, p. 23 right, p. 26, pp. 32–33, p. 36, pp. 38–39, p. 40, pp. 40–41, p. 50, p. 52, p. 61, p. 66, p. 67, p. 73, p. 79, pp. 80–81, p. 83, p. 92, p. 93, pp. 94–95, p. 100, p. 101, p. 130, p. 132, p. 133, pp. 142–143, p. 145, p. 146, p. 147, p. 148, p. 149, p. 150, p. 151, p. 152, p. 154, p. 156, p. 158, p. 160 left, p. 160 right, p. 161, p. 162, p. 163, pp. 164–165, p. 181, p. 182, p. 183, p. 187, pp. 188–199, p. 219, pp. 238–239, p. 242, p. 243, p. 246, p. 252, p. 253, pp. 260–261, p. 262, p .263, p. 264–265, p. 266–267, p. 271, p. 273, p. 278, p. 279, p. 280, pp. 282–283, pp. 286–287.

The drawings of the geographic areas are by Gianfranco Casula.

The publisher asks to be notified in case of any credit needing correction.